Burden of Service

Reminiscences of Nigeria's former Attorney-General

Mohammed Bello Adoke

Clink
Street

London | New York

Published by Clink Street Publishing 2019

Copyright © 2019

First edition.

ISBNs
Paperback: 978-1-912850-90-7
Ebook: 978-1-912850-91-4

To my late parents, Bello Abdullahi Adoke and Sefinatu Bello Adoke,
for their tough love, wisdom and sacrifice to make me a man.

CONTENTS

ABBREVIATIONS

ABU	Ahmadu Bello University
ACJA	Administration of Criminal Justice Act
ACN	Action Congress of Nigeria
ADC	Aide-de-camp
AGF	Attorney-General of the Federation
ALSCON	Aluminium Smelter Company of Nigeria
ANPP	All Nigeria Peoples Party
APC	All Progressives Congress
APGA	All Progressives Grand Alliance
ASCL	Ajaokuta Steel Company Limited
BL	Barrister-at-Law
BUK	Bayero University Kano
CJN	Chief Justice of Nigeria
CNMC	Cameroon–Nigeria Mixed Commission
CPC	Congress for Progressive Change
CPC	Consumer Protection Council
DPP	Director of Public Prosecution
DPPF	Director of Public Prosecution of the Federation
DSS	Department of State Services
EFCC	Economic and Financial Crimes Commission
FAFT	Financial Action Task Force
FCPA	Foreign Corrupt Practices Act
FCT	Federal Capital Territory
FEC	Federal Executive Council
FIOD	Fiscal Information and Investigation Service
FIRS	Federal Inland Revenue Service
FJSC	Federal Judicial Service Commission
FOIA	Freedom of Information Act
FWLR	All Federation Weekly Law Report

GIABA	Inter-Governmental Action Group against Money Laundering
ICC	International Criminal Court
ICPC	Independent Corrupt Practices and Other Related Offences Commission
ICSID	International Centre for the Settlement of Investment Disputes
INEC	Independent National Electoral Commission
IOCs	International Oil Companies
JAMB	Joint Admission and Matriculations Board
JSC	Justice of the Supreme Court
LLB	Bachelor of Laws Degree
LPPC	Legal Practitioners' Privileges Committee
MDAs	Ministries, Departments and Agencies
MLAT	Mutual Legal Assistance Treaty
NAE	Nigerian Agip Exploration Ltd
NAPTIP	National Agency for the Prohibition of Trafficking in Persons
NBA	Nigerian Bar Association
NCC	Nigerian Copyrights Commission
NDLEA	National Drug Law Enforcement Agency
NFIU	Nigerian Financial Intelligence Unit
NGF	Nigeria Governors' Forum
NIALS	Nigerian Institute of Advanced Legal Studies
NIOMCO	National Iron Ore Mining Company Limited
NIPSS	National Institute for Policy and Strategic Studies
NJC	National Judicial Council
NNPC	Nigerian National Petroleum Corporation
NWLR	Nigeria Weekly Law Report
NYSC	National Youth Service Corps
OML	Oil Mining Lease
OPL	Oil Prospecting Licence
PCA	President of the Court of Appeal
PDP	Peoples Democratic Party
PSC	Production Sharing Contract
SAN	Senior Advocate of Nigeria
SAPETRO	South Atlantic Petroleum
SDPC	Shell Petroleum Development Company
SERAP	Social-Economic Rights and Accountability Project

SGF   Secretary to the Government of the Federation
SNEPCo   Shell Nigeria Exploration and Production Company
SNUD   Shell Ultra Deep Limited
TPA   Terrorism (Prevention) Act 2011
UNCAC   United Nations Convention against Corruption
WASSC   West African Senior School Certificate

INTRODUCTION

If you can't stand the heat, get out of the kitchen —**Harry S. Truman**

I woke up distressed.

As I dragged myself out of bed, I began to think it was time to end it all. Life was no longer attractive. I was descending deeper and deeper into depression. Christmas 2016 was approaching and I normally would have my family in one place to enjoy the season. But my mood was nothing festive. A wave of sadness swept through my soul and my heart was struggling to pump blood. Life tasted like sand. There was no longer any meaning or colour to it. What was there to live for again?

To wake up every day and see my name being unjustly maligned on the internet was no longer bearable. Being hunted for what I did not do felt like a death sentence on its own. *It is time to force my exit from this world,* I told myself.

I walked to the terrace of my rented semidetached maisonette in The Hague, the Netherlands. I looked down. Plunging a few metres seemed to offer instant relief instead of waiting endlessly for my vindication. I would become totally blank to shame and sorrow within seconds. I would never have to worry about the lies and the persecution again. My blood would be on the hands of those who hounded me to my death. They would live the rest of their lives with a bleeding conscience, assuming that they had any such thing.

Death, rather than life, seemed very attractive to me now.

Then I came to my senses. If I ended things abruptly, who would tell my own side of the story? Would my wife, children, relatives, friends and well-wishers not live their lives carrying a baggage that is not theirs? Would it be fair for me to take the easiest route out and subject my family and friends to a lifetime of stigma? Above all, how would I, as a Muslim, face my God on Judgment Day? Would I tell Him that I could no longer trust in His ability to deliver justice to the oppressed as He promised in the Qur'an?

1

If I succumbed to the thoughts of suicide, the false and wicked reports against me in the media – home and abroad – would go eternally unchallenged and my death would be framed as an escape from justice. The vultures were looking for a carcass. My traducers wanted me out of the way and I would have offered them their wish on a platter of gold. They would go to town and blow the trumpet in celebration. Suicide is cowardly, I said, and, slowly, I walked into the kitchen, brewed a cup of coffee and sat on the sofa in the living room thinking things through again.

I decided to live to tell my story.

That moment, there seemed to be an inflow of fresh energy into my blood. Rather than spill my blood on the ground like a coward, I would fight with it to the last drop to clear my name. It is better to shed your blood on the battlefield, confronting the enemy and defending your integrity, than to walk away cowardly and get shot in the back.

After all, the day I accepted to serve Nigeria, I became a soldier. I literally signed up to die for my country. Nobody ever said leadership was a bed of roses. There is the glamour of holding public office, which many leaders love to enjoy, but there is more to service than glitters. The real service is not glamorous. It is arduous. There is a heavy burden that comes with the package. The burden of service. But if you can't stand the heat, what are you doing in the kitchen?

I have decided that the story of my service to my fatherland must not be reduced to the malicious allegations against me in the OPL 245 transaction. I, as the Attorney-General of the Federation (AGF), implemented the Settlement Agreement between Malabu Oil and Gas Ltd and the Federal Government of Nigeria which was entered into four years before I assumed office. I would not allow that to define my life. I did the best for my country. I saved my country from a certain liability of a $2 billion claim by Royal Dutch Shell at the International Centre for the Settlement of Investment Disputes (ICSID), an organ of the World Bank.

More so, the $210 million signature bonus paid for OPL 245 by Shell and Eni is the highest in the history of Nigeria. I did nothing wrong. I did not take a bribe, not even a cup of water or a slice of cake. Along the line, the narrative about my role has been severely twisted, but the dust will settle someday and the whole truth will come out as straight as an arrow. Truth is so stubborn it refuses to give up until it triumphs.

This book is not entirely about the OPL 245 conundrum. There is far more to my service to my fatherland than that. Of course, I want to tell my own side of the story with all sincerity. I have been viciously maligned. There is a need to set the records straight. By being a frontline minister in the government of President Goodluck Jonathan from 2010 to 2015, I was in the line of fire throughout. I have faced even more fire outside office. It is logical for me to tell the story from where I stood, believing that those who read it with an open mind will come to well-informed conclusions.

However, I would also wish to contribute to the discourse on public sector reform in Nigeria. I witnessed the intrigues that go on in the corridors of power. I was right there, in the middle of things, as a player, not a spectator. I saw things. I saw people. I saw places, inner sanctuaries. The public does not enjoy the benefit of knowing most of what goes on inside there. I thought I knew a lot about Nigeria, having been a senior lawyer and having interacted closely with top government officials for decades. I was wrong. Being an insider unlocks more secrets than an outsider can ever glimpse.

For ease of reading, I have broken this book into five themes. Part I is about the journey of a little boy from Nagazi, Kogi State, to the position of Nigeria's Chief Law Officer. It is a story of pain and gain, of toil and triumph, and of grass to grace. In Part II, I narrate all you need to know about the OPL 245 transaction. I spare no details. In Part III, the historic 2015 general election and all the intrigues before, during and after it are well captured. The myths and the half-truths already in the public domain are addressed in detail. Part IV highlights my key challenges and the major controversies I experienced as Attorney-General. In Part V, I lay out my legacies as well as advance my thoughts on reforming Nigeria.

Why 'Burden of Service' as title of the book? Isn't that negative framing? Not at all, since I do not suppose that it was all bad news while I served Nigeria. Using my position as the AGF and deploying the instruments of law, I helped shape the development of our democracy and our laws in several ways, some of which are highlighted in this book. I helped commit the government to the path of constitutional sanctity. I tried my best to insulate the Office of the Attorney-General from politics. I worked hard to improve the justice system. I did all I could to further the national interest, to build a system that would endure and outlive my generation.

Yet, it has to be said that it was not a piece of cake. There was a burden that came with my service. It was the burden of hard work and patriotic passion. I was pitted against entrenched interests, with all the temptations and threats that are served in cold blood. I stepped on toes. I should not now feign ignorance that I never knew I would pay the price someday. Leadership is a heavy load for those who want to leave their footprints on the sands of time. It is how leaders handle this burden that propels, or pulls back, the progress of the country. I chose the path of progress.

No doubt, I expect this book to be controversial. I am recounting sensitive events and mentioning names, telling stories that many would want buried, especially those who have forever been grandstanding as champions of truth and transparency in public. I am not running away from any controversy. Any book of this nature that is not controversial is not relating the truth. My hope, however, is that even if the truth hurts, lessons will be learnt and Nigerians will be energised to continue to contribute to the progress of Nigeria in whatever capacity they find themselves.

PART I

•

THE CALL OF DESTINY

CHAPTER ONE

A MISSED OPPORTUNITY

Drama. My journey into public service was full of it.

Chief Michael Kaase Aondoakaa, former Attorney-General of the Federation and Minister of Justice, is a friend and a brother. I rejoiced with him when he was appointed into President Umaru Musa Yar'Adua's government in July 2007. I gave him maximum support and advice to help him succeed in office. I had high hopes that he would leave his mark in the annals of Nigeria's history.

A year after his appointment, in July 2008 to be exact, I got a call from Dr Wale Babalakin, a senior lawyer and businessman, which started reverberations that shook me to my feet. The urgency in Dr Babalakin's tone was laced with foreboding. I could not figure out what he wanted to discuss. But since I had arrived office as early as 7:30 am to clear my desk, I invited him in 30 minutes later.

Although I was curious as to the reason for his visit, I disguised my anxiety by brewing coffee for both of us. He told me that he had just left the house of Aondoakaa, who was "weeping like a baby." I had been with Aondoakaa until the early hours of the morning. It had been a purely convivial meeting, devoid of any hint of acrimony. I struggled to make sense of Babalakin's disclosure, but listened attentively to get to the root of such a calamitous state of affairs. Little did I expect what came next.

"Aondoakaa said his best friend is trying to take his job," he dropped the bomb. I was not fast enough to unravel the identity of the said 'best friend'. But Babalakin was on hand to help me out. He said I was the one. Stifling a knowing smile, Babalakin revealed that I was supposed to have been making overtures behind the scenes against Aondoakaa's interest, including submitting my CV to his boss, President Yar'Adua.

The last thing on my mind, at that particular time in my life, was becoming part of government since I had a thriving legal practice. Besides, the person who had barely spent one year in office was my friend. That he would imagine such a sinister motive on my part fairly knocked the wind out of me. Then a huge fury welled up inside of me, which my visitor evidently saw on my face. He urged me to put a call across to Aondoakaa to allay his fears. I lacked the verve to do even that. I was that livid.

Finally, it was Babalakin that made the call and handed the phone to me, protesting that he did not want me to be at loggerheads with my brother. I thundered into the mouthpiece of the phone, avoiding any pleasantries that would have been reminiscent of the night we had spent in more jocular circumstances.

"Mike, what is this nonsense that I am hearing?" I spat those words.

To my surprise, he claimed he got the information from the Presidential Villa after I left his house that morning. He said he was told Dr Andy Uba, a political associate of President Yar'Adua, was promoting my candidacy. Because he couched his comment in a manner that suggested that I might not have been aware of the move, I calmed down a bit thereafter, reassuring him that he was totally wrong and misinformed.

Funnily enough, Aondoakaa then began to speak in a more conspiratorial tone, disclosing that it was Babalakin himself who told him that morning that I was scheming to take his job. He pleaded that I should not accost my guest about it.

That plea I could not take. As I dropped the phone, I shot straight at Babalakin, looking him straight in the eye: "But he just said you are the one that told him I was after his job!"

It was all I could do to control myself. Oddly, Babalakin held my stare blankly. He was like a person hit by an electric volt. As vehemently as he could muster, he denied the accusation, claiming that, on the contrary, it was Aondoakaa who had solicited his assistance that morning.

My confusion was compounded.

We parted with a tepid handshake. I went to see Aondoakaa later in the day and we had a heart-to-heart discussion. All I could glean from the discussion was that he was suspicious of my relationship with Uba. The bond between Aondoakaa and I was momentarily shaken by this incident. We still went past that upset and continued as brothers.

· · ·

It was through Aondoakaa that I first met Uba late 2007.

Aondoakaa had asked me to go along with him to where, according to him, "power resides in the country." I insisted on knowing the location, and he said we were headed to Uba's house. I vehemently objected to the idea. I was mindful of the fact that I supported Supreme Court's nullification of Uba's election as Governor of Anambra State. I was understandably reluctant to pay him a visit.

Uba, who was Special Assistant on Special Duties and Domestic Affairs to President Olusegun Obasanjo from 1999 to 2007, had been elected Governor in the April 2007 General Election. But there was a problem with that process: Mr Peter Obi's tenure as Governor still subsisted at the time. The Supreme Court then ruled on 14 June 2007 that Mr Obi's tenure was yet to expire at the time the Anambra governorship poll was conducted by the Independent National Electoral Commission (INEC). Uba had to vacate the Government House after spending just 17 days in office.

This is the background. In the 2003 governorship election, Obi, flying the flag of the All Progressives Grand Alliance (APGA), had contested against Dr Chris Ngige of the Peoples Democratic Party (PDP), who was declared winner. After the election, Obi filed a petition at the Elections Petitions Tribunal alleging that the results were fraudulently altered. He asked to be declared winner. The litigation went on for nearly three years until the Supreme Court finally declared, on 15 March 2006, that Obi was the lawful winner of the election. He was immediately sworn in as Governor. Having spent only one year out of his four-year term, Obi successfully argued that his tenure was still unspent by the time the April 2007 election was conducted.

Although the judgment was immediately enforced, Uba, canvassing the view that he was not a party to Obi's litigation, had wanted to approach the Supreme Court for a review on the ground of nonjoinder as a necessary party who would be affected one way or the other by the outcome of the verdict, insisting that such a failure constituted an injustice to him. That was the stage at which Aondoakaa sought to introduce me to Uba for my possible involvement with the application for review.

I protested vehemently, but Aondoakaa pleaded with me and we eventually went to see Uba together. When we got to Uba's house, he welcomed us warmly, but I stated categorically: "Before I take a seat, I must tell you that I was one of those who supported the Supreme Court nullification of your election."

Uba embraced me, calling for a "truce." Once they brought up the issue of the review of the Supreme Court judgment, I was unequivocal in pointing out that it was not possible. My candid advice to Uba was that if Obi, who had been willing to participate in the 2007 governorship election, had been allowed to, he would have been estopped from laying claim to the unexpired years of his tenure. But he was not allowed to participate in that election. I said the Supreme Court was right in its judgment and observed that the Supreme Court would not review it in Uba's favour as there were no grounds to support such an application. It would, in my view, constitute an abuse of court process.

I was not sure they agreed with my reasoning. As events were later to show, Uba pursued his application and after a series of attempts and failures, the Supreme Court finally dismissed his case in April 2008. He came to respect my judgment. That was how a bond was established between us. We have remained friends ever since.

• • •

Ironically, not too long after that incident with Babalakin in July 2008, Governor Rotimi Amaechi of Rivers State asked to see me at the Rivers State Governor's Lodge in Abuja. As a close associate of President Yar'Adua, he informed me that the President was seriously looking to replace Aondoakaa. According to him, the President asked him to nominate a suitable replacement. He thought I would fit the bill.

I took a deep breath. The drama with Babalakin immediately sprang to my mind. Agreeing to that suggestion would inevitably become the confirmation of 'treachery'. I was caught between a rock and a hard place. The dream of becoming AGF and Minister of Justice was one I had nursed at the advent of my career as a lawyer. But I would never seek to arrive at that lofty place through subterfuge or by upstaging a friend. I was at the height of my professional career then and could bide my time until much later.

I shared these thoughts with Governor Amaechi, disclosing that Aondoakaa was bound to see this as treachery on my part given our rather close relationship. Amaechi was not convinced. He pointed out that commitment to the nation was a higher calling than loyalty to friends. He stated that the country was facing a crisis and that the President needed to make some strategic changes in order to achieve his Seven-Point Agenda for Development.

Amaechi sounded very convincing but I still could not make any commitment to him. I promised to get back to him after making some consultations. Thereafter, I discussed the issue with my mentor and adopted father, Justice Aloysius Iyorgyer Katsina-Alu, then a Justice of the Supreme Court of Nigeria, to seek his counsel. I shared my dilemma concerning Aondoakaa with him, especially the part about the claim that I was trying to take his job.

Justice Katsina-Alu ruminated on the matter. Far from urging me, as I was praying, to bide my time for the future, he asserted: "Bello, Amaechi is right. Give him your CV."

From there, I proceeded to discuss with my best friend, Damian Dodo. I told him about my encounters with Amaechi and Justice Katsina-Alu. Damian's opinion was going to be vital to whatever path I would toe. We reviewed the situation together. He reasoned that it was an honour to be asked to serve one's country so long I did not go lobbying for it – and that if I was called upon, I should accept to do so.

Thereafter, I also spoke to Uba about my encounter with Amaechi. He was very excited. He took me to see the Senate President, Senator David Mark, who promised to assist with the nomination. Mark took the matter up with President Yar'Adua, who agreed to appoint me but advised that we should see Alhaji Ibrahim Idris, the Governor of my home state, Kogi. Senator Mark called Idris and secured an appointment. Mark, Uba and I thereafter went to Lokoja, the state capital, to see the Governor.

Idris agreed to support my nomination. Along the line, he developed cold feet about it. I was told there was pressure from different quarters regarding the proposed appointment. This was not helped by the disposition of Dr Bukola Saraki, the then Governor of Kwara State, who doubled as the Chairman of the Nigeria Governors' Forum (NGF). Dr Saraki informed Amaechi that he was not comfortable with my nomination because he did not know me well. The NGF chairman was quite influential under Yar'Adua. If I did not have his support, my chances of being appointed would not be great.

On 29 October 2008, President Yar'Adua re-jigged, but did not dissolve, his cabinet. He dropped 21 of the 40 ministers, but Aondoakaa retained his position. Mr Gabriel Adukwu, the Minister from Kogi State, had been dropped from cabinet as far back as March 2008 because of some allegations over the unspent budget of the Ministry of Health. Despite the cabinet reshuffle, nobody was picked from my state to replace Adukwu.

Eventually, in January 2009, Mr Humphrey Abbah was nominated from

Kogi State as Adukwu's replacement. Abbah's nomination generated a lot of furore in the Senate over internal balancing in Kogi State, resulting in his non-clearance for a while. He was from Kogi East Senatorial District, which had produced all the state Governors so far, while I was from Kogi Central, which had produced neither Governor nor Minister since 1999.

The Senate eventually cleared Abbah and he was named Minister of State for Interior. I was disappointed. My disappointment was not, however, with regards to not getting the job. It had more to do with my initial reluctance at jeopardising my relationship with Aondoakaa. To take that plunge and still not get the job appeared to me an unwarranted missing of opportunity. I had to put the disappointment behind me and move ahead with my practice. It was a *que sera sera* moment. My mantra is that what is meant to be will be. Human efforts can only delay or hasten the moment.

• • •

CHAPTER TWO

THE APPOINTMENT

The first time I met Dr Goodluck Ebele Jonathan, I had no inkling that he would one day be my boss. It was one evening in January 2010. He was at the dining table, quietly having his dinner. His trademark bowler hat sat fittingly on his head. His face was calm; his gaze meek. He was eating pounded yam with bush meat. He responded genially to my greeting, inviting me to join him at the table. I politely declined. In a matter of months, however, he appointed me as the AGF and Minister of Justice.

Dr Jonathan was Deputy Governor of Bayelsa State when I first heard of him. In 2005, there was a serious crisis in the state following the arrest of Chief Diepreye Alamieyeseigha, then Governor, by the London Metropolitan Police over alleged money laundering offences. Alamieyeseigha's subsequent impeachment by the Bayelsa State House of Assembly resulted in Jonathan becoming the substantive Governor on 9 December 2005. He would later be named the vice-presidential candidate of the PDP when Alhaji Umaru Musa Yar'Adua was nominated as the party's presidential flag bearer in the 2007 General Election.

As ironies go, I may have turned down President Jonathan's pounded yam, but I would soon be having regular breakfasts and dinners with him. I was to learn that being the Attorney-General of the Federation may, depending on the personality of the President, guarantee you a seat at the presidential table. In my case, I was honoured with more than a cursory welcome. The Office of the AGF and the enormous responsibility it placed on the shoulders of the occupiers made it impossible for them not to be on their toes to offer legal advice and opinions on virtually every decision or action of government. To be close to the President was, therefore, naturally expected.

That chance meeting with Vice-President Jonathan took place in the Abuja home of the Hon. Justice Aloysius Katsina-Alu, who was then the Chief Justice of Nigeria (CJN). I had gone on a routine visit to the Honourable Law Lord. "Daddy" and "Mummy", as I called him and his wife, were used to having me over from time to time. That evening's visit was coloured with the aura of an august visitor. As I walked into the dining area, there was Vice-President Jonathan, the man who was then trending in Nigeria's political theatre. The prevailing episode was the news of President Yar'Adua's illness and his having been flown to Saudi Arabia on 23 November 2009 for treatment.

There had been no official transfer of power to the Vice-President as stipulated in the Constitution. A power vacuum had inevitably been created. Speculations were rife as to the probability that President Yar'Adua did write a letter to the National Assembly, to transfer power in accordance with the Constitution, which appeared to have either been intercepted or lost in transit. So foggy were events surrounding the President's exit that to this day, no one can be sure of the entire truth of what transpired.

But by the time President Yar'Adua had been away from the country for more than one month, amidst conflicting information on his health condition, anxiety peaked among the populace. Important decisions, such as signing the budget, could not proceed without meeting constitutional procedural requirements. The crisis reached a climax with Nigerians demanding to know where their President was. This culminated in a strong public demand for Vice-President Jonathan to be empowered to exercise the presidential powers provided under Section 145 of the 1999 Constitution of the Federal Republic of Nigeria.

Several of his friends had approached me seeking advice on the issue, even before that chance meeting. I had proffered legal opinions to them regarding the ongoing debates but had dismissed their invitation for a meeting with him as totally unnecessary. My opinion had been that the appropriate remedy in the event of the incapacitation of a sitting President in Nigeria was properly stipulated in the Constitution. I advised that the AGF should proactively forward a memorandum to the Federal Executive Council (FEC), being the body of ministers of the Government of the Federation, to trigger the provisions of Section 144 of the Constitution. That would declare the President incapacitated and set the stage for him to be constitutionally replaced.

It was this 'incapacitation' clause in the Constitution that the late Prof. Dora Akunyili, then Minister of Information, sought to trigger in the memorandum she circulated at the FEC meeting on 3 February 2010. But not being a lawyer with an understanding of the workings of the Constitution, she failed to properly articulate the procedure. Consequently, the memorandum suffered a setback as it was instantly shot down. Rather than solve the problem, it worsened the situation. There were public protests and demonstrations. Eminent Nigerians demanded that something had to be done to move the country forward.

There were the 'invisible hands' – a crop of very powerful individuals in government, also referred to as 'the cabal' – that were working against the yearnings of the general public that the letters of the Constitution be obeyed. These individuals were so powerful that it was rumoured that they were even threatening the Vice-President, whom they saw as a weakling from a minority ethnic group. They treated him with absolute disrespect and sought to humiliate him. Their boast of having the Nigerian judiciary "in their pockets" rent the air.

When eventually the Federal High Court was approached for judicial interpretation in an effort to resolve the impasse, it, rather than make a definitive pronouncement on the status of the Vice-President under the circumstance, merely affirmed that the Vice-President had already assumed the position of responsibility as President. This was unsatisfactory to those who wanted to be sure whether, constitutionally, Vice-President Jonathan could exercise presidential powers without resort to the provisions of Section 144 of the Constitution.[1]

The effect of the power vacuum also played out when Justice Katsina-Alu was to be sworn in as CJN in 2009. The tenure of Justice Idris Legbo Kutigi as CJN ended on 30 December 2009 and there was no sitting president to swear in the new head of the judiciary. That was a function traditionally performed by the President, but Yar'Adua had been on a medical trip and the Vice-President did not have presidential powers.

Justice Kutigi saved the day by swearing in his successor. That was unprecedented in the annals of Nigeria's history. It was therefore not surprising that diverse arguments were canvassed as to the constitutionality or otherwise of a predecessor in office swearing in his successor. In the end, common sense and expediency prevailed over legalism. Nigerians reasoned that greater

---

[1] The section says (1) The President or Vice-President shall cease to hold office, if – (a) by a resolution passed by two-thirds majority of all the members of the executive council of the Federation it is declared that the President or Vice-President is incapable of discharging the functions of his office; and (b) the declaration is verified, after such medical examination as may be necessary, by a medical panel established under subsection (4) of this section in its report to the President of the Senate and the Speaker of the House of Representatives.

constitutional crises had been averted through that proactive step taken by Kutigi. The judiciary could not be left indefinitely without a Chief Justice.

The National Assembly also took proactive steps to end the impasse when, on 6 February 2010, they passed a resolution declaring Vice-President Jonathan as the Acting President. The National Assembly relied on the 'doctrine of necessity' to justify their action even though it was strictly a judicial doctrine. The legislature appropriated it in order to break the stalemate confronting the nation. For the second time in Nigeria's history, expediency prevailed over legalism. Vice-President Jonathan officially became the Acting President of Nigeria.

$$\cdots$$

One of the initial actions of the Acting President was to re-assign Chief Aondoakaa from the office of AGF to the Presidency as Minister of Special Duties. Aondoakaa was replaced by Prince Adetokunbo Kayode, a Senior Advocate of Nigeria. If I could hazard a guess, I would say that the Acting President was too quick in replacing Aondoakaa. There had been fears he was about to challenge the invocation of the doctrine of necessity by the National Assembly to make Jonathan the Acting President.

In fact, looking back and knowing Aondoakaa as I did, I believed that if he was better acquainted with President Yar'Adua's health, especially his incapacitation, he would not have hesitated to guide the FEC towards the invocation of Section 144 of the Constitution. I have never doubted that he had the requisite knowledge of the law, personal conviction and courage to do the right thing. His lack of access to the President obviously militated against him as he had to rely on the representations of third parties. He obviously erred on the side of caution.

A couple of weeks later, the Acting President dissolved his cabinet. Unknown to me, Acting President Jonathan had approached the CJN with a request to recommend a lawyer who could serve as the AGF. That was early March 2010. I was later to discover that the CJN's response was that his nominee was out of the country at that moment. I had travelled to London for an arbitration reference. I was an active advocate and arbitrator, and my job involved frequent travels.

Because the President was due to send in his list of ministerial nominees to the Senate the next day, the CJN immediately reached me by phone to convey the development to me. Between my wife and my sister, who are both lawyers, I had my CV rolled out and forwarded to the CJN. He forwarded it to the President. We all kept our fingers crossed and prayed for the best.

In truth, the search for an AGF had been on for a while before then. When Yar'Adua was flown to Saudi Arabia and the power lacuna was staring everyone in the face, Chief Mike Oghiadomhe, the Principal Private Secretary to the Vice-President, had approached the Legal Adviser to the Secretary to the Government of the Federation (SGF), Mr Abba Mohammed, now a Judge of the FCT Judiciary, to source for CVs of lawyers to replace Aondoakaa. From what I gathered, my CV was one of those that were under consideration. This was before Jonathan became Acting President. My appointment was always in the pipeline, as it were.

• • •

The news of my nomination was leaked far afield in no time. Other persons who were interested in the position then moved to stop it. The immediate past occupant of the office, Kayode, a fine gentleman, successful lawyer and prominent politician, obviously wanted to be reappointed. There were persons already pushing his case within the system. It was understandable. But the smear campaign that was launched against me was exceptional. In fairness to Kayode, his name was not associated with that campaign of calumny.

At some point, the whole process became exhausting beyond reason. I was glad to be called to serve my country, but the desperation of those who didn't want me as AGF was getting to me. Ironically, my resolve deepened by the day to beat the odds that were piled up against me. That was my frame of mind when Justice Hassan Lawal Gumi, then Chief Judge of the FCT and now the Emir of Gumi, Zamfara State, intervened on behalf of Kayode.

According to him, he had followed the controversy as it related to a choice between either of us. In his opinion, since I was younger, I should concede the position to Kayode and accept the position of Minister of Police Affairs or any other Ministry. I thanked him for his concern and advice but politely declined the offer on the ground that I was being invited to join government on the specific assurance that I would be appointed AGF and Minister of Justice. If, for any reason, that position was no longer available, I told him I would be willing to drop out of the ministerial list and concentrate on my practice.

Another attempt to stop my nomination was spearheaded by Chief Edwin Clark, the Ijaw leader, whose image loomed large during the Jonathan administration. Chief Clark was not a member of the government but saw himself as the power and protector behind the 'throne'. He was surrounded by a group of younger guys who saw Jonathan's ascendancy as an opportunity to have a say on how Nigeria should be run, on who should serve in the government and on who should benefit from their kinsman's presidency.

So many shocking things were said about me, most of them utter fabrications! One major complaint was that I had acted as Chief James Ibori's lawyer. Clark was a mortal enemy of Ibori, the former Governor of Delta State, his home state. Ibori, himself, was perceived as having taken advantage of his closeness to President Yar'Adua to antagonise Jonathan when he was Vice-President. Ibori was obviously not in the good books of the new powerbrokers in Aso Rock.

As a matter of fact, I did act for Ibori in a court matter at the instance of my colleague, Mr Austin Alegeh, a reputable lawyer with whom I had done many cases in the past. This was when the UK authorities temporarily froze Ibori's assets in August 2007 during the pre-trial stage of a criminal investigation. Alegeh had invited me to be part of the case as an expert on Nigerian law. On the strength of my expert opinion, Ibori's lawyers were able to get the court to unfreeze his assets. In another matter involving the Economic and Financial Crimes Commission (EFCC) and Ibori, Alegeh also invited me to stand in for him in court as the hearing date coincided with his swearing-in ceremony as a SAN. There was no way he could miss the oath-taking ceremony.

My intervention in the matter was to persuade Ibori to talk with EFCC officials, even as he sought to exercise his right of silence. My subsequent brief was to mediate between the two parties to come to some form of agreement and settlement. I had made it clear that if they could not reach any agreement, I would withdraw from the matter. As it happened, the EFCC wanted a custodial sentence against Ibori in addition to the forfeiture of his assets, while the latter insisted that as a politician, this would have far-reaching effects on him. He was, however, willing to forfeit the assets. The EFCC refused this offer. They argued that there must be custodial sentence, otherwise Ibori should be prepared to hand himself over to the UK authorities. The negotiations more or less broke down thereafter. I withdrew at that point and did not represent Ibori at any other point in the matter.

Another allegation was that I was Amaechi's friend and lawyer. Amaechi, who was the Speaker of the Rivers State House of Assembly between 1999 and 2007, was illegally denied the PDP governorship ticket in 2007. He headed to court. I was one of his lawyers. That was meant to be a crime in Clark's court. During the power vacuum crisis, Amaechi, like Ibori, was considered a Yar'Adua man and accused of not supporting Jonathan, who hailed from the same South–South geopolitical zone with him. In the thinking of my opponents, if I became a minister, Hon. Amaechi could use me as a fifth columnist against the Jonathan government. It was that ridiculous.

What I found more disturbing was that there was a close friend of mine who kept coming to assure me that he was in touch with Clark, and that he had been interceding with him on my behalf. It turned out he was interceding for himself! He was not alone. There were also some self-styled human rights activists and civil society profiteers who were interested in the position and who thought pulling me down would lift them up. The nastiest among them was a popular lawyer whose talent for hypocrisy and mischief dwarfed his diminutive frame. But he is a darling of the Nigerian media!

I could not understand what all the desperation was about. The pressure on President Jonathan must have been so overwhelming that he contacted the Senate President, Senator David Mark, and hinted him about the possibility of withdrawing my nomination. I later received a letter inviting me to appear before the Senate for screening. I went for the screening and was asked to take a bow, after responding to questions. I must have done well, going by the demeanour of the senators.

If I thought my travails were over, however, they had only just been reloaded.

Immediately after the screening, those who did not want me to be AGF began to lobby that I should be given another portfolio. The Governor of Akwa Ibom State, Chief Godswill Akpabio, was the arrowhead of that push. His fear was that because I had acted as a lawyer for Rivers State in a matter between the state and Akwa Ibom over the location of oil wells for the determination of derivation payment, I would use the position of the AGF to the advantage of Rivers State. He didn't disclose his prejudice to President Jonathan though. Akpabio himself confirmed his opposition to my candidacy in person. When I eventually became the Attorney-General, however, he congratulated me and offered a hand of friendship. He is actually a great human being.

• • •

Dr Jonathan, as the Acting President, had passed my CV to Alhaji Yayale Ahmed, the SGF, as soon as he received it from Justice Katsina-Alu in March 2010. Minus the obstacles mounted by those who did not want me to be AGF, President Jonathan had to deal with the issue of my state of origin. He thought I was from Benue State, probably owing to my relationship with Hon. Justice Katsina-Alu, who nominated me. Mr Yomi Awoniyi had been promised the ministerial slot for Kogi State, where I also hail from. The President had a decision to make. Awoniyi lost out.[2]

With all the intrigues and high-wire politics that went on, the whole game eventually boiled down to the Acting President choosing between Kayode and me after the Senate confirmation. Many thought that having served as AGF for 33 days, Kayode should be allowed to continue in that position. He had very strong supporters. Some of his supporters were the President's personal friends, including the businessman, Mr Femi Otedola, who was perhaps Kayode's strongest promoter. The Acting President was caught between loyalty to his friends and fulfilling his promise to the CJN.

Some of my friends – including Ms. Chinelo Anohu-Amazu, who was later appointed the Director-General/CEO of National Pension Commission – also got across to Mr Otedola. I eventually met with Otedola and Oghiadomhe. Both men had been directed by the Acting President to have informal meetings with Kayode and me, separately. Otedola was brutally honest in his support for Kayode, whom he already knew. After my interaction with the 'two-man committee', Otedola shook my hands and said he would support my nomination.

It was, therefore, not surprising when, two days before the swearing-in of new ministers, I got a phone call from Kayode congratulating me as the next Attorney-General of the Federation and Minister of Justice. That was how the matter was amicably resolved. Kayode and I remain friends till today. I admire him for his professionalism, open-mindedness and decency.

I began to look forward to the swearing-in ceremony scheduled for 6 April 2010.

The ceremony was, for me, a very sober occasion. As I walked down the long corridor towards the Council Chambers inside Aso Rock Villa, Nigeria's seat of power, Damian was by my side. He was my only guest. Damian is my life-long friend and brother. We were classmates as Law students at the

---

[2] Awoniyi later became Deputy Governor of Kogi State.

Ahmadu Bello University, Zaria, and we have remained friends ever since. Every man needs a Damian: a friend who can tell you the tough truth and pull your ears when you are derailing.

As I was being sworn in, my only regret was that my late mother, Hajia Safinatu, with whom I had shared my dream of becoming the AGF, was not present. There I was taking the oath of office as Nigeria's 21st Attorney-General and Minister of Justice without my mother, who had passionately prayed that my dream would one day be fulfilled. It was tough, but tough times, they say, strengthen the soul.

CHAPTER THREE

THE BAPTISM

"Your Excellency…!"

I heard the salutation, which I had hitherto associated mostly with presidents, governors and ambassadors, being addressed to me. It sounded odd. I had never heard it used for a Minister before then. Not until immediately after my swearing-in at the Presidential Villa on 6 April 2010. I vowed, there and then, not to take such flattery to heart as they were too obviously sycophantic. I could already envision how these same civil servants would turn tail and deride the same persons they pretended to worship soon after they left office.

The charge by President Jonathan to hit the ground running was uppermost in my mind. I decided to hurry to the Ministry of Justice. There was work to be done. As I came out of the Council Chambers, the Permanent Secretary and Solicitor-General of the Federation (PS and SGF), Alhaji Abdullahi Ahmed Yola, who was also at the swearing-in ceremony, was waiting outside with some other Directors of the ministry.

"Your Excellency, your official cars are here sir," I overheard someone say. I immediately turned down the offer. Something was amiss. There was a government policy in place on monetisation. There were no longer supposed to be any official cars for appointees of government. Everything is paid for in cash. I had more than enough cars of my own, I told the PS. I said I would drive behind him and the other Directors.

We left the Villa and went straight to the ministry. On arriving, I went into consultation with Yola on the challenges and the prospects of the ministry. Having carefully listened to all he had to say, I made it clear to him, again, that I would not need official cars during my tenure. I resisted all entreaties to the contrary.

I said to Yola: "Permanent Secretary, you were my senior by three years in the University. I, therefore, expect you to guide me honestly and conscientiously without let or hindrance, and to ensure that under no circumstance would I get what I am not entitled to, even if I demand it."

He did not respond. I was not sure I convinced him of my seriousness in the matter. But having made my point, I left it at that. The heads of the various parastatals under the Ministry of Justice had also rushed to receive me. I scheduled a meeting geared towards the important task of setting the tone for our relationship. After the usual diplomatese and courtesies, I read the Riot Act to everyone. I told them that I was fully aware of the various controversies and ills that bedevilled the ministry, and that my first task would be to sanitise the system and shore up its reputation within 60 days of my assumption of office.

I meant business.

• • •

Before my swearing-in, the EFCC, over which the AGF has oversight responsibilities, had come under heavy weather. Mr Nuhu Ribadu, the pioneer Chairman of the Commission who served under President Olusegun Obasanjo, had been removed by President Yar'Adua and sent on a course of study at the National Institute for Policy and Strategic Studies (NIPSS) in Kuru, near Jos. Following complaints that he was unduly promoted to the rank of Assistant Inspector-General of Police, the Yar'Adua government had also ordered his demotion by two steps, to the rank of a Deputy Commissioner of Police. He was also later charged before the Code of Conduct Tribunal for failing to declare his assets. Ribadu was away in London. He refused to appear before the Tribunal, alleging persecution and threats to his life by powerful forces in the Yar'Adua government. He was subsequently dismissed from service. There was no love lost between him and his successor, Mrs Farida Waziri, either.

Having followed the saga closely, I, on assuming office, deemed it necessary to bolster the relationship between the EFCC and the Office of the AGF by aligning its operational modalities with the Acting President's vision to ensure compliance with due process and strengthen the war against corruption. I decided to personally visit the Commission's headquarters to interact with the Chairman and her officials, and in the process to be properly apprised of their challenges with a view to addressing them. Immediately after my meeting with top officials of the ministry, I told the chairperson, Mrs Waziri, who had earlier come to pay me a courtesy visit, that we were proceeding straight to visit her office.

When I addressed the staff of EFCC, I emphasised the need to ensure that the war against corruption was won and that, under my watch, their mode of operation would be reviewed to ensure compliance with the dictates of the rule of law. I deprecated the EFCC's penchant for filing multiple charges; unnecessary objections to bail applications even where offences charged were bailable; shoddy investigations, which had in the past contributed substantially to trial delays; and general inefficiency in the administration of criminal justice. I was determined to reverse that trend.

Judging from their enthusiastic response to every statement of mine, I was fooled into believing I was on the same page with the EFCC staff. I was to discover many of them had more interest in the ongoing case against Ribadu and whether or not the new Attorney-General would discontinue the suit and facilitate Ribadu's return to the EFCC. The new powerbrokers at the EFCC had an axe to grind with Ribadu and wanted a firm assurance that on no account would the Acting President reinstate him as the head of the Commission.

Shortly after my meeting with the staff, a journalist wanted to know whether or not I would frequently exercise the powers of the AGF under Section 174 of the 1999 Constitution to enter *nolle prosequi* in criminal trials. I had no interest in invoking the power of *nolle prosequi*, even though it was available to me as the AGF. It was my firm view that such a power was intended to be exercised sparingly and in accordance with the dictates of the Constitution in the interest, and for the good, of the public.

• • •

As soon as I returned to my office, I was launched into work by my aide who insisted that I dismissed the throng of well-wishers and friends who had filled the waiting room. Quite a load of work awaited me in the office. As I beheld the mountain of files pending on my desk, I was momentarily terrified. The smartly dressed aide eased me into my job and instantly endeared himself to me by the seriousness of purpose and capacity he brought to the job. Besides being someone I already knew, he had also served Aondoakaa and Kayode, my predecessors.

By his action, he had just passed a job screening to be on my team too. His intervention rescued me that day. He became an invaluable and dependable ally throughout my tenure. We didn't leave the office that day until about

10 pm after treating all the files, approximately a hundred of them. Those files had accumulated during the short period between the dissolution of the Federal Executive Council and the swearing-in of new ministers. That was a period of less than six weeks. The Directors in the ministry could have treated them effectively, but civil servants typically prefer to be directed.

• • •

The morning after my swearing-in, I received a lesson on how the media can be used to serve perverse interests. It was a baptism of fire, and it came barely 24 hours after being sworn in to office. The *Nigerian Tribune* had a screaming headline: "I will not enter *nolle* in Ribadu's case – Adoke." I never said that. Nothing of the sort came out in the course of the question and answer session I had with journalists after the visit to the EFCC the previous day. In less than 24 hours, I had become the target of conspiracy.

I immediately placed a call to Waziri to find out if she knew anything about the report. Although she denied it, I didn't believe her. In no time, I started receiving phone calls from human rights groups, lawyers and, in fact, the Presidency. I was embarrassed. I happened to know the reporter who wrote the story. He was not even at the media briefing at the EFCC. I threatened to sue him for writing a false report.

It is unethical for a journalist to cook up stories. If journalists would sit in the comfort of their homes or offices and publish fake reports, the society itself is endangered. The reporter later confessed to me that the story was based on a statement issued by the EFCC. It was disturbing that the machinery of the EFCC could be used to plant fake news in the media. I invited Waziri to my office and expressed a strong reservation about the approach of her media team in dragging my person into the politics between her and Ribadu. I insisted she should caution her spokesman against using my name to further their narrow interests and politics. I let her know that I took strong exception to his conduct.

Thereafter, Mallam Hassan Tukur, the Principal Secretary to the President, met with me over the Ribadu controversy. He said the President had directed that I should terminate the case and send a memo seeking approval to reinstate him to the rank of Assistant Inspector General of Police and the payment of all his entitlements and possible compensation.

I didn't know what to make of this. I reasoned that if the Acting President wanted to give me a directive regarding such a sensitive matter, he would do so in person. Indeed, on matters of law and procedure, he ought to seek my opinion in line with my constitutional responsibility as the country's Chief Law Officer. I was uncomfortable with the idea of relating with the Acting President through a third party. I therefore resolved not to obey the so-called 'presidential directive' and, accordingly, informed Tukur of my decision.

Two days later, I got a call from the Acting President. He wanted me to see him in his office. It was an interesting meeting. Tukur had apparently reported our conversation to him. He wanted to know why I refused to carry out his directive as conveyed to me by his Principal Secretary. I politely reminded him that it was he, the President, that appointed me to the position of Attorney-General with enormous constitutional powers, the exercise of which had far-reaching implications for him and for the nation at large.

I stated further that in order not to be misled into carrying out actions that could embarrass the government, I considered it only proper that I should take instructions directly from the President. I argued that it would afford me the opportunity of ascertaining the President's position on any given issue and to be in a better position to evaluate any proposed action or directive in line with the dictates of the law and policy.

The President listened attentively. I could not read his mind, but I had had my say. He was quiet and calm. After seeming to think through my words, he finally responded. "My Attorney-General, you are right," he said. "Henceforth, I will give you directives personally. If there is anything, I will make sure I discuss it with you directly. And if there is anything you want to discuss with me, you have 24/7 access to me."

This conversation was to define the relationship between President Jonathan and me throughout his administration. He kept his word.

• • •

CHAPTER FOUR

THE JOURNEY

On the night of my assumption of office as Minister on 6 April 2010, I did not, as already indicated, get home until well past 10 pm. A shower, a dinner and my *Al-'isha* prayers later, I finally had a moment to reflect on the frenetic activities of the eventful day. That I was the Attorney-General of the Federation and Minister for Justice felt ethereal, unreal. I had spent the day in that office receiving visitors and treating files. Yet, it still felt like a far-off experience.

Travelling down memory lane, I relived the story of my life. My journey into the legal profession had been ignited by quite an unusual circumstance. I recalled Chief Reuben Bright Balogun, an Okun man who was our Principal in Government Secondary School, Omu-Aran, in the old Kwara State, and how his attempt to instil discipline started me on my journey into the legal profession in 1977. As I ruminated, memories of that encounter drew tears of nostalgia to my eyes.

I was 14 when Chief Balogun pointed me in the direction of the legal profession. That fateful afternoon, as always, it was sports time in our school, between 4 pm and 6 pm. A disciplinarian of the highest order, Balogun saw six of us loitering on the school compound. Parking beside us, he asked why we were not, like others, on the sports field. When we responded that we were yet to make up our minds on what sports to participate in, he made up our minds for us by shepherding us all into his car, en route to his maize farm. We ended up harvesting corn until it was 6 pm.

When he finally dropped us off at our hostel, all we got was a "thank you." In fact, we had little to eat as other students who arrived the Dining Hall before us had a head start on their supper. Not accustomed to farm work, we went to prep, and thereafter, to bed tired and hungry. We were late to the assembly ground the next morning. Naturally, we were handed over by the head boy to Balogun for punishment. He recognised us among the 15 boys who appeared before him.

"So, you boys went to the assembly late?" he demanded, rhetorically.

Everybody was quiet, awaiting the inevitable punishment with trepidation. I expected the older boys among us to raise an objection to a possible punishment from the same person who caused our lateness. Gathering courage, I raised my hand to speak. I knew my Dutch courage could worsen my situation, but not speaking up against the unjust punishment rankled with me.

"Sir, we were late not because we wanted to be late. We were late because we went to help you on your farm, and by the time we got back it was late. We barely could get a decent dinner to eat because other students had already started eating at the Dining Hall. With the hunger and tiredness, we couldn't wake up early," I blurted out.

Balogun took one long look at me. I had created a moral problem for him. He appeared a bit embarrassed but tried not to show it. He considered my application with approval, separating the six of us who went to his farm from the rest of 15 latecomers. Warning us sternly against future late-coming, he ordered us to return to our classrooms. But I was not done. Buoyed by the success of my application, I intervened on behalf of the remaining nine students who still stood to be punished.

"Sir, may I intercede on behalf of those who didn't go to your farm? If you are going to punish them, then you should punish us all together, and if you are going to set us free, then you should set everyone free. In any case, you are not expected to take students to your farm, Sir."

"Shut up!" he thundered from his seat, knocking a set of papers off his desk.

Meanwhile, my chest was getting constricted with nerves, making it difficult for me to catch my breath. I was that scared. Actually, I knew I had pushed my luck too far. I, however, had no regrets. I must have made an impression on him as he somewhat calmed down and dismissed us all, reiterating his warning against lateness. We thanked him and were about leaving his office when he called me back.

"This is the second time I am observing your sharpness and boldness," he commented with a smile. "You this boy, you have courage."

He went on to recall an earlier incident when a senior student had tried to bully me and I fought back. When we appeared before the Principal, I had argued that I fought back in self-defence. With this second experience, he demanded to know if I came from a family of lawyers. I said no. He then observed that with what had happened that day, and the other incident of self-defence, he was convinced that I would make a very good lawyer. He advised I consider looking to study Law.

In those days, not many teachers, much less principals, would be that proactive. Some others would have felt challenged and humiliated to have a young boy stand his ground against their authority. Not so with Balogun. His words planted the seed in my mind: I could someday become a lawyer. As we stepped out of his office, the other boys thanked and hugged me for saving them. We had all been discharged and acquitted. That was how I won my first case without speaking a single word of Latin and without being called to the Bar.

• • •

Deep in my heart, I was still not sure I wanted to study Law. In Form Four, it was compulsory for students to have a chat with the Guidance and Counselling master. His brief was to advise us on our future careers and fields of study. I told him I was good at History and Economics, and that I wanted to study Economics.

There was so much attached to being an economist for me in those days. The Principal's wife taught us Economics. We nicknamed her 'Mama Teriba' after A.O. Teriba, the author of the famous Economics textbook. She took a liking to me, apparently because I did well in her subject. I always wanted to impress her.

But the Guidance Counsellor observed from my results that I was not good at Mathematics and so I would not be able to study Economics. On my insistence that I made consistently high grades in the subject, he explained that at Ordinary Level, one may get away with not being good at Mathematics, but at Advanced Level, I would have to contend with a part of the course called 'Econometrics'. That, he explained, was pure Mathematics and without proper grounding, I would find it very difficult.

He laughed at my attempt at a joke when I said I would employ people who knew Maths to count my money when I became a millionaire. He insisted I would not be able to study Economics. He also considered that I was good at History. Again, he explained that at the Advanced Level, the syllabus for History was extensive. This, according to him, accounted for the high rate of drop-outs from the course at the University level. Above all, he clarified that studying History would make me a teacher like him or, at best, an administrator in the civil service.

He then went on to analyse my character. According to him, from his observation, I was rather restless, vocal and a bit rascally, which behaviour, he opined, would make it difficult for me to work in the civil service where one was expected to be seen more than heard. He advised I consider a professional course. Since I was good at Literature, History and other subjects, it was his view that I should study Law.

After secondary school, I had to wait for one year before going to the university. Between 1979 and 1980, I was an auxiliary primary school teacher in Agasa, under the Kwara State Schools Management Board, before proceeding to the Institute of Administration, Ahmadu Bello University, Zaria (ABU), for the Diploma in Law programme. The irony was not lost on me: I did, like my Guidance Counsellor, teach in a school.

Banking and Finance was all the rage at the time. I had relations who were in these fields. Banking and Finance, Insurance and Actuarial Sciences were all courses that were much sought after. One of my senior cousins went so far as to advise that I forget about the 'nonsense' called Law and come and study for a Diploma in Insurance and be 'minting money' in no time. There was the late Mr Abdulsalam Ohiare, an accountant with Bank of the North, who was very well celebrated whenever he came home to Okene.

Everybody wanted to be a banker like him. Banking and Finance was a big temptation. I almost changed my mind about reading Law. My father ultimately ruled that I must study Law. My father's friend, the late Prof. Ibrahim Abdulsalami, then suggested that the best way to encourage me was for me to enrol for a Diploma in Law. Within that period, I secured admission to ABU for a Diploma in Law programme. I emerged as one of the best graduating students in 1982.

Despite this feat, I almost didn't secure an admission for the Law degree because I was from the old Kwara State, which was classified as an 'educationally advantaged state' under Nigeria's affirmative action policy. I scaled the hurdle through the gracious intervention of Mrs Aisha Jummai Ango Abdullahi, then the youngest wife of Prof. Ango Abdullahi, the Vice Chancellor of ABU from 1979 to 1986.[3] She had been my classmate during

---

[3] Aunty Jummai, who later became Mrs Alhassan, was appointed Minister of Women Affairs by President Muhammadu Buhari in 2015.

the Diploma programme. Although we were not that close during the programme, I still explained my situation to her. Sad that with the result I had I still could not gain admission into the LLB programme, she collected my credentials with a firm promise to assist with my admission. True to her word, my name made the list. That day was one of my happiest ever.

I graduated from ABU with a Bachelor of Laws Degree (LLB) Second Class Honours Upper Division in 1985. Thereafter, I went to the Nigerian Law School in Lagos and after a successful completion of the Barrister-at-Law (BL) programme, I was called to the Nigerian Bar on 16 October 1986.

• • •

I got called to the Nigerian Bar in borrowed robes. Things were rough for me, financially. Ambassador Mahmud Abdallah, whom we fondly referred to as 'Uncle Mahmud', was a kinsman of mine who worked in the Foreign Service. He, it was, who gave N3,000 to a relation of mine to buy me the wig and gown from the UK. I was disappointed as he didn't buy it. I had to wear someone else's wig and gown on my special day. It was a lonely Call to Bar ceremony. Not a single friend or relation of mine was in attendance. That did not, however, detract from my happiness at achieving my dream of becoming a lawyer.

I was thereafter posted to Kano State for the compulsory one-year National Youth Service Corps (NYSC) programme. An acquaintance had told me that he had the feeling I was going to be posted to Kano and that I should not reject it. I had desired a posting to Lagos. At the time, everybody wanted to be in Lagos or Abuja. I had wanted to serve in Lagos because I had been promised that I could be assisted to secure a job at Mobil, Elf or one of the oil companies. Among lawyers in those days, it was fashionable to work in oil companies and prestigious law firms, such as Kayode Sofola and Co. and Rotimi Williams' Chambers, because of the exposure and prestige that go with it.

When I returned home, I told my mother I was posted to Kano even though I preferred Lagos. She adamantly rejected the idea of my going to Lagos, promise of a job or not. I had to go to Kano. As I was about to leave, my father informed me that the late Alhaji Ibrahim Coomassie, his contemporary in the Nigerian Police Force, was the Commissioner of Police in Kano State. Coomassie, as well as Alhaji Abdullahi Jika, had been our neighbours in Ikoyi in the late 1960s and early 1970s. My father gave me a note to introduce me to Coomassie so that I could feel at home in the ancient city.

My father also gave me a note to Ambassador Aminu Wali, whom he had known from his student days in London. Ambassador Wali studied Business Administration at the North-Western Polytechnic in London, UK, while my father was at the College of Journalism, Fleet Street, London.[4] On getting into Kano late in the evening, I was at a loss as to where I would stay. I, therefore, sought out the residence of the Commissioner of Police. On arriving there, I told his security guards I had a note for him. The note bought me an entrance all right, but it was only so we would stand in the courtyard right in front of his house as he directed that I immediately proceed to the NYSC one-month orientation in Gumel and return to him thereafter. There was no respite for me after a long journey. Hungry and exhausted, I proceeded to Gumel, now in Jigawa State, to the NYSC Orientation Camp.

I was posted to the Ministry of Justice in Kano State for my primary assignment. When I arrived in Kano very late in the evening, I was still smarting from my experience at Coomassie's house and did not want to return there. Rather, I went looking for one Hassan Omolowo, who had done his Master's degree at ABU while I was in my final year. Omolowo and I lived in the same neighbourhood in Okene and our mothers were good friends. He was practising law in Kano. Happily, his house on Zoo Road was easy to locate, but there was a palpable reluctance in the reception he accorded me. I felt uncomfortable and miserable.

Rolling in bed all through the night, I couldn't wait for the day to break. Omolowo himself woke me up first thing in the morning and ushered me out of his house, along with my luggage. He promptly conveyed me to Gidan Murtala, which housed the Ministry of Justice. All I could read from his general inhospitality was the fear that I was about to become a leech on him and remain in his house permanently.

At the Ministry of Justice, I reported for duty along with all the lawyers that were posted there. We converged on the office of the Permanent Secretary. We were given accommodation but without beds. We had to place our mattresses on the floor. When we eventually met with the Permanent Secretary, we complained to him about the state of our accommodation. Rather than address our concerns, he spoke to us in a very condescending manner, reminding us that we were very fortunate to have been given

---

[4] Wali would later be appointed Special Adviser to the President on National Assembly Matters from 1999 to 2003. Later, he became Nigeria's Permanent Representative to the United Nations, Ambassador to China, and Minister of Foreign Affairs.

accommodation as our colleagues who were posted to other establishments had no accommodation. We never really liked him, and I believe the feeling was mutual.

We were asked to report to one A.B. Mahmoud, who was a Principal State Counsel at the Ministry at the time. He would become a SAN 16 years after, and the President of the Nigerian Bar Association (NBA) in 2016. Although, Mahmoud was my supervisor, we really never got along. Apart from my brief stint with the Ministry of Justice, our paths crossed several times and each time, there was something unsavoury about our encounters. Despite this, I have always accorded him the respect due to him as a former boss.

The one positive thing that came from my time at the Ministry of Justice was meeting the one-time Attorney-General of Kano State, Alhaji Aliyu Umar, who later became a SAN. He was then the Director of Public Prosecution (DPP). A great motivator and a wonderful human being, he took great interest in the welfare and aspirations of the younger lawyers.

My stay at the Ministry of Justice turned out to be very unproductive. There was nothing much in terms of assignments or challenges to occupy our zeal. All we did was write legal opinions on road traffic offences. That was not the kind of challenge we yearned for.

But Kano was not all bad news. It was at that juncture that I ran into an old friend, Tokunbo Ajoge, who had built quite a reputation practising law at the magistracy. Both of our fathers attended Government College, Keffi, together. We inherited their friendship. Connecting with him, however, broke the tedium for me and made my stay in Kano more worthwhile.

• • •

As a result of my frequent complaints of not being assigned challenging responsibilities, I was afforded the rare opportunity to appear in court. I received my baptism as a legal practitioner in a High Court in Kano. I remember being given a file to appear before Justice Aloma Mukhtar, who later became the first female Chief Justice of Nigeria. Even though I cannot recollect the details of the case, I still remember what transpired on that day.

Arriving at the court, I had taken it for granted that things would follow the standard practice whereby the senior lawyers would call their cases first before the juniors would have a chance to call theirs. Alas I was mistaken. My case was the first to be called. Her lordship stated her preference for following the order in which cases were listed rather than by the seniority of counsel.

I was called upon to announce my appearance in the matter. I informed the court that the case file was only handed to me by 4 pm the previous day with instruction to appear in court that morning, as result of which I was not conversant with the case file. I, therefore, craved the indulgence of the court to grant me an adjournment to enable me familiarise myself with the contents of the file to be in a better position to present my case. Meanwhile, I was trembling inside, with sheer fright. To my relief, she granted me a 24-hour adjournment to enable me do the needful.

I was prepared to argue the appeal the following morning, or so I thought, having perused the file and checked up on the law. When I came before the Law Lord, I confidently stated: "My lord, I have read through the file, and I am not supporting the conviction."

Thinking that it was all I needed to say, I sat down. I had read all my case law all right, but I didn't think I would need to go beyond declaring my position.

But she prompted me gently by demanding: "Very well counsel! Why are you not supporting the conviction?"

It was then I realised I had to give my reasons too. I went on to state that from the facts disclosed in the file, the conviction was based on suspicion without legal proof. I went further to state that no matter how strong a suspicion was, it could not take the place of legal proof. Since there was no proof to back the conviction, I was of the firm view that it could not stand. I remember citing the case of *Odofin Bello Vs State* in support of my assertion that the prosecution was duty-bound to disclose all material facts to the defence. To my exhilaration, she agreed with me and the conviction was set aside. That was my first experience in a real court, not Balogun's office!

I was spurred on to look farther afield for more challenges. Then one day, I heard that the law firm of Zakari Yaro & Co. was looking for an NYSC member to engage. The condition was that the member must have the wig and gown, and I still didn't have one. Tokunbo came to my rescue with his. I was engaged and subsequently got redeployed from the Ministry of Justice.

At Zakari Yaro & Co., I was thrown deep-end into litigation. Still very much a novice, I was asked to move a motion in court. I didn't realise it was not up to me to give a date for the hearing of the motion. On the next call-over date, which was a Monday, I appeared in court. When His Lordship, the late Justice R.O. Rowland, asked who gave me the date, I replied, "My lord, I gave myself the date." He explained to me that it was the responsibility of the judge to assign a date for hearing and not that of counsel. I had to apologise to the court. I learnt the hard way.

While working as a lawyer at Zakari Yaro & Co., I got an auxiliary job to teach the Law of Contract at the Chartered Institute of Transport. I got another auxiliary job to teach the Law of Contract at the Kano State College of Technology. I had started earning some extra money to complement the N150 I was being paid by the law firm. I was able to support my parents and Ibrahim, my younger brother, who was then an undergraduate.

After youth service, despite the fact that I was taking care of my family, I was still able to have a healthy balance of over N2,000 in my savings account at Societe Generale Bank of Nigeria. That was a lot of money at that time. I was retained as a legal practitioner at Zakari Yaro & Co. – my first major employment – on a monthly salary of N400. I worked there for two years.

I later practised at Ibrahim Boyi & Co. for a while before taking a plunge into private practice. I had made plans to start a law firm with Mallam Sanusi Lamido Ado Bayero, first son of the late Emir of Kano, who was my senior at the Bar by two years. Since Mallam Sanusi was still working in the Ministry of Justice, he was to be a nominal partner until he finally disengaged from the civil service.

Just then, my friend, Tokunbo, came for his wig and gown as he was relocating to Ilorin, Kwara State, to start a practice. With no wig and no gown, I was going to be naked. Luckily, Sanusi later took up an appointment as the Legal Adviser to the Kano State Investment and Property Limited. His wig and gown became my saving grace.

Since the prospect of Sanusi taking up the partnership was extinguished by his foray into the corporate world, I changed the name of the firm to MA Bello & Co, although I was the only one in the chambers. That was the beginning of my solo journey in legal practice. It was not as if I was afraid of going it alone: I loved adventure and innovation. However, the future was not such that I could have predicted. I was yet to know that legal practice would prove to be such a good experience and a commercial success to boot. The firm grew to become an employer of 15 lawyers in no time.

Sometime in 1999, I decided to improve my knowledge of commercial law and equip myself for greater challenges. I took time off for a postgradu-ate programme in International Tax Law at the Robert Kennedy University, Sierra Campus, Geneva, Switzerland. I found the experience very refreshing. By the time I returned to Nigeria, I was beginning to lose interest in practis-ing law in the country. It felt like I had outgrown my environment. Perhaps the time I spent abroad had opened my eyes to new opportunities.

I decided to relocate to the United States. In preparation for that, I trav-elled to the US for the necessary reconnaissance. That was my first visit to the country. I had quite some money with me. Moving around with cash was not a problem then: the 9/11 terrorist attacks had not happened, and there was little fuss about how much cash one could carry around. Besides, Nigerian banks had not started issuing credit cards.

My friend, Audu Nabegu, and I arrived in New York together. He had studied in California and was more familiar with the US. We lodged at the Marriot Hotel at the World Trade Centre. But recalling my fantasy to spend at least one night at the world-famous Waldorf Astoria Hotel, I convinced him that we should move to that hotel. We checked out of the Marriot and went to lodge at the Waldorf Astoria instead. I was grateful to God for bring-ing me to the grand and historical hotel, famous for housing world leaders.

• • •

On the sixth day of that visit, I was shopping on 5th Avenue with Audu when we saw a smallish Asian-American lady who beckoned on us. My friend was sceptical. I said there must be a reason for the lady's call. As much as my friend tried to dissuade me from going to her, I couldn't resist the pull to hear her out.

Taking me to a corner, she took my hands and studied my palms.

"You are trying to relocate to the United States of America," she observed.

Amazed, I nodded in agreement. From then, of course, she had my undi-vided attention.

"You have no future in America. Don't make that mistake because you will regret it for the rest of your life. Your future is in your country, Nigeria. That is where you will make your fame, and everything that God has des-tined will come your way. In fact, if I were you, I would leave America today."

My friend ran away from having his palms read. But I took everything she said to heart. I immediately returned to my hotel room, without shopping, and called up KLM, seeking a ticket for the home-bound journey. They were fully booked: it was summer. I could get a flight for the next day to Amsterdam and from there to London, and then Nigeria. I had to pay $100 as surcharge for the change of itinerary. The next day, I was on my way back to Nigeria. I called the woman from a phone booth in London; she had given me her number asking that I call her as soon as I returned to Nigeria.

"Mohammed, you are still not back to your country," she said, and when I responded that I was in London, she ordered with the finality that brooked no argument: "Go back home!"

Returning to Nigeria, I found myself resolved to concentrate on my practice and to make the best out of it. A year later, I proceeded to the University of Nottingham, UK, for a Postgraduate Diploma in International Commercial Law. I returned to Nigeria in 2002. A book I read in the year 2000 while I was holidaying in the US dealt with the concept of 'intellectual capitalism'. The book motivated me to go for further studies, knowing fully that to gain traction in the world of today and tomorrow, one needed to be intellectually equipped to move to the top of the ladder.

Getting to the top of my game, I analysed, would entail ensuring that I became a Senior Advocate of Nigeria. It was within that period that I resolved to put more efforts into getting the elevation to the rank of SAN. I decided to take my practice to a higher level.

• • •

I had earlier applied for the rank of SAN in 2001. One night I dreamt that my friend, Damian, was participating in the Investiture Ceremony for newly appointed SANs. He was fully kitted with the wig and gown and the silk – in the manner a SAN would be clad. I was also dressed in a SAN ceremonial gown, but the wig was in my hand and not on my head. I shared this dream with my mother. She said my friend would become SAN and that I wasn't going to get it that year, but, having seen myself in the gear, I would get it in the years ahead. My mother did not have extraordinary powers; she just interpreted the dream from the intuition of an elder. She had interpreted several dreams for me in like manner.

When I spoke with Damian, I discovered that he had, indeed, applied for the rank of SAN. I shared both the dream and my mother's interpretation of it with him, urging him to give it his all. I believed my mother's interpretation that it would be his year of taking silk. I wished him the best of luck. I, on my part, took my mind off it.

That was when I decided to go back to school. I returned in 2002 but did not apply for SAN that year or the next. Instead, I contested for the chairmanship of the Kano Bar and won. I decided to reintegrate myself into, and know, the Bar more closely. I went into it passionately too and became very popular across NBA branches in the country. For good measure, I took my Supreme Court and Court of Appeal cases more seriously.

In 2005, all indications were that I would be made a SAN. I had met all the criteria. I went to bed assured of getting it, only for Chief Bayo Ojo, then Attorney-General of the Federation, to inform me that I did not make it despite all efforts on my behalf at the Legal Practitioners' Privileges Committee (LPPC) which awards the rank. I was disappointed I did not get the elevation to the rank of SAN, but I moved on with my life. In 2006, I finally took the silk. In a way, that was mission accomplished.

When Chief Ojo was about to leave office at the end of President Olusegun Obasanjo's tenure in 2007, I was at his office when my friend, Tunde Busari, one of the Special Assistants to the AGF, said to me that he believed I could be the next Attorney-General of the Federation. It sounded like a joke. I had been made a SAN just the previous year. A ministerial appointment sounded too fantastic. But Tunde was adamant. His prediction was to come true four years later.

• • •

CHAPTER FIVE

THE BOY FROM NAGAZI

My earliest memories in life were of the Nigerian Civil War that broke out in 1967. I was approaching my fourth birthday by then, and as such, was too young to remember many things, but two events of that period remain indelible in my mind.

The first was my grandmother grabbing my hand, throwing me on her back, and running into the bush. The other was the image of villagers running helter-skelter, in every direction, in a life-or-death dash for safety. More than 50 years on, these images still play back and forth, now and then, in my subconscious.

I was to learn much later that what happened was that Biafran separatists had bombarded Okene, where I lived with my grandmother. The Eastern Region had, on 30 May 1967, declared secession from Nigeria and proclaimed the Republic of Biafra on the heels of a series of conflicts arising from the bloody but failed coup of January 1966. What followed the declaration was a 30-month civil war.

On 9 August 1967, as I would later learn, the 13th Battalion of the Biafran Army had taken control of Auchi and Agenebode in today's Edo State, South–South Nigeria, and, from there, attacked Okene and Iloshi in the North-Central zone, killing many civilians. It was said that they had come to Okene disguised as federal troops. It turned out to be a brief occupation, as federal troops regained control of Okene the same day. We were in the bush until late into the night. Seven people were reported dead in Okene alone.

My grandmother had good reasons to panic. She had lived through too many premature deaths in the family. My mother's travails in losing her first three babies had naturally heightened my grandmother's trepidation. She didn't want to risk watching another grandchild end up in the grave. Death had hung heavily in the air in my family that when I was born at 4:30 am on 1 September 1963 in Jos, Plateau State, my mother went into fervent prayers to nudge God towards her will, chanting: "This one must survive. This little one must not die."

I was named Mohammed by my father, but my mother also gave me an Ebira name, 'Onipe', which means 'intercessor'. I was to be the jinx breaker, the one on whom God's mercy would fall, to wipe away her tears. I was to become the bridge towards accessing God's favours. God appeared to have harkened to her prayers. I survived. All other children born after me also survived. After me came Ibrahim, Abdullahi, Abdulateef, Bashir, Mukhtar and my only sister, Aisha. Sadly, Ibrahim died on 6 May 2007 in a traffic accident between Lokoja and Okene. His death left me inconsolable, coming, as it did, exactly two months after my mother's.

As I was the first son, I was also nicknamed 'Baba', which means 'father'. But the real 'Baba', my father, Mr Bello Abdullahi Adoke, was born on 11 June 1939 to the Adeika clan in Nagazi, Adavi Local Government Area of Kogi State. It is generally believed that the founding father of Ebira Tao ethnic group was Itaazi. One of his five sons, Adaviruku aka Ohizi, founded the Adavi District. Ohizi also had five children: the progenitors of the five traditional Adavi clans. My lineage is Adeika, one of these clans. The other clans are Upopo-Uvete (Apasi), Uka, Idu (Aniku) and Uhwami.

My mother, born Sefinatu Iyaba Araga, was from Ihima, which was founded by Ochuga/Onotu, one of the children of Itaazi. At her death, we estimated that she had to be 70 or 71. Unlike in my father's case, there was no official record of my mother's birth. We used events that occurred during the era of her birth to estimate her age. Typically, someone's birth date would be described by the timing of an event: the death or the coronation of a king; the building of a monument; or even global events, such as World War I or World War II. The other factor that influenced our estimate was the age of her peers.

• • •

My childhood was just like any other. My father was an Information Officer in the service of the Government of the Northern Region, at the time Sir Ahmadu Bello was Premier. My parents told me that before I was born, life had been challenging for them but after my birth, things improved radically. That, to them, was one of the earliest signs that I would bring them good luck.

Two years after my birth, while my mother was expecting her second child, my father was awarded a scholarship to go for further studies at the College of Journalism, Fleet Street, London, United Kingdom. With my father heading to the UK, my mother and I had to relocate to Okene to live with my paternal grandmother. We were there when my mother gave birth to my younger brother, Ibrahim. My father returned from the UK sometime in 1967, so my mother had to relocate to Kaduna to stay with him. I was left in Okene with my grandmother, to whom I had become particularly attached.

In 1969, after my father had joined the Nigeria Police Force and moved to Lagos, I was reunited with my parents. I can still recall my journey from Okene to Lagos. It was by lorry. The Civil War was still on and there were Nigerian soldiers and military checkpoints everywhere. We kept seeing federal troops all the way from Ore until we got to Lagos. It was perhaps comforting that the checkpoints were there; it offered us a sense of security.

However, the fact that the war was still raging totally chipped away at our peace of mind. Young as I was, I could still feel the cold reality of the likelihood of coming under enemy fire that seemed to wrap us up in its embrace as the lorry laboured all the way to Lagos. I was enrolled at the Ireti Primary School, Ikoyi, Lagos, in 1969, at the age of six. We lived at No. 2 Gerard Avenue, Ikoyi.

If there was something I always remember about my primary school days, it was about one bully called Christopher who used to terrorise us. Everybody was scared of him. One day, I finally got tired of being incessantly bullied. I challenged him. He was surprised that I had the guts to stand up to him. Until then he had always got away with his transgressions. We got into a fight. In those days, once you hit the back of your opponent on the ground, you were automatically the winner. It was more like a wrestling challenge than a gangsters' bloody orgy.

As we held on to each other, struggling to see who would lift the other up first and hit that person's back on the ground, I got lucky. He slipped. I quickly took advantage of the situation and threw him to the ground. I sat on him and filled his mouth with sand, with typical juvenile bravado. The gesture would be the oft-repeated warning a bully would need to behave himself in the future: "I hope you have not forgotten how I filled your mouth with sand! Do you want to taste more sand?"

I became the new champion of the area! Word went round quickly. Anytime he wanted to bully anybody, they would threaten him with the fear of Mohammed and with chewing sand! He found this threat and taunting very humiliating, and was constantly looking for a rematch. I never gave him that opportunity. I was not about to try my luck twice.

I remained in that school until 1973 when my father was transferred from Lagos to Port Harcourt, Rivers State. He was made the Police Public Relations Officer in the state. Not long after assuming duty, he was faced with a massive PR challenge resulting from an assault on a journalist, Mr Minere Amakiri. The man had been arrested, detained and tortured. He had also been given 33 strokes of the cane. On top of all that humiliation, his head was shaven with bits of broken bottles on the orders of the aide-de-camp (ADC) to Commander Alfred Diete-Spiff, then Military Governor of Rivers State. The ADC, Mr Ralph Michael Iwowari, was my father's colleague and of the same rank of Assistant Superintendent of Police (ASP).

Amakiri was the Port Harcourt correspondent of the Benin-based *Nigerian Observer*. The newspaper had published an article about a teachers' strike on 30 July 1973, same day as Diete-Spiff's birthday. For 'embarrassing' the governor, Amakiri was subjected to the most inhuman treatment. My father did not mince words in openly condemning the abuse, even though the culprit was a police officer. My father was, after all, also a journalist and believed that journalists were entitled to the freedom to practise their profession. Although I was young, I remember that he got into an argument with my mother about that outspoken stance. She was not comfortable with my father's devil-may-care approach to the brutality; the repercussions could be grievous, especially under a military government. He remained undaunted by her fear.

We lived somewhere in Old GRA in Port Harcourt. I finished my primary school education in class five, sitting for and passing the Common Entrance Examination in 1974. I gained admission into St Pius College, Bodo, in the Ogoni area of the state. My mother would not allow that I should attend school too far from the mainland. The aftershock of the Civil War, which ended on 15 January 1970, was still very visible. People still feared Biafran attacks. Indeed, there were incidents of people occasionally chanting "Keep the spirit of Biafra alive!"

My mother prevailed on my father, so I was enrolled at the Baptist High School in Port Harcourt. I was there from 1974 to 1975 when my father retired on the rank of Deputy Superintendent of Police shortly after the Murtala Muhammed coup of 30 July 1975. I was in Form One going to Form Two when my father was retired. We immediately headed back to

Okene, where we remained until the late Kokori Abdul, my father's cousin, came and took me to Ilorin, Kwara State.

At first, I was to be enrolled into Government Secondary School, Ilorin, but Kokori thought his son, Sule, who was already in that school, would be a distraction to me. Seeing me as restless and rascally, he suggested that I be sent to a faraway place. That was how I was sent to Government Secondary School, Omu-Aran, also in Kwara State, where my father's classmate, Alhaji Musa Edudaiye, was Principal. It was there that I completed secondary school education in 1979. My O Level results were not great. I could not, therefore, compete with those with better results who sought admission into A Level Certificate programmes at the Kwara State College of Technology, Ilorin, or the School of Basic Studies, ABU, Zaria.

I had no choice but to work to help my parents and to make sure that my younger brother, Ibrahim, also went to school. As an auxiliary teacher on a salary of N120 per month, which was significant at the time, I was able to pay school fees of N30 a term for Ibrahim. Crazy as it may sound, I did share my first salary with every member of my family as a way of seeking blessings from God – in line with our tradition. Indeed, working for that one year with the Kwara State School Management Board in Okene helped stabilise my family in no small way. Then I decided to further my education.

I was billed to go to Bayero University Kano (BUK). The Registrar, Mr Yahaya Ibrahim, invited me to Kano, promising to assist me with the admission process. Travelling by road meant that I arrived in Kano very late at night. I had to sleep inside the bus to await daybreak. Alas, we suffered an armed robbery attack during the night. My box was stolen. Everything I had was in that box, except my credentials, which were in a small bag that I had clutched tightly to my body. My mother always warned me that I should never keep my certificates in my box. That night, I was half asleep when that warning came to my mind. I had, as a result, slept with my head on the small bag and thus saved my credentials.

Needless to say I was deeply wounded by that incident. Unfortunately, too, I didn't end up in the School of Preliminary Studies at BUK as planned. Rather, I went to ABU, Zaria, where I was offered a two-year Diploma in Law programme. As I have recounted earlier, I not only graduated as one of the best graduating students of my set, I was, in fact, the overall best student in my class in 1982. Some of my classmates were Yusuf Pam, who later became the Attorney-General of Plateau State; Afam Ezekude, who was appointed Director-General of the Nigerian Copyrights Commission (NCC) in November 2010; and Hon. Justice Usman Musale, a judge of the High Court of the FCT.

Thereafter, I got admitted into the LLB programme in ABU. On the day of matriculation in 1982, I did not have a suit to wear. It was an expensive piece of clothing for me. Where would I get money to buy one? Many would think that the son of a policeman who retired as a DSP, one who served as PRO for Rivers State Command, should not have problems with meeting basic needs. But there is something to be said for the honesty and integrity with which my father served his country. I remain proud of the fact that he did not enrich himself. We, the children, bore the brunt of that, but there is nothing I would not give for the unquestionable integrity with which he left service.

On my matriculation day, I had a decent pair of trousers. A friend, Bamidele, now of blessed memory, loaned me a jacket, but he too didn't have a shirt to give me. Ezekude lent me a shirt and a tie. I didn't even know how to knot a tie! He helped me knot it. I headed for my matriculation wearing an assemblage of borrowed clothes! But things didn't end well. An argument broke out amongst us at the venue of the matriculation. Bamidele, who could not stomach the very outspoken manner in which I presented my points, decided to give me the embarrassment of my life.

Right there in the presence of everybody, he shouted: "Look at somebody I lent my jacket to... look at him arguing with me!"

It was the height of humiliation for me. I removed the jacket and handed it over to him. But some of our colleagues intervened and persuaded me to take it back from him. That event was a true reminder of the poverty that dogged me every step of the way. But rather than destroy my spirit, it strengthened my resolve to make it in life. After the ceremony, I returned the jacket to him.

Later, I knelt and swore to heaven: "God, a time will come when I will have my own suit!"

• • •

My undergraduate days were remarkable, especially regarding the lifetime friend I made in Damian Dodo. I do not call him my friend; I call him my brother from another mother. That our paths crossed was ordained by God. We were both squatters when we first met in the corridors of Hostel 3 at

ABU. From interacting with each other, we realised we were both studying Law. That was how we became friends. I thought I had other friends who at that time I considered close. It took an occasion of dire hunger for me to realise that I was going to be eternally bonded with him and that he would become my brother forever.

I was an indigent student. I typified those who could not afford to eat breakfast, lunch and dinner, represented by the '1-1-1' formula of our student days. Some settled for lunch only '0-1-0'; or breakfast '1-0-0'; or dinner '0-0-1'. You could switch from day to day or week to week, depending on your financial situation. You could do '1-0-1' or '0-1-1', if your finances got a boost. It was so bad for me at one time that I did not have even money to buy the food ticket. I was on the verge of doing '0-0-0'! Then I remembered I had a friend, or rather someone I thought was my friend. When I approached him and let him in on my predicament, he calmly informed me that he had but could not spare anything for me as he was operating on a tight budget. My disappointment and embarrassment knew no bounds.

I left him and went to the room of my new-found friend, Damian.

"Oh boy, I need a meal ticket," I declared lightly, not expecting much. But he shocked me. Without asking any questions, he simply opened his locker and offered me about three tickets.

"You can have these," he said.

I was over the moon. He just saved my life! I was able to do '0-1-0' for three days non-stop.

That moment touched me and taught me a lesson in friendship. It is impossible for me to forget anyone who came to my rescue in my moment of need. If I were to find myself in a position to assist Damian any day, I would do so without hesitation. I value, and believe in, the fidelity of friendship. I have since learnt there are real friends, there are fair-weather friends, but there are friends that stick closer than brothers.

Damian is more than a brother; he is a friend for all times.

After ABU in 1985, I attended the Nigerian Law School in Victoria Island, Lagos. It was another tough time. Extremely tough time indeed. I would classify those days as the toughest of my life. It got me to understand the saying that it is darkest before dawn. After struggling for so many years and finally arriving at what would seem like a stone-throw away from becoming a lawyer, I was suddenly faced, yet again, with many challenges.

Getting suitable accommodation sparked off fresh challenges. My mother was banking on a kinsman of ours who lived at the 1004 Housing Estate at Victoria Island, which was practically next door to the Nigerian Law School. After we thought the space had been secured, he told us he had no vacant room. I was shattered. Head bowed, I took a bus, along with my mother, from there and headed for Ikeja, where one of my uncles lived. My mother was sitting next to me on the bus. I tried to be strong, but inevitably broke down in tears. It was too much for me to bear. My hopes had both been raised and dashed equally, swiftly.

She comforted me as best she could. "You don't have to cry. Situations like this are what will make you a man in the future," she said. If she had any emotion about the disappointment, she did not show it. Perhaps she was just trying to be strong for me.

I stayed with my uncle, the late Senator A.T. Ahmed, at his Ikeja house for one month. He was gracious enough to offer me a place to lay my head, even though it was very far from the school. I was always short of cash and, sometimes, had to trek from Ikeja to CMS, a journey of about 18 kilometres, before taking a bus to Victoria Island, where the Nigerian Law School was. I used to leave the house as early as 5:30 am for the trek down the lengthy Western Avenue, with all the insecurity Lagos was known for at that time. Thank Goodness, I eventually got accommodation at the 1004 Housing Estate.

Of course, I didn't have a suit as a student of the Nigerian Law School. One of the school's requirements was that we were going to have three dinners and cocktails during which we were to be 'appropriately kitted'. Fortune however smiled on me down the road. My uncle in whose house I was squatting at 1004 was travelling to England. I asked if he could buy me a suit, and he promised to get me one. He got me a black-striped suit for £99. He also bought me a tie and a white shirt.

Mrs Alhassan was also exceptionally kind to me. Apart from being instrumental to my gaining admission for my LLB programme, she was also of help during my Nigerian Law School programme. Both of us were students there, and she lived in the quarters of the Registrar of the Joint Admission and Matriculations Board (JAMB). She would invite me over for lunch, and we would eat and study together. She must have noticed that I didn't have shirts, so she bought me two very good white ones when she travelled to England. Those were the shirts I wore each time I had to attend school dinners and other formal events. She was like a big sister to me. The woman

I would later marry was her relation, although I met Aunty Jummai long before I met my wife.

• • •

I met my future wife by taking a N20 bet. We were both 100 Level students at ABU, Zaria, in 1982. One day, while we were in class, I noticed a beautiful, dark-skinned girl and drew the attention of a classmate to her. Because he instantly agreed with me and expressed his liking for her, I encouraged him to have a chat with her. He did not have the guts to approach her, but rather dared me. He was of the opinion that since she was our classmate, she would ignore us as being beneath her gaze. I insisted I could if he couldn't.

"If you have a chat with her and she agrees to go out with you, I will give you N20," he dared me. That was how the bet came about. That was all the ammunition I needed to fire my zeal. I began to do the arithmetic in my brain.

Two days later, the list for tutorial classes was released. As fate would have it, the beautiful black lady happened to be in the same group with my friend and myself. Her name was Sa'adatu Mohammed Jalingo. The first tutorial class was on the Nigerian Legal System. I was already conversant with both the subject and the lecturer, Dr Musa Agbonika, who had also taught me Constitutional Law during my Diploma programme. I was therefore at home with him and his style of teaching.

During the tutorial, Dr Agbonika posed a question to the beautiful lady of my interest. Not having had previous knowledge of the subject, as I did, she or any other student could not respond effectively to the question. I raised my hand and responded to the question quite casually, like a boss. Afterwards, the lecturer eulogised me and I felt very good about myself.

As I came out of class, Sa'adatu walked up to me and requested to know the books that I read because I seemed to have a good grasp of the Nigerian legal system. I bragged that I was naturally a very brilliant student, that I didn't have the books. I said I was nicknamed 'Onwubiko' in my secondary school days because of my "exceptional brilliance and retentive memory." K.B.C. Onwubiko was a renowned author of History books. She looked impressed. Game on!

"Can we study together please?" she asked.

"Let me think about it," I replied, trying not to give anything away.

I walked away very triumphantly. In my head, I felt like I had already won the first stage of the battle. We were always attending tutorials and I was strategically answering questions, and, in between, exchanging pleasantries with her, without showing much interest. One day, on seeing her at the school kiosk where she was drinking a bottle of Coke, I went over and asked if she could buy me one. She thought it was absurd and curious for me to make such a request. In her view, it should have been the other way round.

"That would have been the ideal thing, but unfortunately, I don't have money to buy you a drink," I replied.

When she demanded if I was not on scholarship, I explained that being from Kwara State placed me on the 'educationally advantaged' list, meaning I was not entitled to such privileges. Sa'adatu was from the old Gongola State, which was classified as 'educationally disadvantaged' with all the privileges that came with it. My explanation did not move her. She stood her ground. Till date, I still remind her of this encounter whenever I want to tease her.

Despite not buying me a drink, she kept coming to me. We would chat, I would visit her in her hostel, and we would walk around the school. Sometimes if I had money, I would invite her out for a meal. One evening, as we had dinner at Shagalinku, our favourite restaurant, I briskly informed her: "This is the last time I will be seeing you."

When she asked why, I got the opportunity to zero in for the kill. I played my card properly and carefully.

"My emotions are running riot," I stated.

"Is that why you are going to stop seeing me? Don't be silly," she replied.

That was all the green light I needed. We started a relationship. The rest, according to the popular cliché, is history.

The history was not smooth, though, as we had to break up. By the time we graduated and went to the Law School, we were no longer dating. In fact, she went on to marry someone else. I was also dating another lady. It was after we left the Nigerian Law School that we came back together.

We had broken up because of culture. In the Hausa tradition under which she was brought up, girls got married very early. There I was, struggling as a student who could not buy her a bottle of Coke, and there she was telling me persistently that her parents wanted her to get married early. I told her I could not afford it. While we were at it, someone else proposed to her and they got married. The marriage did not last beyond seven months.

During the national youth service programme, she fell seriously ill. Nana

Yahaya, a friend of mine who was a junior in the university, told me that Sa'adatu was in Kano and was very sick. Out of compassion, I went to look for her. After that, nothing else came to my mind. It didn't occur to me that anything could happen, even though she was already divorced.

It was now time for her to woo me. Unfortunately, I was at the time in a very serious relationship. But that other relationship had a hiccup – in the form of blood genotype. We both had the AS genotype. My mother vehemently opposed the union because of the likelihood of giving birth to a child with sickle cell. Yet, the lady was such a very nice person who did a lot to shape my life. I recall how she scolded me for my juvenile habits. She even threatened not to go out with me again if I didn't get my act together. She had all the qualities and attributes any man could hope for in a wife.

Meanwhile, Sa'adatu and my mother became inseparable. She was always going to visit my mother. My relationship with the other lady withered away too, naturally. My mother, who had a strong influence on me, encouraged me to do the 'needful' with Sa'adatu. Even when I shied away from the first date I picked for the wedding fatiah, she stood her ground and insisted that I would get married on 26 October 1991. I could not afford to argue with my mother; she was a woman of wisdom and strong will. We used to call her 'Margaret Thatcher'. When she spoke, it was with commanding authority.

Sa'adatu and I eventually got married on that date. We have made a lovely family of three boys: Habib, Abdulsamad and Faisal, and a girl, Husna. We also adopted two girls, Jamila and Binta.

• • •

PART II

•

THE OPL 245 CONNUNDRUM: THE FULL STORY

CHAPTER SIX

THE FACTS OF THE MATTER

I was leafing through a newspaper at the Departure Lounge of Schiphol Airport, Amsterdam, the Netherlands, en route to Morocco in September 2016. I had just completed an Advanced LLM programme at the University of Leiden and badly needed a break to clear my head and de-stress. I noticed a stranger staring intently at me, trying to catch my gaze. My eyes obliged, glancing in his direction. That supplied all the calories his feet needed to spring up and confidently head in my direction as would an old acquaintance. It turned out to be all geared towards making a rather curious demand.

"Good afternoon sir," he intoned politely, and when I responded, he said: "Please I need some money."

I did not know who he was. He did not introduce himself, nor did he lay any sort of foundation which could have passed as a conversation opener. I could smell pure mischief. Confused, I nonetheless explained firmly that I did not have any money. He turned immediately and ambled away, grumbling loudly in Yoruba, one of the most widely spoken languages in southern Nigeria, and one I speak fluently.

"Thief! After all the money he stole in government, he is now saying he doesn't have money. Fraudster!" he spat contemptuously and at full volume, ridiculing my person.

Those words stung me to my bones. As a Nigerian government official, you are automatically awarded the badge of 'thief' even before you take the oath of office. It is assumed that you are going into public office to steal and you are presumed guilty before you commit any offence. That I understand very well. What the stranger said was, therefore, not an innovation.

But my case was atypical. That stranger, like a horde of other impressionable souls, had apparently read the media reports orchestrated against me by the EFCC, Nigeria's anti-graft agency, in collaboration with two UK-based 'anti-corruption' organisations and two Nigerian online news platforms, over Oil Prospecting Licence 245, also known as OPL 245. The media narratives varied. My traducers had a repertoire of scenarios to match whatever viewpoints they found convenient at any particular time. I was accused of stealing $800 million or $1 billion from the deal. In another conjecture, I was supposed to have collected a $2 million bribe. In some instances, I was accused of misleading the Federal Government of Nigeria into making a 'bad deal'. All sorts.

I was a Minister for about five years, from 2010 to 2015. Therefore, I am no stranger to negative media, or to fake news, but things had degenerated to an all-time low in the all-out media trial mounted against my person by the EFCC. What nature of accusations to be levied against me at each moment appeared to be determined by the weather or the position of the planet itself! The narratives went unchallenged. My voice was not heard. Nobody was interested in my own side of the story.

The world was made to believe that Mohammed Bello Adoke was a thief, a fraudster, a bandit! The stranger at Schiphol Airport, a typical Nigerian, only wanted a little slice of the cake. His irritation was not so much that he encountered a 'thief' but rather that the 'thief' wanted to play hardball. I was a 'thief' who refused to share the loot which belonged to no one but which all who were lucky to be present at the sharing could make a bid for. I was breaking a code of honour among 'thieves'!

Encountering the stranger triggered a deep reflection within me. I had a burden to let the world in on my side of the story. I could not really blame every stranger for jumping to conclusions, or for believing popular narratives, unless I gave them the benefit of a counternarrative.

What really transpired in the OPL 245 transaction? What was my role? Was it true I misled the country? Was it correct to say that I took a bribe to facilitate the deal? Was any bribe money traced to me? Was I simply a victim of circumstances? Was this, therefore, not a case of giving the dog a bad name in order to hang it? With the benefit of hindsight, were there things I could have done differently?

• • •

On 11 May 2010, President Jonathan received a letter signed by Rasky Gbinigie, the Company Secretary and Legal Adviser of Malabu Oil & Gas Limited, which was copied to me. It was entitled: "Re: OPL 245 Out of Court Settlement." In it, Malabu requested for the implementation of the 30

November 2006 Settlement Agreement reached between it and the Federal Government of Nigeria when Chief Olusegun Obasanjo was President and Minister of Petroleum Resources. In other words, OPL 245 should be returned to Malabu as agreed upon by the Obasanjo government.

President Jonathan sent the letter to me for my advice in line with my constitutional duties as the Chief Law Officer and Legal Adviser to the Government. My job as the Attorney-General of the Federation was to offer legal opinion on the matters involving the Nigerian government. The simple words inscribed on the copy of the letter by the President were: "Pls advise." This marked my descent into the unknown, a path that initially appeared innocuous.

As things turned out, it was anything but straightforward or simple. Ahead on that course existed many orchestrated bends and potholes, twists and turns! They spring out of nowhere, continuing the nightmarish meanderings, reminiscent of a combination of *Alice in Wonderland* and *Gulliver's Travels*. That journey has been on for over eight years, with no destination in sight.

Before going into recounting my role in the OPL 245 affair, there is a need to rehash the advent of the deal.

Gen. Sani Abacha, the military Head of State from 1993 to 1998, had introduced a policy of indigenous participation in the upstream sector of the Nigerian oil and gas industry. The industry had hitherto been over-whelmingly dominated by foreigners. The new policy, tagged 'Indigenous Exploration Programme', allowed Gen. Abacha to allocate oil blocks to indig-enous companies on a discretionary basis. He lowered the entry point into the industry by fixing the signature bonus at a heavily discounted amount of $20 million. Nigerian companies were required to develop the oil blocks in partnership with International Oil Companies (IOCs) which would act as 'technical partners'. Notable beneficiaries of that policy were Malabu Oil & Gas Ltd. (OPL 245), South Atlantic Petroleum Ltd (Akpo, OPL 246), and Famfa Oil Ltd (Agbami, 216/217), with Mr 'Mohammed Sani', Lt. Gen. T.Y. Danjuma and Mrs Folorunsho Alakija, respectively, as their alter egos.

Malabu was, on 9 April 1998, allocated OPL 245 in the ultra-deep waters of the Niger Delta, reputed to be potentially very lucrative. Abacha died on 8 June 1998, less than two months after that allocation. Malabu had made a part-payment of $2,040,000 for the signature bonus and had, in March 2000, approached Shell to uptake 40 per cent equity stake in the oil block. It offered Shell a 'farm-in' proposal, an arrangement that would see the multinational oil company bear Malabu's share of the cost of acquisition, exploration and development, in addition to its own costs. Basically, it would have the same effect as Shell lending money to Malabu to pay for its own 60 per cent share of the costs. Shell would recover the 'loan' from Malabu's share of oil production. Shell, despite confirming from the Department of Petroleum Resources (DPR) – the industry regulator – that the award papers were genuine and that OPL 245 was not among those revoked by President Obasanjo, decided against Malabu's farm-in proposal.

In October 2000, Malabu returned to Shell with the same offer. After reportedly confirming that there would be no objection to its involvement in the oil block, Shell finally entered into an agreement with Malabu. It set up Shell Ultra Deep Limited (SNUD) as the technical partner for OPL 245 and took up 40 per cent participating interest in the venture. After a Joint Operation Agreement was signed by Malabu and SNUD, the Federal Government issued Malabu the Oil Prospecting Licence (OPL) No. 245, dated 15 May 2001 and effective from 29 April 1998, the original date of award. The title deed was forwarded to Malabu via a letter dated 24 May 2001.

On 2 July 2001, exactly five weeks later, Obasanjo revoked that licence without stating any reasons. The suspicion then, though unconfirmed, was that Obasanjo discovered that 'Mohammed Sani', who owned 50 per cent of Malabu, was actually Mohammed Sani Abacha, son of the former Head of State, while Kweku Amafegha, who owned 30 per cent of it, was standing in for, or was actually, Chief Dan Etete, who was Minister of Petroleum when the oil block was awarded. It would appear, too, that because of the richness of the oil block, some powerful persons in government were beginning to develop an interest in it too. All these are educated conjectures, since government never offered any reasons for the revocation.

In April 2002, less than a year after the revocation, the Federal Government invited ExxonMobil and Shell to bid for OPL 245 as contractors – in a Production Sharing Contract (PSC) with the Nigerian National Petroleum Corporation (NNPC), the national oil company. Shell was awarded the contract eventually. This created a problem. One, Malabu and SNUD, a special vehicle of Shell, had signed an agreement for the development of the oil block before Obasanjo revoked the licence. Two, SNUD already had inside knowledge of the oil block, having served as technical partners to Malabu. Three, Malabu, from indications, suspected that Shell induced the Federal Government to revoke the licence. A crisis was inevitable.

Under the new agreement, Shell was to pay a signature bonus of $210 million. The previous price of $20 million was concessionary to Malabu, but that out of the way, the special rate was no longer applicable. Shell agreed to pay the signature bonus but deposited only $1 million into the account of the Federal Government of Nigeria on 23 December 2003. It paid the balance of $209 million into an escrow account at JP Morgan Chase Bank, London, jointly operated by Shell and the Federal Government of Nigeria. It appeared that Shell expected some legal challenge by Malabu over the revocation, hence the payment of the balance of the signature bonus into an escrow account. I suspect that if Shell was convinced that the Federal Government had done the proper thing, it would have made the entire payment into the coffers of government, not into an escrow account.

• • •

Consequently, Malabu, not surprisingly, petitioned the House of Representatives Committee on Petroleum Resources against the revocation. The Committee conducted a public hearing and concluded that the revocation of the block from Malabu, and its subsequent reallocation to Shell, was done in bad faith. The Committee declared the transaction null and void. The House of Representatives passed a resolution that the oil block should be returned to Malabu. Government refused to comply with the directive. Malabu also filed a suit at the Federal High Court in Abuja, in 2003, to assert its claims to OPL 245. The case went on for three years before it was struck out on 16 March 2006.

Dissatisfied, Malabu appealed against the decision. While the case was pending before the Court of Appeal, the Federal Government, still under President Obasanjo, retreated and agreed to settle out of court and to return OPL 245 to Malabu. The company withdrew its appeal based on that olive branch. The out-of-court settlement was subsequently reduced to a consent judgment of the Federal High Court, Abuja, when Chief Bayo Ojo was the AGF. The terms of the agreement were basically that OPL 245 should be returned to Malabu, but that the company would then pay the revised signature bonus of $210 million, less the $2 million it had earlier paid as advance on the discretionary $20 million fee. That Settlement Agreement was dated 30 November 2006. In it were detailed all the conditions to be met by all parties.

Dr Edmund Daukoru, who was then the Minister of State for Petroleum Resources, in a letter dated 2 December 2006 which he wrote on behalf of

President Obasanjo, the *de facto* Minister of Petroleum Resources, conveyed the decision to return the block 100 per cent to Malabu.

He wrote:

In the Spirit of an amicable settlement and without any admission of liability for an alleged wrongful, unlawful, unjust or any like conduct, the Federal Government of Nigeria (hereinafter referred to as 'FGN') agrees to re-allocate the oil block known as and covered by Oil Prospecting Licence 245 to Malabu Oil and Gas Limited (herein referred to as 'Malabu') within 30 (thirty) days from the date of this agreement;

(ii) The signature bonus in respect of OPL 245 shall be the sum of US$210,000,000 (Two Hundred and Ten Million US Dollars) payable by Malabu to the FGN. In this regard, the FGN acknowledges that Malabu had hitherto paid the sum of US$2,040,000 (Two Million and Forty Thousand US Dollars) to the FGN in respect of this Oil Block which sum shall be deducted from the aforesaid signature bonus leaving a balance of US$207,960,000 (Two Hundred and Seven Million, Nine Hundred and Sixty Thousand Dollars) to be paid by Malabu to the FGN within 12 (twelve) months from the date of the re-instatement of OPL 245 to Malabu;

(iii) The parties agree that Malabu shall, if it so desires, be at liberty to assign OPL 245 or any part thereof in accordance with the provisions of the Petroleum Act;

(iv) Pursuant to this Agreement and in consideration of the foregoing, Malabu hereby forever and absolutely discharges and releases the FGN, its Officers, Agents, Agencies and Privies howsoever described or any person acting for and or on its behalf, from all claims or demands which Malabu has or may have and from all actions, proceedings, obligations, liabilities, losses and damages brought, made, incurred, sustained or suffered by Malabu now or in the future relating to, arising from or however connected with the withdrawal or revocation by the FGN from Malabu of OPL 245;

(v) The parties agree that these terms of settlement shall be made the judgment of the Court.

Shell opted to fight back. On 30 April 2009, it commenced investor-state arbitral proceedings against the Federal Government at the International Centre for the Settlement of Investment Disputes (ICSID), an organ of the World Bank, in Washington DC, claiming at least $2 billion in compensation and damages from Nigeria for alleged breach of contract. It invoked the Bilateral Investment Treaty (BIT) between Nigeria and the Netherlands. It also filed a suit against the Federal Government at the Federal High Court, Abuja, contending that SNUD had the exclusive right to operate OPL 245 as the contractor. It claimed to have spent about$535 million on the block before hitting oil in commercial quantity — and before the subsequent revocation in 2006. With the resultant impasse, high-level meetings were held and several proposals were made to break the deadlock but none was acceptable to the contending parties.

When I reviewed the documents, I found that it was once proposed by President Obasanjo that the interests of NNPC, SNUD and Malabu should be accommodated in the following way: SNUD would be the Contractor-Operator; NNPC would be the Concessionaire Equity Rights holder; and Malabu would hold Concessionaire Equity Interests. That appeared like the middle-of-the-road path to peace, but Malabu would have none of it. As far as it was concerned, it owned the oil block 100 per cent and SNUD could not be imposed as a contractor. It insisted that the 30 November 2006 Settlement Agreement was the basis on which it withdrew its law suit. That engendered deadlock.

On 11 May 2007, Dr Daukoru wrote to President Obasanjo proposing that a committee made of himself, the AGF, the Group Managing Director of the NNPC, the DPR and external solicitors should negotiate with the feuding parties. This was less than three weeks to the end of the Obasanjo Administration and, not surprisingly, nothing came out of it. Everything went back to square one as President Umaru Musa Yar'Adua took the reins of power. He set up an inter-ministerial committee headed by his AGF, Chief Michael Aondoakaa, to look into the issue. Shell's arbitral proceedings at ICSID continued in the meantime.

Perhaps wary of the fact that such an enormously endowed oil block was 'wasting', Shell at some point offered to pay Malabu $500 million in compensation, in addition to giving the Nigerian company some percentage of shares in the block. Malabu appeared interested in the offer but President Yar'Adau did not act on it. It was also possible that because of his ill health, he could not attend to the lingering issue. The new agreement had not been signed when Yar'Adua died on 5 May 2010.

President Jonathan then assumed office. And Malabu wrote to seek the implementation of the 2006 Consent Judgment. And I, as the AGF, was asked to offer legal advice. And I did. And that was how my face came to appear in the OPL 245 picture.

• • •

Because of the controversial nature of the OPL 245 issue, I personally went through all the documents relating to the matter in order to be able to advise the President appropriately. I read the correspondence, the agreements, the court documents, the report of the public hearing by the House of Representatives, as well as letters written by lawyers at different stages. It took my team over one week to come to a conclusion and make a recommendation to President Jonathan. Weighing all the options, my team and I did our best to offer what we considered to be the right course of action for the country. I then wrote to President Jonathan advising that the Settlement Agreement of 30 November 2006 was a subsisting agreement which had already been reduced to a Consent Judgment of the Federal High Court and was, therefore, enforceable.

But there was something else.

Shell still had a claim against Nigeria, and there was the likelihood that the arbitral tribunal could award heavy damages in the range of $2 billion against the Federal Government. This was more so as it appeared Shell had reasonable assurances from the Federal Government in 2002 that it would be allocated OPL 245. This might have informed its decision to proceed to de-risk the block. Without such assurances, Shell would not have had any claim against Nigeria. Thus, when the Federal Government revoked the oil block in 2006 and gave it back to Malabu with a promise to give Shell another oil block of commensurate value, Shell refused the offer and relied on its de-risking OPL 245 to ground its arbitral claim for damages. Shell considered the reallocation of the oil block to Malabu as an expropriation of its asset, hence making it an investor/state arbitration.

These were the knotty issues on the table when I advised the President. He agreed with the opinion, approved the implementation of the Settlement Agreement, and directed it to the Minister of Petroleum Resources, Mrs Diezani Alison-Madueke, and myself for implementation. Mrs Alison-Madueke then issued the licence to Malabu, directing it to pay the signature bonus of $210 million within a period of 180 days. Malabu began the search for technical partners. It was no longer willing to do business with Shell because of the apparent breakdown of trust between them following the revocation of the licence in 2002.

On the other hand, Shell had used its dominant position in the oil industry to issue a caveat to other IOCs that it had an interest in OPL 245. This prevented other IOCs from pursuing any interest in the oil block or entering into a working relationship with Malabu. Effectively, Malabu could not move forward. Neither could Shell. It was a case of who would blink first.

After OPL 245 was returned to Malabu through the "Block 245 Malabu Resolution Agreement" dated 29 April 2011, Agip-Eni S.p.A. of Italy began to show interest in partnering with the Nigerian company. Eni approached the government to confirm if the allocation to Malabu was genuine. This was confirmed. Eni then approached Shell with a proposal to partner and jointly acquire the oil block from Malabu. The Italian company came back with Shell and informed the Federal Government that although they wanted to jointly acquire OPL 245 from Malabu, the crisis of confidence between Malabu and Shell made it inescapable that a third party was needed to help broker the deal.

It was this atmosphere of mutual suspicion that necessitated the intervention of the Federal Government. If there had been no such suspicion, the involvement of the Federal Government would have been limited to giving consent to Malabu to assign the oil block to Shell and Eni. The rest of the transaction, including all payments to Malabu, would have been conducted without the involvement of the Federal Government. This singular factor unleashed a series of events that would later draw global attention to OPL 245 and lead to criminal proceedings in various jurisdictions.

The Federal Government agreed to midwife a settlement between Shell and Malabu on the condition that Shell would withdraw the arbitral proceedings against Nigeria. Shell, in compliance with our demands, terminated the arbitration. Shell had been confident that it would be awarded billions of dollars against Nigeria in arbitration. This thought left me uneasy as the parties kept pulling the Federal Government into becoming more entangled in their deal.

All the parties came together and negotiated directly in 2011. A committee was constituted involving officials of NNPC, DPR, the Federal Inland Revenue Service (FIRS), State House Counsel, and officials of the Ministry of Justice. They deliberated for over three days, successfully negotiating all the terms. They then produced the draft agreements for the consideration and signature of the parties.

I recall that Mr Andrew Obaje, who was then Director of DPR, objected to some parts of the draft agreement which I had sent to him for his comments. His objections were duly considered, especially because DPR, as the industry regulator, had not participated in the negotiations between Shell, Agip-Eni and Malabu. As a follow-up to Obaje's observations, an inter-ministerial committee was constituted with three representatives from DPR to deal with the issues he raised and to ensure that the agreements were truly in the national interest. The resolutions of the Committee formed the basis of the Resolution Agreement dated 29 April 2011. Conveniently, those assailing the integrity of the resolution continue to say Obaje opposed it without reflecting the fact that an inter-ministerial committee was set up and DPR was part and parcel of the final Resolution Agreement that was executed. This is one of the false narratives being repeated again and again by the "anti-corruption campaigners."

In summary, the terms of the Malabu/SNUD Resolution Agreement were that: Malabu waived all interests and rights in OPL 245 and agreed that it should be reallocated to another entity; SNUD agreed that its interest in the oil block be reallocated to Shell Nigeria Exploration and Production Company (SNEPCo), who would reimburse SNUD all costs thus far, including the $335,600,000 incurred by SNUD under the PSC with NNPC in 2003; the Federal Government of Nigeria reallocated OPL 245 to SNEPCo and Eni (known in Nigeria as the Nigerian Agip Exploration Ltd, NAE); and the new licence would be for a ten-year duration and would be converted to an Oil Mining Lease (OML) upon the commencement of oil production.

The other notable terms in the Reallocation Agreement were that Shell would pay a signature bonus to the Federal Government as determined in the Resolution Agreement; the reallocation of OPL 245 would effectively terminate the 2003 PSC between SNUD and NNPC, and the $207,960,000 deposited in an Escrow account by Shell Petroleum Development Company

(SDPC) would be paid to the Federal Government as signature bonus for the reallocation of OPL 245 to SNEPCo and NAE; an escrow account would be opened in the names of the Federal Government of Nigeria and Malabu at JP Morgan Chase in London; NAE would pay an agreed sum into the account, the bulk to be transferred by the Federal Government to Malabu as its pay-off for giving up OPL 245, and a fraction as additional bonus to the Federal Government; NAE and SNEPCO would execute the PSC for OPL 245; and all pending suits and arbitration would be withdrawn by all parties.

The projected effect of the agreement was that Malabu sold OPL 245 to Shell/Eni S.p.A for $1.1 billion (exactly $1,092,040,000) as "full and final settlement" of all claims, interests or rights relating to OPL 245, with the Federal Government serving as an obligor, since Malabu had agreed to settle and waive all claims to the block.

After the requisite presidential approval was obtained, the final Resolution Agreement was signed on 29 April 2011 by the Minister of Petroleum Resources, Mrs Alison-Madueke, the Minister of Finance, Dr Olusegun Aganga, and myself as the Attorney-General of the Federation and Minister of Justice. The Group Managing Director of NNPC, Mr Austin Oniwon, and all the Ministries, Departments and Agencies (MDAs) with oversight over the transaction were all duly represented. This was well captured in the proceedings of the public hearing conducted by the House of Representatives in 2013. I was satisfied that we all played our respective roles to give effect to the directives/approvals of the President.

As usual, the President was duly briefed about the transaction and the $210 million signature bonus that was to be paid, which Shell had warehoused since 2002 in an escrow account jointly managed by it and the Federal Government. Shell wrote to convey its satisfaction with the agreement. It signed off its own portion of the instruction that the Federal Government should take the $209 million in the escrow account, in addition to the $1 million it had paid in 2001. The Minister of State for Finance, Dr Yerima Lawan Ngama, and the Accountant-General of the Federation, Mr Otunla Jonah Ogunniyi, signed off their own portions after the approval of the President.

On 4 May 2011, an escrow agreement was concluded between the Federal Government of Nigeria, NAE, SNEPCo and JP Morgan Chase Bank. NAE and SNEPCo were required to transfer into the escrow account the sum of $1,092,040,000, which was to be used by the Federal Government for the purposes of settling all existing claims in respect of OPL 245. From the records, NAE transferred the sum of $1,092,040,000 into the escrow account on 24 May 2011.

• • •

There was a yet-budding crisis. One of my earliest lessons in government was never to underestimate any problem. The simplest issue could get compli-cated rather quickly, and like a little yeast, could spread *ad infintum*. With the agreement signed and sealed, and with all parties smiling and shaking hands and patting each other on the back, I was of the mistaken belief that my own job as the Attorney-General was done, and that it was time to direct my concentration to other matters of state.

But in August 2011, my attention was drawn to the fact that Malabu had problems with two companies: Energy Ventures Partners Limited, a British Virgin Island Company, and International Legal Consulting Limited, a Russian Company. Energy Ventures had sued Malabu for $200 million together with costs of $15 million in a British court. The Russian company had also sued Malabu for $75 million in England. Both companies claimed to have been consultants or middlemen to Malabu in the transaction and were demanding their fees.

At this stage, I, as the Attorney-General of the Federation, was contacted by JP Morgan for direction. The bank had been served with a court order restraining it from disbursing $290 million from the money in the escrow account. I advised the bank to comply with the orders of the court pending the final determination of the matter. As there was no restraining order on the balance of $801 million, I advised that it could be paid to the beneficial owners. That was the legal and responsible thing to do.

JP Morgan deposited $215 million into the High Court of Justice in England in respect of the Energy Ventures' suit and withheld $75 million awaiting the outcome of litigation by International Legal Consulting. On 17 August 2011, officials of the Ministry of Finance and the Accountant-General of the Federation instructed JP Morgan to transfer $401,540,000 to Malabu's account at First Bank of Nigeria Plc. and $400 million to Malabu's account at Keystone Bank Ltd of Nigeria.

Thereafter, one Lawal Abba came up from nowhere, claiming that he was representing the interest of a former vice-president and the Abacha family. According to him, they all had stakes in OPL 245. He demanded that when the proceeds of the sale of OPL 245 were made to Malabu, we should ensure that the Abachas were also paid for their interest. I found his demand preposterous, because as Attorney-General of the Federation, I didn't have the legal standing to interfere in what I considered to be an individual or at best a shareholder dispute. I reasoned that this was surely a dispute that involved the asset of a private company that could be resolved at a meeting of the company. Where no agreement was reached, the aggrieved party could seek judicial remedies in court.

Then in May 2011, the law firm of A.A. Umar & Co. brought a letter signed by Aliyu Umar, its Principal Partner, informing me that they were lawyers to one Mohammed Sani, whom they asserted was a shareholder in Malabu, and further alleged that Malabu's ownership structure had been altered without authorisation. From the look of things, there was an internal issue in the company. Although Etete had become the public face of Malabu as far back as 2001, Umar claimed that 'Mohammed Sani' had been short-changed by other shareholders and requested the Federal Government to intervene to bring the shareholders to the table to resolve the matter 'amicably'. He also threatened that if we did not ensure that Malabu paid 'Mohammed Sani', they would embarrass the government.

I dismissed the threat as inconsequential. Ordinarily, the government was not supposed to have been involved in the Malabu/Shell/Eni negotiation in the first place. It had felt compelled to do so in order to make Shell withdraw its $2 billion arbitration claim against Nigeria and also to get OPL 245 back on course. It should have stopped at resolving the long drawn-out dispute between Malabu and the Federal Government on the ownership of OPL 245. Having restored the OPL to Malabu in compliance with the 2006 Consent Judgment, the government had discharged its responsibility. Beyond the regulatory oversight, there wasn't more left for it to do.

Therefore, if Malabu had internal problems, that was not the business of the government. The Federal Government of Nigeria did not own Malabu. Shareholders' disputes were private to the companies concerned and the courts were there to adjudicate on issues, if no agreement could be reached amicably. Thus, if there were allegations of falsification of records, that would be the responsibility of relevant law enforcement agencies to investigate and deal with accordingly. The Federal Government could not be resolving internal matters in companies it did not own. Nor was I working for Malabu. I was neither their lawyer nor an arbitrator in their dispute. My duty was to

Nigeria and I had discharged my responsibility to the best of my knowledge. I had finished my assignment and had to move on.

From that moment on, articles sponsored against me practically flooded the media. I was not in the country when the first article was published. The Solicitor-General did a rejoinder, which he ran as an advert in the newspapers, explaining the nature of the transactions to Nigerians. I was later made to understand that the Abacha family had 50 per cent of OPL 245 which was awarded while Abacha was Head of State. As I told Mohammed Abacha, if I knew they actually owned 50 per cent of the company as they claimed, I would have got a court order to forfeit those shares to the Federal Government in accordance with the dictates of Decree No. 53.

Under Decree No. 53 made during the administration of Gen. Abdulsalami Abubakar, the Abachas were made to disclose all their assets and liabilities and forfeit them to the Federal Government. They were supposed to be transparent about that. In other words, they were in violation of that decree by not declaring their interest in OPL 245. It was unfortunate that I was not aware of it until the settlement had been completed. Since I refused to accede to their request, the Abachas set off an avalanche of attacks on the OPL 245 settlements – true to their threats – just to tarnish my reputation. They also orchestrated bogus public hearings and all manner of sponsored articles in pursuit of their quest.

One day, Mohammed came and informed me that they were behind the public hearing by the House of Representatives and that if they could get one or two concessions from me, they would stop it. I told him to go ahead with the public hearing. I had no concessions to grant him. I made it clear to him that my actions were not as a result of any ill feelings towards him, but in discharge of my duties as the AGF.

Meanwhile, Lawal Abba also came to tell me that his principal said if I could help him get what he wanted, I would get a share. I also declined his offer and reiterated my position that their claim was at best a shareholder dispute which was beyond my call of duty. But because he was essentially a commission agent, he probably thought that it was impossible for a public officer to turn down that kind of offer. He probably then concluded that my refusal was because the other party had offered me more money.

I found it surprising that he would think that way, considering he had sought to influence me in like manner in the past but in vain. He ought to have known me better! During the probe of the Yar'Adua Expressway contract, there were allegations that Julius Berger inflated the contract. I was a member of the Committee that investigated it. The then Secretary to the Government of the Federation, Alhaji Yayale Ahmed, a very respectable man, asked me to write the Committee's report. Lawal Abba approached me to say that he knew the powers-that-be at Julius Berger, and that if we wrote a favourable report, I would be 'rewarded'. I told him off. He should have known that the uncomplicated event would have been an easier inducement to accept than in the case of OPL 245. If I wasn't amenable on that occasion, what convinced him I would be on the subsequent one? It was, indeed, baffling!

While this controversy raged, I prepared a comprehensive position paper on the OPL Settlement and sent it to the heads of EFCC and ICPC in order to fully brief them on the transactions, especially in view of the orchestrated media campaigns by those who were determined to impugn the transaction. I had nothing to hide and was glad that the anti-graft agencies informed me that they were convinced I did nothing wrong. At that juncture, I had prepared my mind to expect aspersions to be cast on my person. I knew dirt would be hurled at me. It was the price to pay for being a public officer. It is the burden of service. But, like Atlas, I was poised to bear my burden with equanimity.

• • •

CHAPTER SEVEN

THE WITCH-HUNT

We were in our last days in office. President Jonathan had lost his re-election bid and was preparing to hand over to the President-elect, Gen. Muhammadu Buhari. The handover ceremony was nine days away – 29 May 2015 – when an operative of the Department of State Services (DSS), Nigeria's secret police, walked up to me at the Presidential Villa as I arrived for one of the meetings preparatory to our exit from government.

In a rather soft but stern tone, he cautioned me that I should leave Nigeria before 29 May because, according to him, 'they' were coming for me. I reflected on what had happened in the last five years while I was in office, and as far as I was concerned, there was nothing I had done in office that could not be defended, and so I decided to dismiss the caution at that time. I did not think that the incoming government of President Buhari that had promised 'change' would try to do anything that would undermine the rule of law. However, the security agent returned to me with the same message, reiterating the need for me to leave the country latest by 28 May.

On the morning of 28 May, I was back to the Presidential Villa. The same operative drew me to a corner and begged me to run for my life. He desperately pleaded with me to leave the country that day. To allay his fears, I assured him that I had already booked my flight. I could tell he was not convinced. The disappointment on his face was plain. Indeed, in the evening, I was again at the Villa for the dissolution of FEC. The operative saw me again and declared in alarm: *"Oga, you've not left?"* He dismissed my attempted excuse and stubbornly insisted that I leave the country by 29 May.

On the morning of 29 May, I went to the Nnamdi Azikiwe International Airport in the company of the National Security Adviser, retired Col. Sambo Dasuki, to await the arrival of President Jonathan. Vice-President Namadi Sambo joined us shortly before the arrival of the President. While waiting for him, I noticed that some mischief was afoot. First, the holding room, where the President usually sat pre-departure, was locked up. That was patently out of place.

President Jonathan was supposed to get to the airport after the handover ceremony and was scheduled to use that waiting room before his flight. But by the time he arrived, the official that was supposed to open the place had disappeared. The environment was hostile. And we weren't even up to three hours out of office, at the maximum! I was very downcast. That experience sent some shivers down my spine and for the first time, tears dropped from my eyes. I went to my residence after Jonathan's departure.

After running into the same security officer for the umpteenth time, I was forced to think that, perhaps, God was the one speaking to me through him.

"I beg of you," he pleaded, becoming quite emotional, "please leave tonight."

Picking up my bag, I went to the Nnamdi Azikiwe International Airport, Abuja, and bought a Lufthansa ticket and left Nigeria. It was supposed to be for a few weeks, but it turned into months and years.

• • •

Before the 2015 elections, I had made up my mind to go back to school, whether or not President Jonathan got a second term in office. I opted to study Public International Law since I was an elected member of the International Law Commission. After the election, I got the admission and went on to study for the Advanced LLM in Public International Law with specialisation in International Criminal Law at the University of Leiden, the Netherlands, starting August 2015.

In November 2015, Mr Ibrahim Magu was appointed Acting Chairman of EFCC. Soon enough, I got a call from the Director of Public Prosecution of the Federation (DPPF) at the Ministry of Justice. He said the Office of the Solicitor-General was in possession of a letter from the EFCC inviting me for questioning in connection with OPL 245. I found it curious, funny and suspicious that I was being summoned by the EFCC, whereas they could have contacted my successor in office who had access to the files. Government is a continuum, after all. More so, I had already sent a comprehensive brief on the OPL 245 transaction, unsolicited, to the EFCC while I was in office, which they received with satisfaction.

As a law-abiding citizen, however, I got my lawyers to write to the EFCC stating that I was preparing for my examination and would not be able to honour their invitation. I promised to do so around 28 December 2015, by which time I hoped to be done with the exams.

But before the invitation, I had received a call from a friend who said that one George Ugboh, an ex-convict in the US, had approached him that he had some information on me and was told that my friend was the only person that could link us up. My friend promptly dismissed him with the admonition that my stewardship while serving as AGF was properly documented and that I was capable of defending my actions.

Another of my aides also received a request to talk me into "settling" the EFCC operatives in order to avert "serious problems." Although he said he found the request funny, he was compelled to pass the information to me all the same. I reassured him he had nothing to worry about, emphasising that I had no money to give to anyone. But that put me on the alert. By 21 December, having finished my exams, I chose to take my family on a well-deserved vacation to Dubai. I wanted to reward them for the time lost while I served in government.

The plan was that I would proceed to Nigeria from Dubai, visit the EFCC and return by 2 January 2016 to resume my studies. I booked my ticket to be in Nigeria on 27 December. While in Dubai, I kept getting credible calls from Nigeria warning about a plot to humiliate or even eliminate me, which I still did not take seriously. I prepared to travel as planned, never for one minute imagining that what they insinuated was possible in Nigeria. I assured myself that we were running a constitutional democracy, not a military dictatorship.

In the evening of 26 December, one of my sons drew my attention to a news flash from *Sahara Reporters*, a news website which is unofficially affiliated to the EFCC and which serves as the media trial arm of the agency. It said: "Former AGF Adoke to honour EFCC invitation on December 28, to be arrested, detained and charged to court." That was so precise. This bit of news jolted all of us in the family. The children were alarmed and insisted that I should not honour such an invitation whose sole aim appeared to be my humiliation. Inasmuch as I wanted to return home to honour that invitation, I was compelled to listen to the plea of my family.

Quite fortuitously, the lawyer that I had asked to write to the EFCC to say that I would be honouring their invitation called to inform me that the agency had been calling to confirm if I was still coming as scheduled. The desperation was alarming. He observed the rather heightened level of excitement within the EFCC. He had a premonition that it might not be any ordinary invitation. That was how I finally resolved to stay back and watch as events unfolded.

On 27 December 2015, I ran into Vice-President (VP) Yemi Osinbajo at the lobby of the Kempinski Hotel in Dubai while I went to visit a friend. I couldn't believe my luck. I greeted him and he received me very warmly. He was very pleasant. I told him I had been hoping to see him, so I used that opportunity to secure an appointment. He asked his ADC to arrange the meeting. I took advantage of the proposed meeting to prepare a detailed brief for him.

I further sent a letter with all necessary attachments to the VP through Senator Andy Uba. These were acknowledged by the VP. I also copied the Director-General of DSS and the Office of the Attorney-General of the Federation. I took these precautions mindful of the funny games that were at play at the Ministry of Justice, especially during the period when Yola held sway pending the appointment of a new Minister. I was told that the EFCC came to the Ministry of Justice in search of the files on the OPL 245 transaction and Halliburton bribery scandal. They were, however, given the impression that I must have carted the files away. It took the intervention of my former confidential secretary, Mrs Clementina Ogunniyi, to debunk the claim. She was able to show from the records that Yola had requested for the files and that they were in his custody. The files subsequently surfaced from his office.

I was long aware of the friendship between Lawal Abba and Yola, but became particularly apprehensive about their closeness because of Abba's demonstrable interest in the Malabu transaction. When, therefore, I heard that I was alleged to have taken away the files, I concluded that it had to be the handiwork of Abba. Indeed, Abba was reported to have gone to town bragging that I was mistaken if I thought my briefing the VP would avail me any succour. He claimed that they had already reached the VP and that he was hand in glove with them. I was surprised he knew about my encounter with the VP.

I had been informed that investigators from Milan had already visited President Buhari over the Malabu issue and that he had referred the matter to the VP. I was confident that since Prof. Osinbajo was not only a Senior Advocate of Nigeria but had also handled similar transactions (the Enron power project, for instance) during his tenure as Attorney-General of Lagos State, he was in a position to dispassionately review the Malabu transaction, especially with respect to the role I played as the Attorney-General of the Federation, in order to appropriately advise the government. As it turned out, my optimism was misplaced! I never heard from the VP again.

My not returning to Nigeria was, therefore, informed by my belief that the invitation extended to me was in bad faith. There was a grand, sinister design. It was not about assisting the EFCC with investigations. In any event, all documents related to the Malabu transactions were available in the files.

Actually, I discovered that an operative of the EFCC had been stationed around my house to alert them if I arrived without being noticed. Some operatives were waiting at the airport also. I was not to be allowed to enter my house if I came through the airport route. I was to be whisked away and taken into detention. But if I came by some other route, the operative at my house was to inform them so that they could come and grab me with a lot of media publicity.

These highly credible pieces of information filtering to me made it imperative that I had to take measured steps and be strategic in my approach to the issue. I was not going to allow my traducers to permanently silence me without an opportunity to tell my own side of the story. This required rational thinking, especially as I was already a victim of orchestrated media attacks by the EFCC.

I was still battling to understand the game when an official of the Ministry of Justice confirmed to me the definite plot to witch-hunt me over the Malabu issue. However, he said somebody was requesting that if I could come up with $3 million, they would take me to see a certain 'big woman' in the Presidential Villa. I would also be accorded access to the VP and others. I was to rest assured that it would be the end of the matter. To my query regarding where I was expected to find that amount of money, his reply was that "no matter how small," I should find "something." This was a man accused of taking a bribe of $2 million being asked to pay a $3 million bribe to close the case! Obviously, they must have believed I was a more virulent thief than they imagined. Just like the stranger at Schiphol Airport.

However, I was later made to understand that this was the standard protocol that was used to extort money from Ministers that served in the Jonathan Administration. They would be harassed and someone would offer them reprieve only if they were willing to part with large sums of money. As for me, I knew I had not gone beyond the presidential directives in the implementation of the OPL 245 Settlement Agreement and had no cause to seek reprieve from anyone. In any case, I didn't have money stashed away to pay for protection. I, therefore, resolved to ignore such entreaties from the agents of the EFCC and fight my traducers with nothing but the truth.

• • •

The desire to humiliate me knew no bounds. One day, at the library of the International Court of Justice in The Hague, I instinctively felt an urge to go home. I usually took two tram rides. During my first ride, I suddenly became conscious of the fact that someone was trailing me. Indeed, there was a young man that appeared to stick to my peripheral vision. I became alert. The second tram stop was right in front of my house. When I got off and noticed that the suspicious young man remained on board, I thought perhaps I was becoming paranoid.

But as I made my way through the electric gate of my residence into the common area, I heard a quiet: "Excuse me." The man flashed his badge. He was from the Fiscal Information and Investigation Service (FIOD), the Dutch anti-fraud agency. Before I could take that in, two more persons had joined him, seemingly out of nowhere. They were detailed to search my house. That was the first Gestapo-like experience of my life. I let them into my house. They refused to let me answer my phone when it rang. They requested that I switch it off.

"Can I call my embassy?" I asked.

"Not at the moment," they responded.

"Can I call my lawyer?" I made a second request.

"No," they responded.

There, they had made the first tactical mistake, but then I kept mum about it. I wasn't going to argue with them about the fact that it was my fundamental right to call a lawyer. They took my laptops and my iPad which I was using for my academic work. After some time, an Italian investigator joined them, followed by some Dutchmen. Finally, the young man that was in the tram showed up. I was psychologically destabilised.

"What exactly are you looking for?" I summoned the courage to ask.

Money laundering and corruption investigation, they claimed.

I kept quiet but I could feel my blood pressure shoot up. I was allowed to take my drugs. I could even eat if I wanted, they said. They were very patient.

"What are you waiting for?" I asked.

They were waiting for the judge.

"What is the matter?" I then asked pointedly.

They said they were investigating OPL 245.

Then the judge arrived. Her opening comment was to the effect that she was sure I had been informed about why they were in my house. She asked me if I had any money or documents at home.

"Yes, I have plenty money and documents," I told her.

The excitement on their faces was discernible! They were about to make a catch! The EFCC had informed them that I stole millions of dollars and, therefore, had a lot of money! The EFCC had put their media troops on standby, waiting to break the news that an operation was going on in my house in The Hague and that they were about to catch a corrupt former public officer with huge sums of money. I took the investigators to the cloak room and showed them my coin box. In it was roughly €60 in coins.

"That's the money," I told them.

"No, no, no, not this kind of money," they protested. I told them that was all I had at home.

Then I said: "You are looking for documents on OPL 245? Then come with me."

I took them upstairs. I still had three bundles left from the 12 bundles I had prepared and distributed earlier to various agencies and individuals. They were going to take away the three bundles, but I protested. The reason they found any bundle with me was because the others didn't collect everything. The judge advised that they should collect only one bundle. But they refused. It took the intervention of my lawyers before the two other bundles were later returned to me.

It turned out that the Dutch authorities had been misinformed by the Nigerian Government that I owned the house. That was a most unfair lie. The Embassy was aware that I had rented the property, and with their assistance too. In fact, the Embassy introduced me to the housing agent from whom I leased the accommodation. The investigators were shocked when they saw the lease agreement and discovered that it was a rented accommodation.

They took my credit cards, screened them immediately and returned them to me immediately. The cards had saved my life. If it hadn't been for them, I was sure I would have died of hunger in The Hague. Yet, by EFCC propaganda, I was supposed to have corruptly enriched myself to the tune of about

$800 million, or $1.1 billion, or $2.2 million, depending on the version of the story that caught the tale-bearer's fancy.

The investigators stripped the house clean and found nothing. They said I should sign that they took some documents. They took my bank statement, which showed that I had about €18,000 in my account. Of the €18,000, the school had transferred €15,000 to me. For the Dutch to issue you a student visa, you must show evidence that you have transferred your maintenance allowance for the duration of your studies to the school that offered you admission. The school will then transfer the money back to you once you have opened an account in the Netherlands.

The experience of the search left me traumatised for days. I was glad the EFCC media troops were disappointed, and in my view, disgraced. Shamelessly, though, they still reported a few lies but nothing compared to their expectations. Four days later, the investigators called to say they wanted to come and have a friendly chat with me. I had no problem with that, even though I insisted that my lawyer would be present. When my lawyer came, she said since I was under suspicion for money laundering and corruption, I had nothing to tell them. The lawyer, a brilliant young lady, said anytime they were ready for proper, formal investigation, they should let us know.

I later got a letter from the Italian prosecutor, Fabio De Pasquale, inviting me to Italy to be interviewed with regards to OPL 245. My lawyer got an Italian lawyer to reply, informing them that I was preparing for my exams and had no free period within which to make the trip. They opted to come to The Hague instead. On the appointed day, in May 2016, with my final exams behind me, the Dutch authorities indicated that I would be making a witness statement. I cooperated with them as best as I could.

I gave a witness statement on the first day. On continuing the second day, De Pasquale, the main prosecutor for the Italians, who was not at the inter-rogation meeting the previous day, opposed the Dutch investigators who had reiterated that I was continuing my testimony as a witness. He insisted I was under investigation by the EFCC and, therefore, a suspect. My lawyer then declared that the interrogation was over, that I would exercise my right to silence and would say nothing further.

De Pasquale, an arrogant and condescending fellow, accused me of not having respect for law officers. I told him if that was true, I wouldn't have cooperated with them in the first place. I stated that he was the one who went from interviewing me as a witness to branding me a suspect. I had the right to change my position too.

It was at that point he made a Freudian slip. He said: "It is all about your life!"

"My life?" I caught the edge of that utterance. I insisted that now that I had been made aware of the threat to my life, the Dutch authorities owed me the duty of protection. He realised the gravity of his statement. He looked embarrassed. At that point, I stood up and left, with my lawyer reiterating that I would not give any further testimony.

To the Dutch officials, I promised: "You have treated me very well. Any day, any time you need information from me, please call me and I will talk to you without the Italians." True to my word, I went out of my way to acquire and forward to them any document that I felt would be of assistance to them. I have not heard from them since then.

• • •

It was not just my residence in the Netherlands that was searched.

Sometime in 2016, my friend's wife called me frantically to warn me that security agents were searching my house in Abuja and that they were looking for money to prove that I was corrupt. She was distressed. I reassured her she had nothing to worry about. It later turned out that it was not even my house that was searched. Apparently, somebody misled them. They had, so far, successfully recovered money from residences of former government officials. Thinking I was one of those, they happily followed up on any lead that would 'expose' my hidden billions. It was laughable.

If, indeed, I had the kind of money they were talking about, I wouldn't have been living on handouts from friends in my self-exile. Before I came to office, I had a successful law practice. I was also an international arbitrator. The hounding by EFCC had ruined my legal practice. The negative stories had affected my position locally and internationally. I had suffered double jeopardy for serving my fatherland.

The witch-hunt continued unabated. On 12 April 2017, my house in Kano was subjected to another attack under the guise of a search. They had subjected an innocent person to media trial and must desperately search out evidence to justify their infamy! The EFCC operatives swooped on the house, purportedly acting on a tip-off by an imaginary whistle blower. They spent two hours at the house turning things upside down. They searched all the rooms, the ceiling, the water tank and even the septic tanks but found nothing.

I was informed by those who should know that the EFCC raid team was looking for documents on OPL 245. When President Obasanjo denied any knowledge of the Malabu Settlement Agreement executed during his tenure and a document surfaced in the media putting a lie to his claim, the authorities most likely believed the leak came from me. That gave them the false assurance that I still had documents that would implicate many others, including myself. They could not find anything.

Not satisfied, they invaded the home of my younger brother, Bashir, in Nagazi, Adavi Local Government Area, Kogi State, on 6 May 2017. They were described as 'unidentified gunmen' in media reports, but they were EFCC operatives, for sure. They were clad in black when they stormed the house in a Hilux van. They did not have a warrant; if they did, they didn't show it to anybody. They merely claimed they were looking for dollars. Perhaps, the famous $1.1 billion was in my brother's house! It was that ridiculous.

It was possibly another 'whistle blower' who gave them the fake lead. The security operatives beat up the caretaker of the house, most likely out of frustration – or out of drunken cruelty. They broke doors, shouting: "Where is money kept in this house?" They upturned the furniture and ransacked every part of the building in mad desperation. They vandalised everything when they could not get any cash. I did not steal any money. I did not collect any bribe. If they searched the whole world for the next 200 years, they would find nothing. Truth is constant. This is my truth.

The witch-hunt was becoming a pastime for them. On 14 July 2017, the baton of the never-ending search appeared to have been passed on to the Police. The EFCC was probably frustrated; perhaps they were finding it difficult to mask their too obvious witch-hunt as something noble or praiseworthy. It was policemen that were instructed to search my country home in Okene. There were about 20 police officers. They invaded my residence around 3 pm and left at 5 pm, with the same old and tired story: still in search of concrete evidence to justify my ongoing vilification in the media. They turned my house upside down and searched septic tanks (again!), but all they got was the stench of their iniquity. That was the fourth search.

They searched everywhere in the world looking for evidence to justify my persecution. They upended bank accounts and security fund accounts. They breezed through everything that could be traced to me in the world. Still they came up empty-handed. Money is arguably the easiest thing to follow in the world. Mohammed Bello Adoke was famed to have stolen his country dry, yet no one, both at home and abroad, could find any money! If indeed I stole, they wouldn't need a microscope to find evidence of the booty. Millions of dollars cannot disappear without trace. That is a natural fact.

Frustrated and fagged out, my traducers invented another strategy: to abduct me from abroad and haul me into Nigeria for castration! On 20 August 2017, I issued a statement raising an alarm about that new plot. The information I received was that on the orders of the Presidency (President Buhari was on sick leave at the time), the EFCC was working to abduct, detain and humiliate me for challenging my continuous persecution, intimidation and harassment. I was more convinced than ever that what I had been dealing with was not mere prosecution but persecution. I resolved to remain in self-imposed exile until I had certainty of a fair trial – if, indeed, I was properly accused of any crime.

I have ample evidence of the evil plan against me. At a restaurant outside the country, I met a young Nigerian who recognised me and revealed knowledge of the plot to eliminate me in Abuja between the airport and my residence if I had returned in December 2015 as I had promised the EFCC. The young man had even gone out of his way to pray for me not to return into the waiting arms of my killers. I could still feel his relief that my story did not end like that of many other Nigerians.

● ● ●

CHAPTER EIGHT

THE WITCH-HUNTERS

Chief among my purported infractions as a Minister was that I wielded too much power. I was accused of being too assertive in putting forward my viewpoints and arguments. I was said to be dogmatic and always insistent on my own interpretations of the law in giving legal advice to the government. I had long sensed that even many of my colleagues did not like my guts. Some of them accused me of arrogance. Those feelings were not unknown to me. My closeness to President Jonathan had further attracted envy and resentment. Meanwhile, outside of government, there were those who felt I had not employed the trappings of my office to their benefit while others felt that I had checkmated their greed.

After President Jonathan lost the 2015 elections, I was in no doubt that I was a marked man. Some of my colleague Ministers were going to tell the new government that Mrs Alison-Madueke and myself were President Jonathan's star Ministers. They curried favour using our names as bargaining chips, thinking that by so doing, they would be free of prosecution. However, all they sought was to be integrated into the new government, to get back on the gravy train no matter whom they had shot in the process. In fact, some of them defected to the All Progressives Congress (APC) as 'insurance' against arrest and prosecution. They, thereby, positioned themselves comfortably to concoct lies and fantastic stories against President Jonathan and their erstwhile colleagues.

I, therefore, knew the new government would come for me. The signs were there as soon as the election was lost. What I could not foresee was that there would be such a broad coalition of interests against me. The OPL 245 conundrum proved to be the fortuitous rallying point they needed to express their repressed aggression. It was, and is, a coalition of the aggrieved. They surely could not have had the opportunity to sit down to draw up a battle plan. It had to be a case of "the enemy of my enemy is my friend." They found a common target in me. Mohammed Bello Adoke was the juicy bone thrown to the hungry dogs. The dogs would remain engaged until that bone was picked clean of both flesh and marrow!

Mr Ibrahim Magu, the Acting Chairman of EFCC, led the field operations to destroy me. Initially I had felt he was an innocent tool in the hands of my tormentors. It so happens in life that some people are used to prosecute vendetta battles but they would not know. They would think they are doing humanity a service. But Magu's subsequent utterances and actions confirmed him to be more than a passive actor in the process.

Yet, I would say that I deserved more from him. I was instrumental to reinstating him to the EFCC from the police, where he had been vegetating. When Mr Ibrahim Lamorde was appointed EFCC Chairman in 2011, I asked him what he needed to succeed in his new assignment. He pleaded that he needed some crack officers he had worked with in the past in the EFCC. Under my direction, he applied to the Police Management requesting that they be reposted to EFCC. The police authorities were reluctant to release some of them for their own reasons. Among those they didn't want to repost was Magu. There were so many negative comments about him but I had already promised Lamorde that I would help facilitate the reposting. I couldn't go back on my words. I thought he was being victimised or that some officers were envious of him and were out to run him down.

I made the request for Magu's return to the EFCC. The police management was not enthusiastic about it but obliged the request at my insistence. That was how Magu was reposted to EFCC. I never told him the role I played. I never asked him for any favours. If I were the corrupt person he has been used to portray me as, would I not have capitalised on this to demand favours from him while I was AGF? How he allowed himself to be goaded into using the EFCC machinery to demonise and persecute me when he became the Acting Chairman was baffling.

From what I have been made to understand, he said that he had no personal problem with me but that there were many powerful forces that were after me. I was in government for over five years and I understand how these things work. But I believe Magu went beyond his brief. My mother used to tell me: "If you are sent to deliver a message as a slave, you should deliver it as a freeborn." Magu was delivering the message with such a slavish disposition.

I was told an influential Governor from the North-West geopolitical zone once asked Magu why he was after me so vindictively. Magu reportedly confessed to him that it was the Vice-President, Prof. Osinbajo, that directed him to do so. He further advised the Governor to tell me that I should go and sort out whatever issues I had with Osinbajo. On receiving that information, I recalled that one of Magu's top aides had also voiced a similar sentiment to someone that the VP had given the marching orders to get Adoke at all costs.

Still I would not blame the VP alone.

Magu also had his own agenda. A Senator once asked him if he had any personal issues with me, and Magu replied that I owned half of the Centenary City in Abuja. Ironically, I had, on record, opposed the Centenary City project right from the beginning. Senator Anyim Pius Anyim, who was Secretary to the Government of the Federation, is my very good friend. We never had any disagreement until the issue of the Centenary City came up. I had opposed it to no end, in spite of my relationship with Anyim. Yet Magu would claim authoritatively that I owned half of it. How could he come to such a strong conclusion without proper investigation? He was boasting that he would deal with me, he would finish me, he would disgrace me. That was how power-drunk he got, forgetting that he could end up with a hangover someday.

Magu, in one of his moments, told his associates that I collected £25 million from the recovery of Abacha Loot from the Island of Jersey and shared it with my friends. He could simply have gone to Jersey to initiate an investigation into that recovery. It would have been an easy accomplishment for him to expose the facts. Rather, he chose the route of scandalising my person. I had become the easy target, the fall guy on whose doorstep all trash must be dumped. Of course, Magu and his henchmen later discovered that the entire money went into the Federal Government account in Basel, Switzerland. Nobody ever talked about the Jersey recovery again.

But on record my name had been scandalised simply because a so-called human rights lawyer, known to be teleguiding Magu, had asked for the Jersey brief to be given to him when I was AGF and I refused. I had given him many briefs before then and hadn't been entirely satisfied with his output. I also doubted his capacity to handle the intricate multi-jurisdictional issues involved in the case. This was a serious legal job, not the art of issuing press statements and granting media interviews which are his forte. The loquacious lawyer had conveniently failed to disclose that I gave him the case of Enron in the US and paid him handsomely for it. This was in addition to several favours I had done him while I was in office, including appointing his wife to the board of one of the MDAs under my supervision.

I am also aware that Senator Ali Ndume, who is from the same place as

Magu, played an inciting role in the EFCC war against me. There is a story behind it. After the re-election of President Jonathan in 2011 and Anyim Pius Anyim was appointed as the SGF, we were looking for a lasting solution to the Boko Haram insurgency, including adopting the carrot-and-stick approach. One evening, I received a call from Anyim who asked for a meeting. He said he thought we might have made a breakthrough in resolving the Boko Haram crisis as we might have found someone who could serve as a link between the government and the insurgents.

He was referring to Senator Ndume. He linked both of us up. We met and resolved that I would take him to see the President for a discussion. I had to quickly brief the President because of his eagerness to have the matter resolved. Ndume had told me he could solve the problem and that the prime promoter of the militant group was a former Governor. He had been a known associate of that former Governor. He told me it was not a matter of speculation that the former Governor had a link to Boko Haram. He told me firmly that he had the evidence.

I went to inform the President of the new development and he was excited about it, requesting that I come with the Senator at 6 pm the next day. I told Senator Ndume that we should meet at the pilot gate so that I could take him to see the President. I got to the pilot gate and waited. I didn't see Ndume. After some time, I placed a call to him and he said, astonishingly, that he had seen the President. That was not the arrangement. I proceeded to see the President. As I walked in, I saw a little frown on his face. He asked if he was the same person I was talking about and I said yes. He said the security report on the Senator was not good. With that caution, I made sure that I did nothing further.

Not long after that, I started receiving calls from strange people threatening that if I did not help to remove the Governor of Borno State, Alhaji Kashim Shettima, they were going to do me harm. I passed the information and the phone number to the security agents. They did their job, the individual was apprehended, and when he was interrogated, he said it was Ndume that gave him my number to be calling me. That was how Ndume was arrested and subsequently charged to court. The prosecution suffered adjournment for one reason or the other until we left government. Thus, when Magu started his war against me, he had another aggrieved person to incite him.

Also, the EFCC, as an establishment, already had a grouse against me. It was very easy to railroad them into carrying out a hatchet job. They could hardly be counted upon to be fair-minded in matters concerning me. As AGF, I had proposed the creation of a "Proceeds of Crimes and Asset Management Agency" which would be independent of the EFCC and be charged with the management of recovered assets. That agency was part of a proposal made by our development partners which I had bought into completely.

In my opinion, the creation of such an agency would be in the interest of the country. Their operation would have ensured transparency of the EFCC operations too. I believed strongly that it didn't make sense for EFCC to be allowed to manage the assets they recover unsupervised for the obvious reason that accountability would be jeopardised. That proposal set the EFCC leadership against me. Had they listened to those suggestions, the crisis that eventually engulfed the agency over the mismanagement of recovered assets would have been averted.

Another point of disagreement was the proposal to make the Nigeria Financial Intelligence Unit (NFIU) autonomous from the EFCC. Until recently, the EFCC was the NFIU for Nigeria. This was against the best practice recommendations of the Financial Action Task Force (FATF), which required the NFIU to enjoy financial and operational autonomy such that they would be able to provide untainted intelligence to all the stakeholders in the country. The EFCC apparently wanted to retain the NFIU as a Department within the EFCC so as to have control over the intelligence emanating from it. Several attempts to present an Executive Bill to establish the NFIU were frustrated by the EFCC.

The most fundamental of our disagreements was over the regulations I made pursuant to the powers vested in the AGF by the EFCC Act. The regulations sought to ensure that the AGF was properly informed of all high-profile cases and those involving sums in excess of N50 million. It also provided the procedure for the disposal of assets recovered by the EFCC and the payment of the proceeds of such sale into the Consolidated Revenue Fund of the Federation. The EFCC completely opposed the regulations and sought to frustrate its implementation under the guise that I was trying to prevent them from fighting corruption. A lot of sponsored articles appeared in the media to misinform the public about the objectives of the regulations. But I stood my ground and gazetted the regulations.

The sour relationship between the EFCC and myself reached a crescendo when the Delta State Government sued the EFCC for the recovery of the $15 million 'bribe' allegedly paid by Chief James Ibori to Mallam Nuhu Ribadu, the former EFCC Chairman. The EFCC had retained the services of Rotimi Jacobs who successfully defended the suit. In line with extant policy of government that the AGF should approve all fees for legal services rendered to any agency or para-statal, some top EFCC officials came to my office to seek approval to pay about $1.5 million to the lawyer, being 10 per cent of the $15 million claim. I promptly rejected the request on the grounds that the service rendered by the lawyer was not a recovery to warrant payment of 10 per cent of the recovered sum but a defence *simpliciter*. They were visibly disappointed at my position on the matter. That further worsened the wedge in our relationship.

I will, however, continue to relish the fact that I contributed to the building of the EFCC as an independent institution. At some point, the agency was having financial constraints and could not meet its commitments. I raised a memo to the President asking for an intervention fund of N500 million for the commission. That gave the EFCC a lot of comfort and it was able to continue to do its job unimpeded. If I were corrupt as the institution has been used to portray me globally, I would not have gone to this length to strengthen the body.

• • •

The bizarre role of Vice-President Osinbajo in my persecution remains incomprehensible to me. But three possibilities suggest themselves. First, it was possible some persons who were fighting me gained his confidence and persuaded him that, indeed, I was floating on a sea of stolen loot that needed to be recovered. It could, as a matter of fact, be a well-meant and altruistic fight against corruption based on the purest of intentions on the VP's part. I know too that the ubiquitous dealmaker, Lawal Abba, who was also deeply involved in the OPL 245 saga on behalf of Mohammed Abacha, was hand-in-glove with close associates of the VP. Abba, as I have already recounted, had boasted that if I thought the VP could assist me, I was mistaken, that they had reached the VP before I got a chance to. Lawal is also obviously connected to Magu.

Second, I was told that Vice-President Osinbajo, in an effort to impress President Buhari, had informed him that the signature bonus paid on OPL 245 was too meagre. He was of the opinion that if the transaction was to be reviewed, he could get the beneficiaries of the block, Shell and Eni, to pay up to $500 million as signature bonus. To accomplish this objective, all efforts were made to malign the Settlement Agreement of 2011 with allegations of corruption. This was a worthless effort because he obviously was not aware that OPL 245 was a discretionary allocation made pursuant to government policy to encourage indigenous participation in the upstream operations of the petroleum sector. But for the controversies surrounding its revocation and re-allocation to Shell in 2001, the signature bonus payable on the Block 245 should have been the same $20 million paid on similar allocations such as OPLs 244 and 246. Interestingly, the $210 million paid by Shell/Eni is still the highest in Nigeria's history!

The third possibility was that in an interview I granted *THISDAY* in 2016, I did make reference to the Halliburton case in which we retained the services of Nigerian lawyers to prosecute the foreign companies that allegedly bribed Nigerian officials in respect of the NLNG project. I did make the case that we adopted the template that was used in the Pfizer case to get the indicted companies to pay the fees of the lawyers in addition to the monies recovered from them. In the Pfizer case, the amount recovered was $65 million, but Pfizer, in addition, paid the lawyers the sum of $16 million as fees.

In that interview, I mentioned the names of the lawyers who got paid by Pfizer to include Chief J.B. Daudu, Prof. Osinbajo, and a host of other Nigerian lawyers, including Mrs Mariam Uwais, now a Special Assistant to the President on Social Investment Programme in the Office of the Vice-President. Their fees, I had pointed out, were paid to them by Pfizer through Mr Tunde Irukera, an associate of Osinbajo. Irukera is now the Director-General of the Consumer Protection Council (CPC).

I was told that Osinbajo was very bitter that I mentioned his name. He didn't fancy being portrayed as having benefited from certain transactions as he sought to maintain a clean public image. It appeared I had inadvertently blown open that holy lid. That could possibly account for his hate and contempt for me. This consideration, however, remains speculative. I have not been able to confirm it. If that be the true position, then the VP was possibly trying to get his pound of flesh by supporting those aggrieved by the Malabu transactions to come after me, using the EFCC over which he has enormous control. Magu would then be his puppet in the cheap drama that has unjustifiably rendered me a fugitive.

All said and done, the biggest masquerade in all the EFCC charade remains Mohammed Abacha. The others only seized the opportunity to trample upon me.

I confess that I did give him hell in the battle over the recovery of the public funds looted by his family when his father was the military Head of State from 1993 to 1998. I made Mohammed Abacha forfeit stolen monies hidden away in several jurisdictions across the world. He hates me to no end. I undermined every attempt to compromise the case and turned down several overtures and tempting offers made to me by both him and his agents. He thought he had outplayed the Federal Government, but I uncovered about $1 billion that had been well hidden.

Perhaps his biggest grouse, to my mind, was the OPL 245 case. He said he owned 50 per cent of Malabu Oil & Gas Ltd. He claimed that the registration documents of the company had been tampered with and his name removed. That meant that he did not benefit a dime from the $1.1 billion the company had made from the sale of the oil block to Shell and Agip-Eni. But he had not come out openly to assert his shareholder's rights. The political atmosphere did not appear favourable then. He only started making his claims after Malabu had been paid in 2011. When he approached me for assistance, I told him clearly that it was a shareholder issue and that the Federal Government could not get involved.

President Buhari was misled into thinking I was not fair to the Abacha family in the Malabu transaction. That Mohammed Abacha suddenly began to grow in confidence under the Buhari government is not in doubt. He has gone on to file a case in court over Malabu. Something, or someone, had given him the confidence that the courts could be used to get back the oil block. The bird dancing on the way path obviously has a drummer in the nearby bush. Yet, by virtue of Decree No. 53, now an Act of the National Assembly, the family was expected to honestly declare their assets and forfeit them to the Federal Government. The non-disclosure of their interest in OPL 245 is a violation of the decree. Meanwhile, why has the EFCC not gone after Mohammed Abacha to ask how he acquired an interest in OPL 245?

Obviously, for the Abachas to dare raise their head to make claims on their loot, today's political environment is conducive to them. Clearly, they have sympathisers in the Buhari government. For the eight years that President Obasanjo was in power, the Abachas never came out to make a claim to OPL 245. They never tried it under President Yar'Adua either. Under President Jonathan, they never came out boldly to assert any claim. But under the government of President Buhari, they feel so comfortable to make such an audacious claim, even going on to file a suit in court. The Abachas have become sure-footed enough to step forward to go after OPL 245!

I must also not fail to point out that in 2016, an American professor, John N. Paden, wrote the authorised biography of President Buhari, *Muhammadu Buhari: The Challenges of Leadership in Nigeria*, in which he made reference to corruption cases and corrupt people. He mentioned my name and OPL 245 as an example, using *Sahara Reporters* as his source! A newspaper editor, who read the book immediately it was published and who is very close to the corridors of power, called me and asked: "Oga, have you read the book?" I said no. He said: "Please read it. It is very clear now that your issue is from the highest political authority. Whatever you do, don't come back to Nigeria any time soon. They are after you."

I immediately recalled the Freudian slip of De Pasquale, the Italian prosecutor. While trying to bully me, he had told me during my interrogation over the OPL 245 transactions at The Hague that "this is about your life." I was, thus, further convinced that my life was indeed in danger.

In sum, I was the hunted mouse being offered as sacrifice to appease the Abacha family because of the perception that I had "not been fair" to them. State institutions were clearly working for them, with the help of those who felt I had stepped on their toes one way or the other when I was the Attorney-General.

The witch-hunters are having a ball.

• • •

CHAPTER NINE

THE MISCHIEF

Google 'Mohammed Bello Adoke'. You would be sure to find allegations of fraud and money laundering associated with the name. Given a gun, you would happily shoot the bearer of that name. You would deny him a decent burial too. Going by what has been planted in both foreign and local media about him, you would conclude that he should remain a *persona non grata*.

It has taken the combined onslaught against my person by the EFCC and its Nigerian media propaganda arm – in collaboration with some sinister elements in the Civil Society Organisations (CSOs) – to paint me this black. The media and civil society collaborators may not altogether be blamed, considering the extensive grand plan of the EFCC. But they can't be totally absolved either for not independently digging deeper. They have failed in their role to closely interrogate whatever they are being fed with. They must take responsibility for abandoning their sacred duty to humanity. They failed me by swallowing twisted facts hook, line and sinker, despite unassailable documents that I had placed at their disposal. My story here will, hopefully, offer the public the opportunity to ask pertinent questions and set the records straight.

But first, it is important to understand the modus operandi of the EFCC as exemplified by the media reportage on the case they filed in court in respect of the OPL 245 transaction. On 21 December 2016, the EFCC filed a nine-count charge against me and eight others at the Federal High Court, Abuja. Curiously, it was only my name that appeared in the headlines of most news reports. That alone would make it appear to the undiscerning public that the entire court case was about me. The EFCC typically spins the focus of reports to suit certain narratives and leaks them to their trusted media propaganda arm, which in turn insinuates them through highly publicised channels. Soon their quarry makes the 'Breaking News' and then operatives of the EFCC will jump from their vantage corners to play heroes of anti-graft wars!

In order to appreciate this analogy, let's analyse the case.

It is interesting to note that my name was mentioned only in two out of the nine charges on the record, being Charges No. 7 and No. 8:

That you Dauzia Loya Etete (aka Dan Etete) and Malabu Oil and Gas Limited and Mohammed Adoke Bello (SAN) sometime in 2011 in Abuja within the jurisdiction of this Honourable Court conspired among yourselves to commit money laundering offences contrary to Section 18 of the Money Laundering (Prohibition) Act 2011 as amended in 2012 and punishable under Section 15(3) of the same Act.

That you Mohammed Adoke Bello (SAN) on or about the 10th August 2011 in Abuja within the jurisdiction of this Honourable Court aided Dauzia Loya Etete (aka Dan Etete) and Malabu Oil and Gas Limited to commit an offence of money laundering by facilitating the payment of an aggregate sum of $801,540,000 only to Dauzia Loya Etete (aka Dan Etete) and Malabu Oil and Gas Limited through the Federal Government of Nigeria Escrow Account No. 41451493 IBAN GB 30CHAS609242411493 with JP Morgan Chase Bank in London which you reasonably ought to have known that the said funds formed part of the proceeds of an unlawful activity to wit; fraud and thereby committed an offence contrary to Section 18(a) of the Money Laundering (Prohibition) Act 2011 as amended in 2012 and punishable under Section 15(3) of the same Act.

It is crystal clear, from reading these charges closely, that I was not accused of benefitting from the alleged fraud. Stripped of the verbosity, the charge against me was for 'conspiring' with and 'aiding' payments to Malabu Oil & Gas Ltd. Nowhere on the charge sheet was I accused of stealing. Nowhere was I charged with making payments to myself or to any agent or proxy traceable to me.

Still the media reports gleefully painted me as the fraudster and money launderer.

The truth about that EFCC suit, though, is that the EFCC needed to give the Italian prosecutors something to work with as evidence to charge Shell and Eni to court. An impending suit by Nigeria's anti-graft agency would apparently strengthen their case. The mischief succeeded to a large extent; albeit based on twisted narratives.

It would take an unbiased mind, a mind that has not been irreversibly poisoned against me, to see through the trumped-up charges. There is no truth in the claim that I facilitated payments to Malabu. I was asked to give, and I did give, a legal opinion on a Settlement Agreement/Consent Judgment reached between the Federal Government and Malabu under President Obasanjo in 2006 – four years before I ever became Attorney-General. I found that Settlement Agreement/Consent Judgment to be subsisting and legally binding. The President directed the Settlement Agreement to be implemented. How that translated to "aiding money laundering" in the court of the EFCC is difficult to comprehend.

To be taken seriously in the comity of nations, states have a cardinal responsibility to respect agreements. That is what the noble and internationally recognised concept of *pacta sunt servanda* is about. How does advising the Federal Government to honour its agreement amount to 'aiding' money laundering and fraud? Moreover, at the time that I gave the advice, there was a pending ICSID arbitration against Nigeria at the instance of Royal Dutch Shell, where it was claiming the sum of over $2 billion as damages over the revocation of OPL 245.

Shell had a strong case against Nigeria because of the assurances given to them by government officials to proceed to de-risk the block even when proceedings were pending in court. Shell had paid the bulk of the signature bonus into an escrow account pending the outcome of the dispute. I am surprised that the EFCC and the media are not interested in ascertaining who gave Shell the authorisation to de-risk the block while court proceedings were pending. But for the assurances it got and subsequent de-risking of the block, Shell, in my view, would not have had a strong case against Nigeria.

The implementation of the Agreement by the Federal Government had the effect of bringing all the contending parties to the negotiating table. This facilitated amicable resolution of the dispute leading to the termination of the ICSID arbitration. At the end of it all, Shell and Eni paid a signature bonus of $210 million to the Nigerian government, much higher than the initial $20 million approved when the block was first allocated to Malabu Oil & Gas Limited. In the light of these facts, did I aid "money laundering and fraud" by offering legal advice that led to the withdrawal of a claim of over $2 billion against Nigeria, and the payment of $210 million signature bonus for an oil block to the Federal Government of Nigeria? The reasonable answer must be in the negative.

I was also accused of "facilitating the payment of an aggregate sum of $801,540,000 only to Dauzia Loya Etete (aka Dan Etete) and Malabu Oil and Gas Limited" although the EFCC's propaganda machine had reported "facilitating" as "authorising" payments to Malabu Oil & Gas Ltd. Has it ever been part of the schedule of the Attorney-General to 'authorise' payments on behalf of the Federal Government? What was the function of the Ministry of Finance and the Office of the Accountant-General of the Federation? It is apposite to note that JP Morgan Chase Bank, in its defence filed in a London court on 29 March 2018 in respect of the suit brought against it by the Federal Government of Nigeria, listed in detail the authorising officers for the Escrow Account from which all payments were made to Malabu. My name was not listed as one of the authorising officers for the Escrow Account at JP Morgan!

According to the bank, a letter issued from Dr Yerima Lawan Ngama, then Minister of State for Finance, dated 3 August 2011, intimated the bank of the Federal Government-designated new Authorised Officers for the purposes of the Depository Terms with the bank for the OPL 245 payments. From the terms of that letter, instructions in connection with the Depository Account were required to be given by one "Category A" signatory and one "Category B" signatory. The "Category A" signatories were Dr Ngama and Mr Danladi Kifasi (Permanent Secretary of the Federal Ministry of Finance). The "Category B" signatories were Mr Otunla Jonah Ogunniyi (the Accountant-General of the Federation) and Alhaji Babayo Shehu (Director of Funds in the Office of the Accountant-General of the Federation). Not once did the bank mention my name in the transactions, yet EFCC spoon-fed the media and 'anti-corruption' campaigners with the fable that I was the one who authorised the transfers.

My only involvement in the payment process, if it could be termed 'involvement' at all, was when some judgment creditors sought to attach funds in the Escrow Account with JP Morgan Chase as a result of the court orders they had secured against Malabu Oil & Gas Limited. JP Morgan got in touch with the Federal Government asking what to do. I advised that the court orders restraining the disbursement of $290 million from the sum ought to be obeyed. I certainly could never advise otherwise. No lawyer worthy of their call would ever advise that court orders should not be obeyed. I also advised that the balance that was not restrained by court orders could be disbursed. Again, what was I supposed to advise?

There is an aspect of the whole transaction that I need to clarify again.

Although the entire sum of $1.3 billion was paid into an escrow account jointly operated by the Federal Government and Shell, it would ordinarily not have been so. Since the oil block reverted to Malabu in 2010, following the implementation of the Settlement Agreement, what Shell/Eni should have paid to the Federal Government was $210 million only as the signature bonus for OPL 245. The balance of $1.1 billion was what Shell/Eni agreed to pay to Malabu to take over the oil block from them. Ordinarily, I have to repeat, Shell/Eni could have paid that sum directly to Malabu. The Federal Government would then not have been involved at all. Perhaps, all the controversy would have been avoided.

However, as I explained in Chapter Six, after Malabu got its oil block back, Shell remained in arbitration with Nigeria while Eni was showing a strong interest in taking a stake in OPL 245. Malabu and Shell were technically not on 'speaking terms' because of trust issues. All parties needed to come to a closure. The Federal Government merely served as a mediator between the feuding parties who agreed that the payment should be made to the Escrow Account at JP Morgan.

Shell had already paid a deposit of $209 million into the account in 2002 when Obasanjo gave it the oil block. Resolving the trust issues and releasing the Federal Government of Nigeria from the contingent liability of over $2 billion in damages was the cord that tied the three parties – Shell/Eni, the Federal Government and Malabu – together in that deal. Otherwise, it would have been a straight deal between Shell, Eni and Malabu.

There was also that 'urban legend' about the deal: that the $1.1 billion paid to Malabu should have gone into the Federation Account instead. That was the weightiest of the prevailing mischievous narratives being peddled by the EFCC. Indeed, it commanded the most widespread following ever among 'economic analysts' as 'clear evidence' of Adoke's fraud. One organisation even designed an infographic illustrating how many hospitals and roads could have been constructed by the 'fraudulent' payment to Malabu. According to that legend, all the payments made by Shell and Eni into that escrow account should have gone to the Federal Government. That would automatically mean that Malabu should not have received a dime from the deal. In view of my foregoing account, was there any sense in that contention?

The oil block was allocated to Malabu in 1998, revoked in 2002 and returned to it in 2006. The Federal Government implemented the 2006

Agreement in 2011. With the oil block now 100 per cent restored to Malabu, Shell and Eni agreed to 'buy' it from that Nigerian company for the sum of $1.1 billion. Does it accord with logic that Malabu's money should have been paid into the Federation Account and shared by the three tiers of government?

A further illustration will simplify the situation, hopefully. Hypothetically, Malabu was allocated a plot of land by the Lagos State Government and asked to pay "Capital Development Fee" of N210 million. Shell agreed to buy the land off Malabu for N1 billion, and based on that sale agreement, Shell paid the "Capital Development Fee" of N210 million to the Lagos State Government. Would it make sense to claim that Shell should have paid the entire N1.21 billion to Lagos State Government? This illustration typifies the scenario in business. It is commonplace. It cannot become the basis to ground a charge of fraud in the OPL 245 case. Well, except where an agency like the EFCC desperately needs to 'discover' fraud!

Still on the hypothetical Lagos case, just as the state would earn more revenue from the land deal by way of annual land use charges and taxes, etc., so also would the Federal Government earn more revenue from OPL 245 by way of royalties, petroleum profit tax, VAT, withholding tax and PAYE as soon as production starts. This is in addition to the $210 million signature bonus already in its pocket. But for politicisation of events, this appears quite straightforward and uncomplicated! Vindictiveness and prejudice blind both the eye and the mind!

It is completely inaccurate to say Nigeria was short-changed in any way in the OPL 245 deal. We need to be reminded that OPL 246 was awarded to Lt. Gen. T. Y. Danjuma's South Atlantic Petroleum (Sapetro) on the same day OPL 245 was awarded to Malabu. OPL 246 is practically next to OPL 245. Sapetro paid the concessionary signature bonus of $20 million only. In 2006, Sapetro sold 45 per cent of OPL 246 to CNOOC of China for $1.7 billion. Nobody muted the idea of the Federal Government getting paid the said $1.7 billion. Nobody insinuated that the money ought to have been paid into the Federation Account. Not even the almighty EFCC, its righteous media wing and its principled 'anti-corruption' campaigners made any fuss about Sapetro.

Malabu's $1.1 billion take from selling off 100 per cent of OPL 245 was even lower, compared with Sapetro's $1.7 billion haul from selling just 45 per cent of OPL 246. The fact that exploration had not started in OPL 245, of course, accounts for the much lower value of OPL 245. Sapetro was close to exploration when it sold the stake to CNOOC. Unlike OPL 245, nobody raised any eyebrow about how Danjuma got his own oil block. No one cared about how much he made from it personally. He is a very powerful Nigerian: a hero of military coups, a key figure in the Nigerian Civil War, former Chief of Army Staff and financier of presidential candidates. He was a Minister in the Obasanjo government that revoked OPL 245.

Chief Etete could not boast of such an intimidating CV. Apart from being a minority from Nigeria's oil-rich region, he had fallen out of favour after the death of Abacha in 1998. Of course, many moral issues were being raised on the propriety of awarding an oil block to a company in which Etete had beneficial interest while he was Minister of Petroleum Resources. However, legally speaking, the case filed by the EFCC in court was about fraud and money laundering, not about 'conflict of interest'.

The most ridiculous of the allegations against me was that I 'misled' the Federal Government in my legal advice on the Settlement Agreement. This was tantamount to giving a dog a bad name in order to slaughter it. Nothing could be more malicious than saying somebody should be jailed for giving 'wrong' advice. If this were to be the standard for criminal prosecutions, Special Advisers all over the world would be in jail. Advisers only proffer advice to their principals. The principal remains responsible for whatever cause of action he chooses to adopt. In any case, the EFCC could not have expected me to advise President Jonathan to repudiate the Consent Judgment willingly entered into by the Federal Government under President Obasanjo in 2006. Could I have, in all conscience, advised President Jonathan to tear up the Settlement Agreement? Government is a continuum.

If I were in a position to advise the Federal Government again on the status of the Settlement Agreement signed in 2006 which was later reduced into a Consent Judgment of the Court of Appeal, Abuja Division, I would adopt the exact position I did in 2010 in view of the circumstances of that case. My advice would remain: respect the agreement you willingly entered into. Respect the Consent Judgment that was subsisting. Your word should be your bond. A sane society can only thrive on the rule of law and sanctity of contracts. Nigeria should not be an exception.

That, in a nutshell, was the reason I was branded a money launderer and fraudster by the EFCC, acting out the script of a consortium of very power-ful Nigerians determined to do me dirt and damage my reputation.

• • •

Since the case was filed against me by the EFCC in December 2016, quite a number of interesting incidents have taken place. Many overtures have been made to me. One was that I should pay the sum of $3 million so that my name would be removed from the case. The request was conveyed by a retired Air Commodore of the Nigerian Air Force, purportedly acting on behalf of the goons at the EFCC. Where did they imagine I would find that amount of money? Apparently, my reputation for having stashed away quite a fortune as Minister was not peculiar to the stranger at Schiphol Airport! Every scum out there would also like to milk me for their bit of the national cake!

The court case was blackmail, pure and simple. It was clear to me that many people who served under President Jonathan were being extorted likewise. In my case, in the absence of any concrete evidence to put me on trial, the EFCC became desperate. From what I have gathered, some former ministers have had to dispose of their assets in order to meet up with the bribes being demanded by the EFCC and to forestall the sort of media trial I have had to endure. From the beginning, I had vowed not to succumb to any form of blackmail. But that has exerted a heavy price. The cross I have had to bear is evident all over the internet. Just Google my name…

I refused to play ball with the blackmailers, choosing rather to go to court to seek judicial interpretation of the constitutional provisions relating to my role in the transaction. From the charge sheet, it was very glaring that the EFCC had nothing on me. All they could do was to twist the facts and use the online media to amplify the defamation of my character. It was nothing short of a well-orchestrated mischief, indeed. I issued a statement announcing my resolve to clear my name. I listed the names of prominent Nigerians and government officials who were part of the negotiations from 1998 till 2011 and wondered why those people were not charged to court as well for 'conspiring' to commit and for 'facilitating' fraud.

The EFCC then pulled the next trick from their repertoire of infamy.

On 30 January 2017, the anti-graft agency filed a five-count charge against Alhaji Aliyu Abubakar, a property developer, and me at the Federal Capital Territory High Court, in Abuja. According to sensationalised media reports, I was charged with collecting a bribe of $2,267,000 in the Malabu deal. The bribe money was purportedly paid to me by Alhaji Abubakar through a bureau de change in September 2013.

The international wing of the EFCC propaganda machinery went crazy on a defamation binge, tearing at that new succulent bone with gusto! The only problem, though, was that EFCC did not charge me to court over Malabu or OPL 245. It was its media spinners that added OPL 245 and Malabu to their imaginary charge sheets. There, again, was yet another concrete evidence that the Commission was merely fishing for anything they could use to destroy me.

The charge sheet read that:

(1) I committed money laundering offences contrary to section 18 of the Money Laundering (Prohibition) Act 2011;

(2) I took possession of "two million, two hundred and sixty-seven thousand four hundred dollars" when I "reasonably ought to have known that the funds formed part of an unlawful activity to wit: fraud";

(3) I converted $2,267,000 to N315,200,000 as part of an "illegal activity";

(4) I used the money to offset a loan I took from Unity Bank "to conceal" the illegal activity;

(5) the $2,267,000 exceeded the threshold for cash transactions allowed outside of a financial institution…

The desperation was unmistakable. There was not one mention of Malabu or OPL 245 in the charges! In truth, the EFCC knew there was nothing linking me to the contrived sleaze in that transaction. The EFCC could not approach the court to claim that "Adoke collected $2,267,000 in the Malabu deal." It still cannot do so because I did not collect a dime from that transaction. Not one kobo. Not one cent, much less a dollar. In the fullness of time the truth will prevail. My truth will remain unimpeachable.

To start with, it is strange for someone who allegedly 'aided' the OPL 245 'fraud' and 'authorised payments' of $801 million to Malabu in August 2011 to wait until September 2013 to collect his 'share' of the booty. Of all the cases of bribery that I have ever heard of in my life, I am yet to learn of one where a person would bide their time for two solid years after a transaction was concluded to receive their share. Those who collect bribes would usually demand to be paid upfront. I may be wrong. Those who collect bribes would also argue that for a deal worth $1.1 billion paid to one of the parties, a gratification of $2.2 million would be nothing short of an insult. I may be wrong, of course.

Whatever the case may be, I did not collect any bribe from anybody for the five years that I was a Minister. I repeat: I never took a kobo, a cent or a dollar bribe from anybody throughout my tenure as Minister. It probably appeared strange, by Nigerian standards, to believe that there could be people who would advise the Federal Government on the execution of an agreement worth $1.3 billion and not make demands on the parties. They had to resort to twisting facts in an effort to rope me in. Yet in all the charges, they still could not provide any evidence linking me to sleaze. Unfortunately, with the help of the media and the 'anti-corruption' campaigners, the EFCC has sustained its infernal campaign to ruin my name.

And now, I will tell the inside story of the $2,267,000 'money laundering' case.

In 2011, after I was re-nominated as minister, my security detail advised me that it was no longer safe for me to continue residing at my terrace apartment. According to him, it would be difficult to secure me in an environment where several other persons were residing and shared common facilities. They reminded me that one of my predecessors, Chief Bola Ige, was assassinated rather easily in December 2001. He said they would be failing in their duty if they did not adequately secure me. I turned down their request. I told them it was their duty to secure me. But the pressure to relocate kept mounting. My net salary was less than N500,000 monthly, after all deductions, from a gross of roughly N990,000. There was no way I could afford to move houses based on my income, except I wanted to dig into my savings.

When, however, the pressure would not subside, I approached my bankers seeking a mortgage to buy a house. Alhaji Aliyu Abubakar, a builder and a developer whom I had been acquainted with for a long time, had earlier approached me with an offer to sell me a house for N500 million. The bank, the Chairman of whose Audit Committee I used to be, agreed that I should make an equity contribution of N200 million for a mortgage loan of N500 million that they would extend to me. The mortgage was approved and the payment made directly to the developer, not to me.

I had hoped to raise the N200 million from the sale of a piece of land I owned in Abuja. However, it turned out that I could not secure a buyer for that price. Meanwhile, interest was accumulating on the N300 million loan from the bank. At a point, I had to pay interest of about N40 million from my savings which predated my ministerial appointment. The bank also informed me that the CBN was raising issues against the loan, especially the mounting interest, as I was a politically exposed person (PEP).

As I was ruminating over how to sort that problem out, the developer contacted me, offering to return the money paid to him by the bank. He had got wind of the interest of the CBN in the property and wanted to take it back. I was too glad to let go. I suggested Abubakar should approach the bank and offer to pay back the loan since I was unable to sort it out. I asked him to retrieve the title documents which he gave to the bank upon receipt of their N300 million.

All I know beyond that conversation was that he paid off the loan to the bank and retrieved the title documents. I have no inkling of how he paid or how much he paid. I have no idea if he made the payments in dollars, neither do I know if a *bureau de change* was involved. I merely recall that both the developer and the MD of the bank confirmed to me that the loan had been repaid and that the title documents had been returned. I asked that the bank account be closed. That ended the matter as far as I was concerned.

EFCC's fishing expedition took them through the accounts of the said developer. On sighting the said payment from Unity Bank, they promptly summoned him to quiz him about the transaction. Typically, they brought out the brute force: "Where is the house?!" This would be followed by the aggressive caveat – "KEEP OFF! HOUSE UNDER INVESTIGATION" – that the EFCC employs to terrorise hapless Nigerians.

It was from Abubakar that they got the information that the house was no longer mine; that the CBN had bought it as I couldn't meet up with payment; and that he had repaid the Unity Bank loan and retrieved the Certificate of Occupancy. He further told them that he paid the bank in dollars, which they changed into naira at a *bureau de change*.

I have just described the failed transaction that the EFCC classified as "unlawful activity" and "money laundering" over which I was charged to court along with Alhaji Abubakar.

Irrespective of the facts on the ground, I was told one of the EFCC operatives screamed: "We must find something to pin on him!" From what I was told, Lawal Abba, nosing out that Abubakar was an Ebira man like me, pushed the EFCC to pin the *bureau de change* transaction on me. That was how frantic they got in their shameful pursuit of an innocent man.

. . .

Success came on 13 April 2018. I won the case I instituted against the Attorney-General of the Federation on 21 December 2016. I had taken an originating summon wherein I asked the Federal High Court, Abuja, to interpret certain provisions of the Constitution, particularly sections 5, 148 and 150, as they relate to the extent of presidential powers under the Constitution and the delegation of such powers to a Minister in the Government of the Federation. I sought to know whether a Minister could be held personally liable for carrying out the lawful directives/approvals of the President.

The court declared that I had no case to answer over my involvement in the OPL 245 transaction (this is discussed in detail in Chapter Ten). This judgment effectively killed any criminal action instituted against me on the implementation of the OPL 245 Settlement Agreement. Also, obviously unable to criminalise me for the aborted mortgage transaction between Abubakar and Unity Bank Plc, my traducers were beginning to look stupid. They were always bound to bite the dust in any event.

Yet, it is not over until it is over.

I was still celebrating the forthrightness of the Nigerian judiciary in my case when my tormentors struck again with another mischief, using the *Premium Times*, an online news website. Nigerians woke up 5 May 2018 to a screaming headline: "I knew Malabu was a 'presidential scam', ex-AGF Adoke admits on tape."

To be honest, I was jolted. It was as if as I was quenching one fire, another one was blazing away! This time, though, my tormentors claimed to have a recorded tape in which I confessed that I knew the OPL 245 deal was a scam. Anybody who had wanted to give me the benefit of the doubt would begin to have second thoughts. After all, this was not just an accusation floating in the air; there was now a "tape" to prove it. Finally, it appeared my enemies had found a concrete piece of evidence of my complicity!

In the report, *Premium Times* claimed that one Ms Carlamaria Rumor, of RAI Television in Italy, had a phone conversation with me in which I admitted knowing that the Malabu Oil deal was a "presidential scam." The recorded telephone call, the website reported, was the latest material to cast light on my role as a "principal player" in the "questionable deal." It was reported that the audio tape was filed as an exhibit before an Italian court by prosecutors in the trial of the executives of Shell and Eni over allegations of bribery in the OPL 245 transaction. The phone conversation, said to be one-hour 17-minute long, allegedly took place on 5 November 2015.

I was said to have told Ms Rumor that "Etete collaborated with some Italian oil workers" to "divert some funds to foreign accounts" in an "illegal" move that "betrayed" the spirit of a tripartite agreement which the Nigerian government entered into with Italian oil giant Agip-Eni and Royal Dutch Shell on the one hand, and Malabu Oil & Gas on the other. The audio "marked the first time" I admitted personal knowledge of the "unspeakable corruption" in the transaction, according to *Premium Times*.

It was alleged that Ms Rumor had called me to get the insights into the deal and had assured me that the discussion would not be published. "Although the conversation, the filed audio shows, frequently broke into Mr Adoke demanding to have 'a personal relationship' with the journalist, he managed to give out some of those he believed illegally benefited from the deal, mentioning Mr Etete, Aliyu Abubakar and Emeka Obi," the report alleged. "When Ms Rumor sought to know the whereabouts or personal contact of Mr Etete, Mr Adoke told her he would not disclose any information until the two became close enough as he had repeatedly demanded in the minutes preceding this mark."

The truth, of course, is that this is a fake tape. Absolutely fake. If this is what the Italian prosecutors would be relying upon in their case against Shell and Eni, then they have nothing. As at 5 November 2015 when the alleged phone conversation was supposed to have taken place, I was already marked for persecution by the Nigerian government. As someone who worked at the top level in government for over five years, and was privileged to be a member of the National Security Council, I would be a complete moron not to know that telephone lines were bugged and conversations recorded. I knew very well that the new government was digging for dirt over the OPL 245 deal. I was fully aware of the clandestine plans to nail me at all costs. I was a person of interest. I knew very well that Italian prosecutors were fishing for evidence. How would I talk so recklessly on the phone to some Italian journalist I had never met in my life! Was that the best those dirt-diggers could do?

The publication by *Premium Times* placed heavy reliance on a so-called recorded telephone call that I never had. My traducers had sunk to manufacturing evidence against me. The appropriately named 'Rumor' is unknown to me and had never spoken to me. I could not have granted her such a lengthy phone interview. When the news was published, I immediately checked RAI Television's website but could not discover any listing for the name 'Rumor' whether as a TV or print journalist with the outfit. *Premium Times* claimed to have contacted one Michael Nomah, said to be a lawyer, to react on my behalf. I had never heard of that name before. They even went to the extent of manufacturing a lawyer for me! How infantile!

The mischief became quite evident when *Premium Times* wrote:

> Mr Adoke, AGF from 2010-2015, admitted that Mr Etete, an ex-convict, was actively involved in the talks held between Nigerian government officials, representatives of Agip-Eni, Shell and other players. This indicates that Mr Adoke recognised Mr Etete as the owner of Malabu Oil and Gas, and dealt with him accordingly, thereby sidestepping Mohammed Abacha and other beneficial owners of the controversial oil firm.

The impression the publication wanted to impart was that I deliberately chose to deal with Etete to the exclusion of other known beneficial owners of Malabu Oil & Gas Limited. They, however, did not reckon with the fact that since 2001, Etete had been the only person that engaged successive governments on behalf of Malabu. He was effectively the alter ego of the company to the knowledge of all government officials involved in the negotiation and implementation of OPL 245 Settlement Agreement. 'Mohammed Sani' Abacha only appeared on the scene when the Settlement Agreement had been executed and implemented in 2011.

Premium Times also went to great length to impute improper conduct on my part by alluding to the so-called "cozying up and offering millions" to the non-existent Ms Rumor. However, any discerning mind would see through the tissue of lies. What will be the motive for asking for a "relationship" with a person that I had never met, or spoken to, in exchange for information that was not exclusive to me but was already in the public space? Nigerians know that I am not a stakeholder in Malabu, Eni or Shell. I did not benefit from the proceeds of the sale of OPL 245 by Malabu. If indeed I was given $2.2 million for the OPL 245 transaction as alleged by the EFCC, why would I be offering the same millions to the imaginary journalist? Offering millions of dollars just to be "close" to someone I had not met? Could anything be more bizarre?

To be sure, I first heard of the existence of the tape in a publication by *Vrij Nederland* on 26 October 2017 with the title: "Shell in Nigeria: Corrupt Constructions." When the highly libellous publication was drawn to my attention, I had instructed my solicitors to write to the Dutch magazine protesting against it. I had also requested that they disclose the tape and the details of where the alleged interview took place, including relevant dates. *Vrij Nederland* declined on the ground that they were protected sources. They responded to the lawyers that they would correct the libellous aspects of the story. This they attempted to do, in their online version, although not entirely to my satisfaction. If they were sure of their facts, they would not have attempted to correct the libellous aspects of their story. They would have claimed justification.

The disclosure I requested was to afford the parties interested in the so-called tape recording an opportunity to subject it to forensic analysis to ascertain its authenticity. I was informed by sources familiar with the Italian proceedings that the contents of the recording "appear (on the face of it) wrong and out of question to such a point that many top officials believe the tape was manipulated." I was later informed that they were seeking technical expertise from phonic court experts to authenticate the voice.

I also learnt that the number of the telephone that was supposed to have been used in the purported telephone interview was a Nigerian line. As at 5 November 2015 when the conversation reportedly took place, I was in the Netherlands. Furthermore, I had stopped using a Nigerian telephone line as far back as August 2015. But *Premium Times* did not deem it necessary to exercise caution in the publication because of the burning desire to satisfy those looking to smell my blood.

I read many possible motives into that publication. One, it was aimed at pitching me against my boss, President Jonathan, with a view to causing ill will and disaffection between us. Or two, it was to downplay the significance of the judgment delivered by Hon. Justice Binta Murtala Nyako, of the Federal High Court, Abuja, which upheld the extent of presidential powers under our Constitution and declared that I acted within the confines of the presidential directives/approvals given to me as a Minister of the Government of the Federation and therefore incurred no personal liability for implementing the OPL 245 Settlement Agreement. Or three, it was to denigrate my person, attract public opprobrium to me and further lower my estimation in the eyes of right-thinking members of society.

The truth remains that I had no such telephone conversation with anyone, much less a Ms Rumor.

• • •

CHAPTER TEN

THE VINDICATION

When I read the EFCC charges against me for my role in the OPL 245 settlement, I was relieved that, indeed, it was clear they were unable to establish any criminal case of money laundering against me. I was certain that resorting to the claim that I 'aided' the transfer of $801 million to Malabu Oil & Gas Ltd would never ground a prosecution in any court of justice in the world. I could see through the make-believe.

The only role I played was offering legal advice to the Federal Government on the validity of the Terms of Settlement reached between the President Obasanjo Administration and Malabu, an agreement sealed between the parties three-and-a-half years before I took office. I also offered legal advice on the need to obey UK court orders restraining the disbursement of $290 million from the escrow account at JP Morgan Chase Bank. Those orders were obtained by middle men engaged by Malabu in their negotiations with Shell and Eni in 2011. I was not involved in any other aspect of the transaction.

If the EFCC was seriously seeking those who 'aided' payments to Malabu, there were at least 1,000 former government officials they could charge to court. It was on the basis of that Settlement Agreement signed by all parties in 2006 that I 'aided' the Federal Government to obey the Consent Judgment.

Most of those who 'aided' the Settlement Agreement are still alive. The Minister of Petroleum Resources was President Obasanjo; the Minister of State for Petroleum Resources was Dr Edmond Daukoru; the AGF and Minister of Justice was Chief Bayo Ojo; Mr Funso Kupolokun was the Group Managing Director of the NNPC; and so on. I could list a thousand officials who possibly 'aided' the Malabu transactions on OPL 245 for which Shell and Eni agreed to pay the Nigerian company $1.1 billion to take over ownership. I was the only one picked out as the easy target for persecution in EFCC's ploy of working to an answer and appeasing the witch-hunters.

On conferring with my lawyers, we decided to seek judicial interpretation of the role I played in the implementation of the Settlement Agreement of 2006. On 24 May 2017, we filed an originating summons against the Attorney-General of the Federation at the Federal High Court, Abuja, seeking the following reliefs:

(1) A declaration that my involvement in the negotiations leading to the implementation of the Settlement Agreement between Malabu Oil and Gas Limited and the Federal Government and the eventual execution of Block 245 Malabu Resolution Agreement between the Federal Government and Malabu Oil and Gas Limited of 29 April, 2011,was in furtherance of lawful directives/approval of the president in the exercise of his executive powers.

(2) A declaration that my involvement in the negotiation and eventual execution of the Block 245 SNUD Resolution Agreement between the Federal Government and Shell Nigeria Ultra Deep and Shell Nigeria Exploration and Production Company Limited was in furtherance of the lawful directives/approval of the president in the exercise of his executive powers.

(3) A declaration that my involvement in the negotiation and eventual execution of Block 245 Resolution Agreement between the Federal Government; and SNUD; and NNPC; and Nigeria Agip Exploration Limited; and SNEPCO was in furtherance of the lawful directives/ approval of the president in the exercise of his executive powers.

(4) A declaration that any correspondence/instruction to JP Morgan from me in furtherance of the implementation of all these Agreements were in furtherance of the lawful directives/approval of the president in the exercise of his executive powers.

(5) A declaration that any correspondence/instruction to JP Morgan Chase or any other entity and ancillary actions and processes taken by me in furtherance of the implementation of the Settlement Agreement were in furtherance of the lawful directives/approval of the president in the exercise of his executive powers.

(6) A declaration that my prosecution by the Economic and Financial Crimes Commission on account of carrying out the lawful directives and implementation of the approvals of the president is illegal, null and void and inconsistent with the intendment of section 5 (1) of the Constitution of the Federal Republic of Nigeria 1999 as amended.

(7) A declaration that I cannot be held personally liable for carrying out the lawful directives/approvals of the president while I served as a minister of the government of the federation.

On Friday, 13 April 2018, Hon. Justice BFM Nyako, of the Federal High Court, Abuja, granted all but one of the reliefs I sought. According to the court, I could not be held personally liable for carrying out the lawful directives and approvals of the President while I served as a Minister. The relief that the Court did not grant was the one seeking to stop my trial by the EFCC. The court saw that as a mere "academic exercise" since the current AGF, Mallam Abubakar Malami, had already written to President Buhari and the EFCC to state that there was no case against me.

Questions have been asked as to why the EFCC was not joined in my suit. We had reasoned that the EFCC was prosecuting on behalf of the Federal Government of Nigeria. By virtue of Section 174 of the Constitution, such prosecutions were subject to the overarching powers of the Attorney-General of the Federation. There was, therefore, no compelling need to join the EFCC since the Attorney-General of the Federation was already a party representing the Federal Government.

• • •

For the avoidance of doubt, I reproduce below AGF Malami's letter to President Buhari, dated 15 September 2017, giving his legal opinion on the EFCC prosecution.

RE: FORWARDING OF CASE FILE IN RESPECT OF CHARGE NO. FHC/ABJ/CR/268/17 AND FCT/HC/CR/124/2017 MALABU OIL & GAS LTD

May I refer Your Excellency to the above subject matter, please.

2. This case file was received from the EFCC in a letter dated 21st December, 2016 for vetting and further directive. Having fully examined the entire case file I am inclined to request you to note the following and direct accordingly.

3. A curious observation of the entire Malabu story clearly indicates that there are the civil and criminal aspects to the case.

4. The civil aspect borders on the skirmishes between the directors of the company which led to the claims that shares of the same directors were divested without their consent thereby taking over their interest. Having examined the cases it is important to note that the cases are pending before the courts and therefore subjudice; the FGN should await the outcome of the cases- Suit No. FHC/ABJ/CS/201/2017 MALABU OIL & GAS LTD vs. THE FEDERAL GOVERNMENT OF NIGERIA AND & 6 ORS; and Suit No. FHC/ABJ/CS/206/2017 MALABU OIL & GAS LTD vs. MR KWEKU AMAFAGHA & 9 ORS.

5. In the criminal case, the aggrieved parties through their lawyers petitioned the EFCC against some directors of Malabu Oil and Gas alleging fraudulent divestment of their shares and subsequently depriving them of their benefits in the sale of OPL 245. EFCC investigated the case and filed nine-count charge dated 16th September, 2016.

6. Attached to the charge are a proof of evidence, case summary and list of witnesses in support of the counts which border on fraud, conspiracy and money laundering.

Regarding the criminal charge. Your Excellency is invited to note that the charge as presently constituted may most likely not succeed against the parties for the following reasons:

(a) There is nothing to show that the parties as constituted were at all times working together and having a 'meeting of minds' to wit: to forge CAC documents and use same for the purpose of divesting the shares of the complainants and thereafter, enter into a settlement agreement with FGN and other parties to take delivery of the proceeds of sale of OPL 245.

(b) There is also nothing in the proof of evidence to support the charge money laundering and it is therefore impossible for the prosecution to prove the elements which include illicit funds, transfer for such through various channels to re-introduce same again into the regular financial system as legitimate funds in financial institutions etc. Without the express proof of these elements, the count may not be sustained on the premise of the attached proof of evidence.

(c) The EFCC investigation and attached proof of evidence do not appear to have clearly revealed the case of fraud against the parties who claimed to have acted in their official capacities with the approval of three consecutive presidents of the federal government of Nigeria at the time with further claim that the matter was intended to be resolved in national interest thereby saving the nation acrimonious litigations resulting in high legal fees and the dormancy of the oil field while litigation lasted.

(d) In this regard, the Public Officers Protection Act CAP P41 Laws of the Federation of Nigeria, 2004 limits liability of Public Officers to a period of three months much naturally come to mind considering their claim that the acts which are complained of were authorised by the three presidents before this current administration.

7. Your Excellency, the beneficial approach I counsel in the circumstances is for the federal government to take advantage of the terms of the agreement under clauses five and 11 to acquire a stake in the OPL 245 converting it to a production sharing contract (PSC) between FGN/NNPC, Shell and Agip after negotiating with the ENI/Shell to absorb the cost of the FGN/NNPC entry under the said clauses five and 11 through the PSC mechanism,."

8. The idea of revisiting the settlement agreement which resulted in the sale of the oil field to SNUD, SNEPCO and NAE is not workable. It is important in this regard for His Excellency to note the following:

(a) The agreement was executed by the highest authority in Nigeria and remains sacrosanct unless it is eventually set aside by the decision of a competent court of law and denying the parties immediate benefit of reaping the fruit of their investments. The agreement has its mechanism for compensation in the event of any of the rights conferred to ENI or SHELL are challenged or violated. For the FGN to revisit the agreement, the consent of Shell and ENI will be required.

(b) It is very unlikely that the consent will easily be obtained but rather they would rely on the protection afforded in the contract, and any unilateral effort by FGN to vary the terms of the agreement would probably open up a new bout of litigation, deter further investment, give rise to a claim for damages and payment of huge legal fees. Your Excellency may wish to note some of the FGN's representations and assurances in the clauses 12, 13 and 17 of the agreement.

(c) FGN confirms that the terms of this FGN resolution agreement have been agreed by all the appropriate agencies of the FGN including the Ministry of Finance and the Federal Inland Revenue Service.'

(d) FGN acknowledges that, in entering into this FGN resolution agreement, the other parties have relied on its expressed or implied representation before the signature of this FGN resolution agreement regarding the efficacy of the terms thereof.

(e) FGN shall indemnify, save and hold harmless, and defend SNUD, SNEPCO and NAE from and against all suits, proceedings, claims, demands losses and liability of any nature or kind, including, but not limited to, oil litigation costs, attorneys' fees, settlement payments, damages, and all other related costs and expenses, based on, arising out of, related to or in connection with: (i) this FGN resolution agreement. (ii) the resolution agreement/ (iii) the issuance of the oil prospecting license in respect of Block 245 jointly in the name of SNEPCO and NAE and arising out of any asserted prior interest in Block 245.

9. The above commitments are binding on the FGN. ENI/Shell legitimately expects that the FGN would respect the commitments. Failure by the FGN to respect them would cast Nigeria in a very bad light internationally and negatively impact the FGN's quest for foreign investments. Clearly, potential investors will not have the confidence to invest in Nigeria if the government of the country is perceived as one which does not honour its commitments (captured in an agreement signed by three of its ministers).

10. ENI/Shell claims to have invested in excess of US $2.5 billion in OPL 245 from 2011 to date and as such would seek the protection of international law, including applicable investment treaties which prohibit the unreasonable, unfair and inequitable treatment of their investments and could expose FGN to international arbitration involving multi-billion dollars claims.

11. As the FGN/NNPC relies on the provisions of the resolution agreement, charges preferred against ENI/Shell companies and employees would necessarily have to be withdrawn as continuing with the charges will be inconsistent with the spirit of the relevant clauses of the resolution agreement which will enable FGN to obtain immediate interest in OPL 245. Regardless, as submitted in paragraph five and six above, the charges as constituted and filed by the EFCC are unsustainable.

12. Accept the assurances of my warm regards and loyalty, always.

Abubakar Malami, SAN
Honourable Attorney-General of the Federation & Minister of Justice.
September 27, 2017.

The import of the letter is that the interest of Nigeria is best served by the Settlement Agreement and that I did not commit any crime.

• • •

Furthermore, in a letter to the EFCC dated 20 September 2017, Malami provided a legal basis for the termination of prosecution. The letter was in reply to the one written by Magu in which he said he was forwarding the case file in respect of charges against me and eight others over the OPL 245 transaction. Magu said he was seeking "vetting and further directive."

The AGF's reply to the EFCC is reproduced below.

Having fully examined the entire case, I am inclined to request you to reconsider the charge in relation to the composition of the parties, the offences, the proof of evidence and the case summary in view of the fact that nothing in the proof of evidence appears to have directly linked the parties to the offences as charged.

A curious observation of the entire file clearly indicates the proof of evidence is unlikely to support the count which borders on fraud, conspiracy and money laundering. The following reasons are apt:

There is nothing to show that parties as constituted were at all times working together and having 'a meeting of the mind' to wit: to forge CAC documents and use it for purpose of divesting the shares of the complainant and thereafter, enter into a document agreement with the FGN and other parties to take delivery of the proceeds of sale of OPL 245.

There is also nothing in the proof of evidence to support the charge of money laundering therefore it is unrealistic for the prosecution to prove the elements which include illicit funds, attempt to conceal/concealment of illicit funds, transfer of such funds through various channels to introduce same as legitimate funds, in financial institutions, without express proof of these elements, this count may not be sustainable.

The EFCC investigation and attached proof of evidence does not appear to have clearly revealed the case of fraud against the parties in view of their claimed acting in their official capacities with the purported approval of the President of the FGN at the time and with claimed intentions that the matter be resolved in the national interest to save the nation from acrimonious litigations resulting into high legal fees and the none (non) production of the oil field while litigation lasted.

I view, and rightly so, that there are other key players, non-public officials who are very relevant parties given their actions in divesting the complainant's shares by the alleged forgery, you are to also forward your comments explaining the reason for not charging the principal players such as – Rasky Gbinigie, who was the Company Secretary of Malabu Oil and Gas Ltd and instrumental in the filings of all CAC forms that fraudulently changed the Directors and the share structure of the company: Seidugha Munamuna and Kweku Amefegha, who are consistent Directors of the company who hold various shares allotments in the company shares.

The EFCC investigation and attached proof of evidence to the 9 count charge does not appear to have clearly reviewed the case of fraud against the parties who claimed to have acted in their capacities with the approval of 3 consecutive Presidents of the FGN at the time and with claimed intentions that the matter be resolved in the national interest saving the nation from acrimonious litigations resulting into high legal fees and non production of the oil field while litigation lasted.

Furthermore, I am of the view that the Public Officers Protection Act CAP P41, Laws of the Federation of Nigeria, 2004 limits liability of Public Officers to a period of 3 months following the acts which are complained of unless if the acts were not within the mandate of the functions of the Public Officer, and your investigation needs to have covered that eventuality in view of the claim that the acts were authorised by the 3 Presidents before this current administration.

On the above grounds, I am of the considered view that there is the need to consolidate on the charges and the matter be thoroughly investigated especially regarding the allocations of the wrong doing in connection with the $1.1billion dollars in order to satisfy the constituent elements of offences. You are to also take steps to urgently file an application for a worldwide mareva injunction and or the forfeiture of the assets of the beneficiary of the $1.1 billion dollars pending the conclusion of investigation of the areas above stated.

Abubakar Malami, SAN
Honourable Attorney-General of the Federation & Minister of Justice.

From the foregoing, Malami essentially acknowledged that there was no legal basis to prosecute me. There was no proof of evidence linking me to money laundering and fraud. On the other charges relating to the other accused persons, he advised the EFCC to conduct further investigation.

Needless to say that Malami came under heavy attack from you-know-who! They could not fault the logic of his legal opinion, so they resorted to their trademark tactics of blackmail against his person. Insinuating that he was attempting to protect me, they mounted tremendous pressure on his office to sanction the prosecution. He, however, could not find any genuine ground to do so. Since Magu cannot manipulate the courts, his only option to continue my persecution remains the ill-informed and sometimes compromised online platforms that purport to focus on anti-corruption. I have been hardened by media trials. I certainly will survive the blitzkrieg.

• • •

Dr Ibe Kachikwu, Minister of State for Petroleum Resources, also wrote to President Buhari, through Mallam Abba Kyari, the Chief of Staff, on 13 December 2017, asking the Federal Government to abide by the Settlement Agreement of 2006. While Malami's position was a legal argument, Kachikwu's was an economic case. Reproduced is the full text of Kachikwu's memo to the President.

> *I am writing further to your letter dated 8th November, 2017, Ref SH/COS/24/A/7921 to advise that I have considered the letter of the Attorney-General and Minister of Justice to His Excellency, the President in respect of the above subject and am of the considered view, following the advice of the Attorney-General, that the Federal Government is obliged to respect the resolutions of the Settlement Agreement entered by the Federal Government with respect OPL 245 given:*
>
> *The consistent role of three (3) predecessor Presidents in the matter, and*
>
> *The potential negative view of Nigeria that may follow should international arbitration ensue from the matter.*

My experience is that the potency of bilateral investment treaties upon which a claim could be made on Nigeria is such that, any attempt to abrogate the Settlement Agreement or take any steps that will undermine its integrity could prove costly to the country.

In the circumstances and following the advice, I respectfully recommend that the Federal Government should take advantage of the Settlement Agreement to acquire an interest in OPL 245 and ensure its conversion to a Production Sharing Contract (PSC) between the FGN and relevant parties as per paragraph 7 of the AG's letter. This will not only ensure that Nigeria will bear no funding obligations for the development of the block, but will be a strategic, yet commercial, approach and solution to the OPL 245 issue which will ensure Nigeria is focussed on obtaining an immediate benefit from OPL 245.

Please accept the assurances of my warmest regards.

Dr Ibe Kachikwu,
Hon. Minister of State for Petroleum Resources

• • •

In sum, I have won my case in court against the Federal Government. This has effectively sounded the death knell to my trial by the EFCC for "facilitating" money laundering. I have been vindicated and I am gladdened by this fact. In addition, the letters written by Malami to President Buhari and the EFCC, as well as the one by Kachikwu to the President all confirmed that I did nothing wrong in the OPL 245 transaction, particularly on the basis of legal evidence and common sense. I broke no laws. I have been vindicated after all the mudslinging and persecution. Injustice cannot last forever.

There is a second trial for 'money laundering' instituted against me by the EFCC. The media spin on the trial was that I was charged to court for collecting a $2.2 million bribe two years after the OPL 245 deal had been signed, sealed and delivered. The headlines said so. However, there is no such thing as "OPL 245" or "bribery" in the court papers. "OPL 245" and "bribery" were invented in media spins to give a dog a bad name in order to hang it. Not a dime has been traced to me. In an increasingly sophisticated world, a money trail is one of the easiest things to find and follow. Nothing can be traced to me because I did not collect any bribe. Truth is eternal.

The $2.2 million case being used to malign me was a loan I got from Unity Bank. True, I got a mortgage from the bank. The money was disbursed directly to the developer, not to me. When I couldn't meet my part of the obligation, the developer took back his property, sold it to the CBN and repaid the mortgage to Unity Bank. I was not involved in the repayment process. I even lost money because I had to pay interest on the loan. But the EFCC desperados twisted the facts to say I collected a bribe, just to satisfy their puppet masters. This is what 'campaigners' are relying upon in their miscalculated attempt to impugn my integrity.

Since 2015, the EFCC has been used to destroy the integrity of many Nigerians. Many have caved in to blackmail to avoid the media trial but I have resisted every attempt to extort me by the EFCC. I have stood my ground and paid a heavy price for it. My reputation has been damaged globally. But I am happy to have fought a good fight using nothing but the instruments of truth and the laws of the land. I am happy to have been vindicated. I pity other victims of the EFCC. Our experience in Nigeria, though, is that tyranny never endures. Power-drunk individuals like Magu always live the rest of their lives in regret for allowing themselves to be used to fight other people's battles.

For me, I will be back on my feet again. It is just a matter of time.

• • •

PART III

•

2015: THE ROAD FINALLY TAKEN

CHAPTER ELEVEN

THE CONSPIRACY OF EVENTS

With the benefit of hindsight, it was obvious that the politics to oust President Jonathan in 2015 commenced almost simultaneously with his winning the presidential election in 2011. Gen. Muhammadu Buhari, his main opponent who ran on the ticket of the Congress for Progressive Change (CPC), had challenged that election all the way to the Supreme Court and lost. Before that election, he had vowed that it was the last time he would contest for the presidency of Nigeria having made unsuccessful bids in 2003 and 2007. He reneged on that pledge, perhaps because he believed his destiny was positively beckoning or because his supporters got him to believe that nobody else had the kind of followership and clout to wrest power from a sitting President.

The 2011 presidential election had been peaceful until the results started rolling in. That was when violence broke out in some Northern states, particularly in Kaduna and Bauchi, leading to significant loss of lives and destruction of property. Many political watchers insisted that Buhari's style of campaign was responsible for the ensuing crisis. He was quoted as inciting his supporters to "escort the ballot, protect the ballot and kill if need be." After losing the election, he did not concede, thus triggering violent reactions from amongst his supporters in the North. Innocent people were killed. Most notably, 12 NYSC members lost their lives in Bauchi State.

The newly elected Jonathan government came under pressure to arrest and prosecute Buhari. Reasoning that any move against the latter, no matter how legal and altruistic, would only lead to more needless deaths, Jonathan refrained from toeing that line. Rather, on 9 May 2011, he inaugurated a 22-man Presidential Committee on the 2011 Election Violence and Civil Disturbances to investigate the causes of the post-election violence in parts of the country and make recommendations to forestall a reoccurrence.

The Committee was chaired by Sheikh Ahmed Lemu, a retired Grand Khadi of Niger State, with Honourable Justice Samson Uwaifo, a retired Justice of the Supreme Court, as the Vice Chairman. The Committee made a general condemnation of the political class in the country. It attributed the violence to the widespread desire for change in the political make-up of the country and that when it became apparent to many people that the change was not forthcoming, they resorted to violence. Other notable findings of the Committee included: the subsisting culture of impunity, bad governance, inciting political statements, insecurity, poverty, corruption, unemployment and the extravagant lifestyle of political office holders.

Although the Committee's findings did not specifically indict Buhari, the fact that he was associated with the making of "inciting political statements" led to the clamour for his arrest and prosecution over the loss of lives and property that followed the elections. Despite the clamour, government refrained from arresting him. Our consideration was the mood of the nation. We noted the bitterness in the core North. President Jonathan decided to cultivate him, given his cult-like followership in his part of the country. The strategy was to gain his confidence so that he would rein in his supporters for the necessary conducive atmosphere to govern the country.

Even within our party, the PDP, some members felt that President Jonathan had stolen the slot meant for the North. It was even rumoured then that some senior PDP members from the North backed Buhari against Jonathan based on the sentiments regarding power rotation, which should have seen power return to the North based on a gentleman's agreement that the PDP had adopted. That implied that on the death of President Yar'Adua after three years in office, the North should have had the pleasure of taking power for the remaining four years before passing it to the South again. Jonathan, being from the South, was, therefore, usurping the slot of the North, in their opinion. But Jonathan did not break any Nigerian law when he contested in that election. He only broke with the party's tradition. The repercussions, however, ended up reverberating beyond the PDP. Nothing Jonathan did, it appeared, was adequate to appease his adversaries.

The effect was that preparations for the 2015 elections commenced immediately after the 2011 elections, even among members of his own party. Some prominent PDP members went around the states canvassing that Jonathan had made an "irrevocable undertaking" not to contest in 2015. They latched on to a statement credited to President Obasanjo at the 2011 PDP National Convention to support their position. Indeed, it was touted that Obasanjo had praised Jonathan for being a great man who had promised to run for presidency for "only one term." When it became obvious that Jonathan might run for office again, some PDP leaders protested vehemently against that possibility, thus precipitating the first crisis in the party.

The crisis festered and worsened due to the disrespectful disposition of some governors towards the President. A case in point was Mr Timipre Silva, erstwhile Governor of Bayelsa, Jonathan's home state, who spearheaded opposition to that second term bid. These political differences created an atmosphere of mutual and deep suspicion. But Silva, whose first election was annulled, had other worries too, including the fact that he was going to contest in 2012, rather than 2011, as elections in Bayelsa were held on a different timeline from that of the general election. The President would not, therefore, be compelled to support him for re-election for a second term.

The fire of discord was stoked to such a conflagration by various interests that when the time came for Silva's re-election in 2012, the machinery for manipulations had swung into active mode. Some people called for a fresh primary election, even though Silva had already won the party's ticket. The crisis spread to other states too. In Kogi, Jibrin Isah Echocho had also won the PDP governorship primary election, but Governor Ibrahim Idris decided he preferred Alhaji Idris Wada.

Alhaji Kawu Baraje, then Acting Chairman of the PDP, called for caution as the party faced imminent implosion. But all he advocated was that Jonathan had the ultimate decision to make on the issue. Because of the sensitivity of the matter, I refrained from tabling it for discussion with the President. In my humble view, succession to political positions within the party did not fall within the remit of the Attorney-General. I had to watch, helplessly, as the fragile fabric of the party was being torn into shreds.

Some governors tried to intervene on behalf of Silva. They asked the President to support his re-election bid. The President could not make a firm commitment in that regard. At one point, Silva was reported to have threatened to kill President Jonathan, an allegation he denied. The security personnel made meat of that rumour, further stirring up the already boiling pot of trouble. The Governors became very bitter and felt that the President did not keep his words. Eventually, Chief Seriake Dickson was picked as the PDP candidate and he was elected the Governor of Bayelsa State.

There were other fires also burning up the polity: chiefly, the controversies over the management of the Excess Crude Account and the creation of the Sovereign Wealth Fund. Amaechi, then Governor of Rivers State, led some of his colleagues to war against President Jonathan, notwithstanding the fact that he was a member of the PDP.

• • •

On 1 January 2012, the President, under intense pressure from the Governors to remove the subsidy on petrol, caved in. The Governors regarded the subsidy regime as inefficient and a drain on resources that could have been better utilised on social services. In return for bending to their will, they promised to support the President "all the way." Nigerians woke up in a New Year to be jolted by the heart-rending news that the pump price of petrol had gone up. It was not the best New Year present to give!

With the subsidy removal, Jonathan played into the hands of his enemies. He had walked unknowingly into a trap. There was nationwide protest. The Administration never recovered from that massive blow. A President that had become so popular with the people, one who had won 23 out of 36 states in his election, had overnight been portrayed as an enemy of Nigerians. The Governors who promised to support the President over the subsidy removal betrayed him. They became experts at saying one thing to him and another behind him.

There was also the issue of single-term tenure, which was deliberately twisted to antagonise the President. It was part of the conspiracy of events ahead of the 2015 elections. I was at the Obudu Cattle Ranch Retreat with President Jonathan and Elder Godsday Orubebe, among others, shortly after the 2011 elections when the President made a statement regarding the single-term tenure. He had stated that the political straits of the nation appeared to him to be connected with the quest for second tenure by incumbents. According to him, in order to critically face Nigeria's development challenges, there was a need to amend the Constitution to allow for a single term of six years for the President and Governors. He reasoned that if the National Assembly were to agree to such an amendment, and if serving Governors would accede to it and decide not to seek a second term, he too was ready to serve only one term.

Having agreed on the spirit of the amendment, a draft was prepared and circulated among the leadership of the National Assembly for their input. However, the first-term Governors, being in greater number, felt threatened by the proposed amendment which would halt their second-term ambitions.

The proposal was killed on arrival. Opinion was divided between whether the President wanted to extend his tenure through the backdoor and the need to insert a transition clause so that the President would complete a six-year tenure. But that was not the intention of the President. In fairness to him, President Jonathan had truly intended to serve out his first term and forgo the idea of seeking a second term if the idea of a single six-year term had been agreed upon. But that was made impossible by the agitating first-term Governors.

With the proposal effectively killed, it became glaring to all that Jonathan would go on to seek a second term. Dissatisfied politicians orchestrated all manner of tactics to ensure he would not be able to seek re-election, including instigating legal actions against him, arguing that he was not qualified to run again having been sworn in twice as the substantive president. Mischievous constitutional interpretations were promoted all over the media space.

But section 137 (1) of the Constitution clearly states: *"A person shall not be qualified for election to the office of President if (b) he has been elected to such office at any two previous elections."*

Jonathan had been elected only once – in 2011 – and not twice. He had assumed power in 2010 because of the death of President Yar'Adua. Justice Mudashiru Oniyangi, who was then judge of the High Court of the FCT, made a profound ruling on the position of the Constitution, stating that Jonathan had not participated in the electoral process more than once. I thought that had settled the matter, but alas, it had not! Instead, the campaign that Jonathan couldn't seek a second term was accelerated. Oniyangi's judgment apparently gingered Jonathan's interest in that race.

• • •

The mounting pressure within the PDP, to my mind, led to many avoidable errors. One of such was the election of Alhaji Bamanga Tukur, former Governor of the defunct Gongola State, as National Chairman of the party in March 2012. That fundamental slip by the party struck a deadly blow on the PDP. Tukur, coming into office with a mindset that the Governors' excessive powers needed to be curtailed, openly confronted them. He started by dissolving PDP State Executive bodies, perceiving them as loyal to the Governors, particularly in his home state, Adamawa, where it was rumoured that he wanted to install his son, Awwal, as Governor.

It appeared that the President initially fully backed Tukur. He did not heed the Governors' entreaties. By the time he realised what was happening, irreparable damage had been done to the party. Tukur was not working cohesively with the PDP National Working Committee. He was also not at peace with the National Secretary, Prince Olagunsoye Oyinlola. Matters degenerated to such an extent that Alhaji Kashamu Buruji was rumoured to have been goaded to institute a court case against Oyinlola. In a jiffy, there was an order removing Oyinlola as the National Secretary. Oyinlola appealed against the order and won, but he was not reinstated. This further aggravated the problem on the ground.

Several PDP Governors began to gang up against the President. Seven of them formed a group they called the G-7, which openly attacked Jonathan at every turn. The G-7 was instrumental to the break-up of the PDP at the August 2013 mini-convention. The seven Governors walked out in protest. The former Vice-President, Alhaji Atiku Abubakar, joined them on their way out. The 'new PDP', led by Baraje, was, thereafter, formed. That was the last straw in the conspiracy of events that broke the back of the PDP and paved the way for the emergence of a strong opposition party.

The G-7 governors who walked out were: Dr Babangida Aliyu (Niger), who served as their Chairman, Rt Hon Rotimi Amaechi (Rivers State), Alhaji Rabiu Musa Kwankwaso (Kano), Rear Admiral Murtala Nyako (Adamawa), Mr Abdulfatah Ahmed (Kwara), Alhaji Magatakarda Wamakko (Sokoto) and Alhaji Sule Lamido (Jigawa). The President, under pressure from his political associates, failed to immediately confront and address the grievances of the Governors. Among the dissenters were people who also wanted to replace Jonathan as President. It was near impossible to appease them. The only thing they wanted to hear was that Jonathan would not seek a second term. At that juncture, there could only be a stalemate.

By the time Jonathan finally withdrew his backing for Tukur in January 2014, the damage had become irreparable. In November 2013, five of the governors had defected to the newly formed All Progressives Congress (APC), which was a merger of four parties: the Action Congress of Nigeria (ACN), the CPC, the All Nigeria Peoples Party (ANPP) and a faction of the All Progressives Grand Alliance (APGA). Although Lamido and Aliyu remained in the PDP, it was obvious that they were not enthusiastic about the Jonathan candidacy. There were constant speculations that they too would join the new opposition party, but, eventually, they did not.

• • •

While the defections to APC were quite devastating, the PDP hawks decided to hit back at the Governors. Some Governors went to the President to demand the removal of their colleagues who had defected. They were trying to rely on the judgment of the Supreme Court in the case of Amaechi. Indeed, the Supreme Court had ruled in that case that it is a political party that is voted into power, not the individuals who stood for elections. In that case, Amaechi had been picked as the PDP governorship candidate in Rivers State for the 2007 elections but it was Chief Celestine Omehia that was eventually presented by the party. Amaechi went to court and the Supreme Court ruled in his favour that he was the rightful candidate of the party. And since it was not the individual that canvassed for votes but the party, the Supreme Court directed that Amaechi be sworn in as Governor.

It was, therefore, the argument of the Governors that their colleagues who had defected to the APC were mere trustees of the PDP and could not defect to the opposition with the trust of the electorate. Essentially, they were canvassing that the affected Governors be removed and their Deputies who had not defected with them be sworn in as Governors. They canvassed that as for those who left with their Deputies, the Speakers of the respective State Houses of Assembly should be sworn in as Acting Governors pending elections.

With the abandonment of the party by the Governors, it could be argued that they were no longer Governors and their party should be allowed to replace them. I believed very firmly that what the Governors did was wrong. They certainly had the right to freedom of association. They were also free to cease to be members of the PDP, but they had no right, in my view based on the provision of Section 221 of the Constitution, to take with them the mandate that was entrusted to them by the party.

When the President sought my opinion on the matter, I advised that the party should not resort to self-help but seek judicial intervention on the matter. I also advised that it was not within the remit of the Attorney-General to institute such actions and that the party was best suited to commence the legal action. The PDP went to court but the contending issues were never determined because of the antics of the Governors that were involved in the matter.

It is, however, pertinent to emphasise that Section 221 of the Constitution states clearly that *"nobody can canvass for votes other than a registered political party."* This presupposes that it was the party that was voted for. And if that is the case, a Governor becomes, by implication, a trustee of the party. Can such a trustee run away with the trust? If a Governor, as trustee, decides to leave the party, what should be the right thing to do? Should he not resign from the office of Governor so that the party can either conduct a byelection or have him replaced by the Deputy Governor? Does it not amount to violating the spirit of the Constitution for a Governor to abandon the electorate that voted him into office under a particular party, and on top of that, still be able to retain that mandate? Unfortunately, the court never got the chance to adjudicate on any of these issues.

Another mistake made by the PDP was attempting to adopt the American model where a sitting President from the ruling party does not get challenged. Aspirants were not allowed to participate in the 2015 presidential primary. They should have realised that Nigerian democracy had not advanced to that level of maturity. In hindsight, it would have been better to have had a contentious primary. It would have created a moral burden for any aspirant who considered leaving afterwards. In my view, that would have accorded people the opportunity to ventilate their views by participating in the process to get a sense of accomplishment, even if they didn't win. That would have given the party's primary more credibility.

As soon as only one nomination form was printed for the presidential race, more upheaval was engendered. Many more people exited the party. Even those who remained were not there for the love of the party but for the benefit they stood to reap: campaign funds and more.

• • •

CHAPTER TWELVE

THE BUHARI TEST

Did Gen. Buhari really obtain a secondary school certificate? Should he be disqualified from participating in the presidential race? These questions floated in the air and foreshadowed the 2015 presidential election in Nigeria. The eligibility of Candidate Muhammadu Buhari of the APC was a major topic of discussion. In fact, as soon as he signified his intention to run, speculations became rife that he did not possess a School Certificate, the minimum academic qualification required to run for office, according to the 1999 Constitution of Nigeria (as amended).

Buhari was accused of being in violation of the provisions of Sections 131 of the 1999 Constitution on minimum educational qualification and Section 31 (3) of the 2010 Electoral Act which required that copies of his school certificate be attached to the INEC Form CF001. Buhari did not attach the certificate. Law suits were filed in court. In all, there were 13 court cases challenging his eligibility, the most prominent being the one filed by a certain Chukwunweike Okafor. Indeed, many private citizens went to court to challenge Gen. Buhari's eligibility.

I was informed by my friend, Mr Jimi Lawal, that while they were with Gen. Buhari in his house, Hon. Farouk Adamu Aliyu said I was behind the myriad of suits challenging his candidacy. Buhari looked in Mr Lawal's direction and replied: "Ask Jimi. He is AGF's friend..." But Lawal said he told them I would not need to hide behind anyone if I wanted to take Buhari on in court. That was the truth, in any case. I am not one to hide behind fronts and proxies. I go headlong. I still do not know if Buhari believed Lawal or the Farouk of a guy. I would guess, from what I have suffered since I left office, that he believed that Farouk instead.

In the fullness of time, though, President Buhari would come to realise and accept the whole truth: that God used me, and two other high-profile Nigerians whom I will not name for confidential reasons, to make sure he was not disqualified by the courts from running in 2015. The two individuals have, like me, also suffered indignity in the hands of Buhari and his men. It must be emphasised here, though, that I did not oppose the disqualification because I wanted to help Buhari. Rather, I was being faithful to the Constitution. I would argue on the side of the Constitution any day, no matter my political sentiments – even though there was the option to legally strangulate Buhari if we were desperate to hold on to power.

While the controversy was raging, a West African Senior School Certificate (WASSC) purportedly issued by the Katsina State Ministry of Education suddenly surfaced on the internet. On the face of it was the picture of a 72-year-old Buhari. It was dated 21 January 2015 (meanwhile, Katsina State was created in 1987). The certificate also contained a grading scheme that was not in use in 1962, around the time he was said to have sat for the examination. This generated public outrage as people were questioning the authenticity of the certificate and whether, indeed, Gen. Buhari had the requisite qualification or had committed forgery. A lot of petitions were sent to the Office of the Attorney-General of the Federation requesting that Buhari be prosecuted for forgery and INEC be advised to disqualify him.

In one instance, I received a letter from a lawyer asking for a fiat to prosecute Buhari on the ground of certificate forgery. I was constrained to deny the application as the lawyer had not furnished me the requisite material upon which I would exercise such discretion. Beyond applying for a fiat, the lawyer was also required to show evidence of having made a complaint to the police. A report detailing the outcome of the investigation was essential to ground such a fiat.

A week later, I met up with Dr Olusegun Mimiko, then Governor of Ondo State, at his request. After the exchange of pleasantries, he brought up the issue of the lawyer's request for a fiat to prosecute Gen. Buhari and appealed to me to grant it. I informed him that, regrettably, I was unable to grant the request for a number of reasons. I reiterated my response to that lawyer. I emphasised to Mimiko that the candidate in question was a former Head of State. In my opinion, even if he had no certificate, being a retired General in the Army, he must have passed Staff College which was more than an equivalent of the WASSC. I added that as a former Head of State, Gen. Buhari's experience would be more than 'an equivalent' of a school certificate. I drew attention to the provisions of Section 318 of the Constitution to support my assertion.

When I left Mimiko, I became worried that there was something going on in the political environment that I was not aware of. I drove straight to the President's residence. After recounting my interaction with Mimiko and the uncanny feeling that was bothering me to him, he calmly responded: "Do what is right."

Having had the presidential assurance to "do what is right", I decided to be pragmatic. At the back of my mind were memories of the violence that followed Buhari's loss in 2011 and his failure to call his supporters to order to avert bloodbath. I knew my job was well cut out for me. I was a member of the National Security Council. I knew the implications of a breakdown of law and order were Buhari to be disqualified. Besides, President Jonathan had persistently assured the world that his ambition was not worth the blood of any Nigerian.

• • •

It was not just the certificate issue that was being used against Buhari. There was also the retroactive sentence and execution of three Nigerian citizens under his watch as military Head of State. At 8:30 am on 10 April 1985, three young Nigerians were tied to the stakes at Kirikiri Prison and executed by a military firing squad. Bartholomew Azubike Owoh, 26, a former employee of Nigeria Airways, Lawal Akanni Ojuolape, 30, a spare parts dealer, and Bernard Ogedengbe, a 29-year-old sailor, had been sentenced to death, separately, by a military tribunal in December 1984.

They were found guilty of illegal possession of cocaine and heroin, punishable by death under Decree No. 20 of 1984. The death penalty was introduced after the offences had been committed. Despite the public outcry, the law was applied retroactively. More than 30 years after, the cry of Owoh as he faced the guns still rang in the ears of many Nigerians: "If I knew I would die for the offence I could have left the country after I was first given police bail!"

In 2015, Buhari was being called upon to account for his past. People were ready to resuscitate the matter by liaising with the three families concerned to institute a suit against Buhari in the UK with a view to getting him arrested and put on trial under the principle of 'universal jurisdiction'. Under this principle, former Heads of State could be prosecuted outside their countries for crimes committed while in office.

General Augusto Pinochet's case provided a good precedent for that contention. On 16 October 2008, the former Chilean dictator was arrested in

London following his indictment for human rights violations by a Spanish magistrate for crimes allegedly committed by him while in office. He was held for over a year by the UK authorities before he was released, most likely on compassionate grounds because of his old age. He had ruled Chile for 17 years and had been accused of committing numerous human rights violations.

I turned down all those who approached me to trigger the universal criminal jurisdiction principle to get Gen. Buhari arrested and put on trial abroad. The political future of Nigeria, I maintained, needed to be developed by allowing healthy contestation for office. I refused to have a hand in the attempt to give Buhari the Pinochet treatment. I briefed the President about it because some mischief-makers were already calling me a Buhari sympathiser for not toeing their line. I was branded a closet APC member too. The blackmail was sickening.

President Jonathan, however, agreed with my position that we should not play the Pinochet card. He thought the government would be seen as encouraging 'bad politics' if we succumbed to that call. He was under intense pressure from some associates to use any means necessary to stop Buhari but he opted to participate in competitive politics in a fair and credible manner, not taking undue advantage of any quick-fix scenario that was presented to him. I strongly believed, on my part, that the electorate should be left the freedom to exercise their political judgment. It was not for us to use our institutions and the instruments of law to hound anybody.

There was also the Lemu Panel Report that some people were eager to use against Buhari. Since 2011, there had been pressure on me to prosecute Buhari after the post-election violence in which over 800 people were killed. He was captured on video appearing to use violent language to incite his supporters during the campaigns. But I felt that those words were uttered in the heat of the moment as passions were inflamed. In any case, having won the election in 2011, Jonathan felt more compelled to build peace and assuage frayed nerves. Putting Buhari on trial would have further polarised a nation in which ethnic and religious sentiments are easily mobilised for political purposes. Based on these considerations, I declined to put Buhari on trial.

The option was available, too, to refer the matter to the Office of the Prosecutor of the International Criminal Court (ICC) for crimes against humanity. It involved loss of lives due to electoral violence. We could have claimed that the political environment was such that would not allow for a fair trial in Nigeria and would have referred the matter to the ICC as governments in other countries were doing to their political opponents.

We chose not to go that route not because we could not, but because it would further fracture the fragile peace in the country. The point is that if President Jonathan was desperate to stop Buhari, he could still have gone ahead with the prosecution and damned the consequences. The best I could have done as Attorney-General was to resign. But he could have appointed another willing Attorney-General to prosecute the matter. It is very important to stick this point at the back of our minds.

• • •

The 2015 elections timetable had to be adjusted to forestall a potential political crisis, as the Boko Haram insurgency raged strongly in the North East. The perception in Buhari's camp was that the change was intended to hurt their candidate. That was preposterous! It would have been to our advantage for elections to have proceeded as scheduled: the insurgency-prone areas were Buhari's strongholds. The PDP would have enjoyed some numerical advantage.

The Boko Haram crisis would have meant that Buhari's supporters would have been deterred from actively participating in the elections by the violence and threats to life. As at early 2015, Borno, Yobe, Adamawa and parts of Bauchi and Gombe had become affected by the insurgency. The only state Jonathan could count on his side was Taraba, which was not affected by the crisis. Some Jonathan supporters had pressed for him to cash in on the situation, but some of us felt that if elections were not held in Borno and Yobe, which were the worst affected states, the credibility could be questioned.

The government was conscious of the fact that it would constitute a huge problem were Buhari to lose the election. Claims of having manipulated the election against Buhari's interest would have been raised and President Jonathan's legitimacy would have been challenged. To avoid that scenario, government insisted on conducting elections in all troubled states as well. Good enough, the military was able to arrest the deteriorating situation when the programme was adjusted by six weeks. As things turned out, the results from Borno and Yobe States were overwhelmingly in support of Buhari. Many people would later criticise Jonathan for being 'naïve'.

For the record, I would like to correct the notion that President Jonathan breached the provisions of the Constitution by sanctioning the adjustment to the election timetable. He did not. The Constitution provides under Section 132(2) for an election to hold on a date not earlier than 150 days and not later than 30 days before the expiration of the tenure of the President or a Governor. This period was not breached. Besides, in the interim, government was able to take delivery of critical equipment for the military that enabled them to ramp up the anti-insurgency war and recover some of the local government areas that were under the control of Boko Haram in the North East.

Moreover, if President Jonathan needed to postpone the general election, as some politicians were urging him to do, there are ample provisions in the Constitution that he could have employed to serve that purpose. Most notable are the provisions of Section 135 (3) of the Constitution which state:

> If the Federation is at war in which the territory of Nigeria is physically involved and the President considers that it is not practicable to hold elections, the National Assembly may by resolution extend the period of four years mentioned in subsection (2) of this section from time to time; but no such extension shall exceed a period of six months at any one time.

Given the potency of this provision and because the country was at war with Boko Haram, members of the National Assembly who had lost out in the nomination process of their party primaries – and they were the majority across party lines – sought to convince the President to deploy the instrumentality of Section 135(3) to postpone the elections for a period of six months in the first instance and every six months pending when normalcy would return.

The security situation in the country was such that Boko Haram had captured Nigerian territories up to 'the size of Belgium', as a foreign journalist put it. Instead of the election holding in March 2015, therefore, President Jonathan could have moved it to September 2015. If still not satisfied that the conditions were good enough for an election, he could have further postponed it by another six months, taking it all the way to March 2016, subject of course, to the resolution of the National Assembly approving the postponement.

To the credit of President Jonathan, he insisted that even if he was going to lose the election, he was not going to postpone it. The President, conscious of his democratic credentials, did not want to lose legitimacy in whatever form. For him, it wasn't just about his political interest. The legitimacy factor was important to him too. Even in adjusting the timetable, the President did not act arbitrarily. He had called a meeting of the National Council of State, made up of all the 36 Governors, former Heads of State, retired Chief Justices of Nigeria, and the Attorney-General of the Federation. He put the whole issue on the table. The National Security Adviser, INEC and other stakeholders, such as the security chiefs, had also been asked to address the Council on the matter.

After they had made their submissions and analyses, it was glaring that the election timetable needed to be adjusted. There were disproportionate collection rates of the biometric voter's card in the states. Indeed, most Nigerians had not collected their PVCs. In order not to disenfranchise the majority of the electorate, there was a need to address these diverse problems and find a common solution. The National Council of State advised INEC to take a second look at it and make the necessary adjustment in the national interest.

Gen. Buhari opposed the adjustment at the meeting. The APC Governors also opposed it. I felt that they thought their party was poised to win and believed the government was hesitating to go ahead with the elections because of that. Little did they realise that they were going to be the ultimate beneficiaries of the adjustment. The timetable was adjusted and the presidential election was held on 28 March, instead of the original date of 14 February.

• • •

CHAPTER THIRTEEN

THE HISTORIC CONCESSION

"Have you come to tell me I lost the election?" President Jonathan asked us.

On Sunday, 29 March 2015, the day after the presidential election, I, along with Col. Sambo Dasuki, National Security Adviser, and Ambassador Hassan Tukur, Principal Secretary to the President, went to the Presidential Villa to see the President as the feedback we were getting on the elections appeared rather bleak. It had become obvious that the political leaders who promised to deliver certain states had failed. Worse still, they had betrayed our confidence. We needed to apprise the President of the situation to prepare his mind for the worst.

It was lunchtime at the Villa but there was no merriment on the menu. The President did not look particularly sad, but, understandably, neither did he exude that much confidence. When he popped the question ("Have you come to tell me I lost the election?") it had the impact of stilling the atmosphere, further chilling out the already fraught state of things. The ensuing silence had an edge to it. You could hear a pin drop! The air of foreboding was acute. Of course, we had not come to tell him he had lost. That would have been too early. Announcement of results was not to be expected before Monday, 30 March. In fact, the winner was not expected to be officially announced until Wednesday, 1 April. Our mission, rather, was to review the situation.

"If I lose, I will not contest the outcome. I will call and congratulate Gen. Buhari," he promised, not for the first time.

Looking at him at that moment, we could see a man who was at peace with himself, a man who was more worried about getting the election process right. It was not about losing or winning the race.

"Mr President," I made to lighten the mood in the room, "nothing is certain yet. We could still hope for a run-off even if we don't win at first ballot."

He did not look convinced. Perhaps I was in denial. Much as we tried to change the topic, we could not get away from discussing our disappointment with politicians whom we had thought trustworthy. What remained clear to us, however, was that the President was prepared to do what no previous presidential candidate had ever done in the history of Nigeria: concede an election while the final result was yet to be announced. Even Alhaji Bashir Tofa who was reported to have congratulated Chief MKO Abiola in the June 12 presidential election of 1993 ended up denying that he did.

On 30 March, a day after our visit to President Jonathan, Chief Mike Oghiadomhe, Chief of Staff to the President from 2010–2014, also went to see him at the residence. He told me that he found his former boss taking down his books from the shelves and packing them, obviously in preparation for his exit from office. Seeing the surprised look on Oghiadomhe's face, President Jonathan said: "Look, Mike, elections have been won and lost. A President has been elected. It is time to go home." From all indications, Jonathan believed he had lost the election. He was prepared to concede to Gen. Muhammadu Buhari.

On 31 March 2015, Alhaji Ahmadu Adamu Mu'azu, National Chairman of the PDP, came to my office at the Ministry of Justice at 10am. Mu'azu was not looking lively. Nobody was. Defeat was staring all of us in the face. It was just a matter of time before it became official.

He said: "My brother, the way the results are going, we are likely to lose the election."

I agreed with him. I had been in denial on Saturday and Sunday, but by Monday I had realised it was a lost battle. Mu'azu said he was deeply worried at the likely turn of events, especially if the President refused to concede or decided to challenge the results. There would be consequences. He reminded me of the violence that greeted the 2011 elections after President Jonathan was declared the winner and feared that the country was at the verge of another bloodbath, especially if the President refused to accept defeat.

He then dropped a bombshell.

"If the President does not concede between now and 5 pm, I, as the National Chairman of the PDP, will have no option than to concede on behalf of the party," he said.

It didn't sound like a joke. I became alarmed. We had a bigger problem on our hands than I had imagined. The tension lines in the country were multifaceted and deeper than ever: Christian/Muslim dichotomy; North/ South divide; Hausa-Fulani/Ijaw tension; majority vs. minority sentiments. Mu'azu was a Northern Muslim like Buhari. If he conceded the election on behalf of the party, it would be interpreted in various ways. He had already been treated with some suspicion in the Jonathan camp. Many people were not convinced Mu'azu was committed to the cause. I had a situation on my hand. I needed to manage the information he just handed to me with tact.

Mu'azu conceding defeat, to my mind, would make him the new hero of democracy. That would have taken victory from the jaws of the President and would have left Jonathan in the cold. It had been widely speculated that Mu'azu was nursing a presidential ambition. Conceding ahead of Jonathan could be interpreted to mean he was already placing himself in a prime position ahead of the 2019 elections. I felt that if the President was going to lose the election, he must not lose his dignity as well. He must be a statesman. There were, of course, the national security implications.

Earlier that morning, I had received a call from a lady who was sounding desperate on the phone. She said with the way results were going, there was a need to act urgently to stop the President from losing the election. She suggested that I should go and get a court injunction to stop further announcement of results. What came to my mind immediately was the 1993 presidential election when the Association for Better Nigeria (ABN) used the courts to truncate the announcement of results. The election was eventually annulled and this plunged Nigeria into a prolonged crisis and led to death and destruction.

I told the lady, without thinking twice, that election had taken place and it was incumbent on INEC to announce the results and declare the winner. I said I was the Attorney-General of the Federation and not the Attorney-General of the PDP. If the PDP had any problems with the conduct of the election, I said, they should collate their evidence and get their lawyers to head to the elections petitions tribunal. I told her, politely, that nobody should call me again. She did not like it, but I was thinking of the larger picture: the peace and progress of Nigeria.

After Mu'azu left my office, I remembered the words of the desperate lady. I decided to act fast. The first thing I did was to go to the office of Col. Dasuki to alert him on the brewing problem. I sought his opinion on how to manage the situation. While we were trying to work out a solution, some hawks within the administration, who had been heating up the polity with careless statements, arrived to say there was still something that could be done to change the situation. They were asking for "support" to facilitate victory for the PDP. Dasuki and I looked at them and told them directly that it would not be in the national interest.

I was still in the office of the NSA when I received a call from Chief Osita Chidoka, then Minister of Aviation, urging me to hasten my way to the Presidential Villa, insisting that I was one of the very few who could douse the conflagration that was raging. Meanwhile, I noticed that more and more people were beginning to troop into the office of the NSA.

As I was about rounding off the discussion with Col. Sambo, Chidoka called for the second time, asking desperately: "AGF, where are you?" The anxiety in his voice and the urgency with which he sought my attention led me to assure him that I would be with him in good time. I immediately left Dasuki's office and rushed to the Villa. As I was stepping onto the red carpet, there was Chidoka to meet me.

"Suddenly, there is so much pressure on the President not to accept the election results," he told me.

I could see the alarm in his eyes. I was disheartened. The President had consistently stated he would concede, that he would not go to court, and that he was ready to go home. Who were the hawks putting him under pressure? Why would they do this to him? My head was bursting with unanswered questions. I could not think straight.

I went into the room where the President was. I could see Dr Ngozi Okonjo-Iweala, the Co-ordinating Minister of the Economy and Minister of Finance, sitting beside him. Vice-President Namadi Sambo was on the other side. There was also the Governor of Akwa Ibom State, Chief Godswill Akpabio, as well as Mr Kennedy Okpara, the Executive Secretary of the Nigerian Christian Pilgrims Commission. Hon. Waripamo-Owei Dudafa, the Special Assistant (Domestic) to the President, was there too. There were other persons there too that I am unable to recall.

The President was talking, looking forlorn. Okonjo-Iweala was speaking to him. What I could gather from my observation was an uncongenial atmosphere – and justifiably so. We all felt betrayed by our political associates and friends who could not deliver on their promises to the President. Also, the President complained about underage voting and massive rigging, particularly in the North West where Buhari got the most votes. While he got 1.3 million votes in the zone, Buhari scored 7.1 million. That was a whopping difference of 5.8 million! It looked incredible. The issue of the uneven distribution of PVCs across the political strongholds of the candidates was also discussed. The President kept venting his frustration and disappointment. But, to be fair to him, he did not at any point say that he would not concede.

As a matter of background, the DG of Department of State Services (DSS), Mr Ita Ekpeyong, had come to see the President earlier in the morning of that day to notify him that the way the results were going, he had lost the election. Ita then advised him to put a concession call to Buhari or issue a statement. The President said it was too early, that there was a need to wait and see the emerging development. After the DSS DG left the Villa, President Jonathan had called Dr Reuben Abati, his Special Adviser on Media and Publicity, and asked him to prepare a speech.

The thrust of that speech was to the effect that he had kept his promise to Nigerians to conduct an election and that Nigerians should go about their activities peacefully while awaiting the final result. He admonished them to eschew bitterness, rancour and a breakdown of law and order while awaiting the final result. He asked Abati to work with Dr Akinwunmi Adesina, Minister of Agriculture, and one other person to prepare the speech. While the speech was being prepared, people kept coming in with various reports about rigging and manipulation, so they made things difficult. All this had happened earlier on 31 March.

At the afternoon gathering to which Chidoka hurriedly invited me, I heard Dr Okonjo-Iweala say that President Jonathan still needed to put a call to Buhari despite all the disheartening reports. Indeed, she was trying her best to be supportive but the President was agitated. I fixed my gaze on the President. He finally noticed that I was in the room. I could see a change in his countenance. We had that kind of bond. I looked him straight in the eye but did not utter a word.

Studying the room and taking stock of the situation, I approached Akpabio and urged him, as the Chairman of the PDP Governors' Forum, to prevail on the President to put a call to Buhari and concede gracefully.

"Let's hold on a bit," Akpabio suggested.

I then approached Vice-President Namadi Sambo.

"I think you should urge the President to call Gen. Buhari and concede," I told him.

"No!" Vice-President Sambo thundered. "Let the results be announced first."

I would later learn from Prof. Abubakar Suleiman, then Minister of National Planning, that the Vice-President told him I was an APC man and was the arrowhead of those who prevailed on the President to hastily concede defeat. According to Prof. Suleiman, he immediately dismissed Sambo's insinuations. It was obvious that the VP did not want the President to concede at that time.

The room was, to put it frankly, full of hawks. They were playing on the emotions of the President and trying to dissuade him from following the path he had carved for himself five years earlier on the mantra that nobody's blood was worth his ambition.

Dudafa, who was standing by one corner in the room, suddenly shouted, like a man possessed: "Daddy, we are leaving this place on the 29th of May."

The room went quiet. Gathering momentum from that, I joined Chidoka and Dudafa to approach the President, who was sitting. We stooped to speak with him. I whispered to the President: "You have been a champion of electoral reforms." The look on his face was like "you are right." Chidoka and Dudafa echoed the same sentiments. This was a little past 3 pm. President Jonathan then got up and went into the study with Dudafa. He came out a few seconds later and told us he had just called Buhari to congratulate him.

President Jonathan had just done the unthinkable! Nigerians had just witnessed that unforgettable, historic moment in their history. The hawks had failed woefully with their last-minute efforts to play on President's emotions and make him renege on his promise. The President demonstrated his will so powerfully.

Chidoka, full of excitement, asked: "Mr President, can I tweet it?"

Jonathan nodded his affirmation. And that was how Chidoka broke the internet with the tweet: "President Jonathan congratulates Gen. Buhari in a phone call this evening."

No single person can claim credit for that historic moment. President Jonathan's key policy and legal advisers offered their own opinions and he could have ignored them. But he was very ready to play the role of a sportsman and a statesman. He was not clearly thinking of the election itself; he was thinking rather of the fate of the country. He was more interested in the electoral reforms bearing fruits in the interest of the citizens of the nation. He was not a man of inordinate ambition.

If there was one person that should be praised and hailed for the unprecedented act, it is President Jonathan himself. No matter the amount of persuasion and intervention, if he was not interested in handing over power, he would not have conceded. But, truth be told, he was not the only hero of that historic concession, given that the hawks were almost overwhelming him at some point.

• • •

There was also the contention that having conceded defeat, he later told the party to challenge the results in court. I was not part of it, but from what I understand, the party leaders had had an expanded meeting during which they expressed their displeasure at the President's action in conceding without consulting them. Some threatened to go court to challenge the election results.

Chief Emeka Nwogu, the Minister of Labour and Productivity, came in from Aba, Abia State, that morning and headed straight to the Presidential Villa. He arrived shortly after the President had made the concession call. He was then asked to join a group of politicians meeting in a different room. They were discussing how to go to the tribunal to challenge the result. Nwogu declined to join them, asking why they would still be discussing litigation after the historic concession.

Those of us who urged the President to concede took cognisance of precedence all over the world and found that a candidate didn't wait for the party in order to concede an election. The practice was always to concede first and later conduct a post-election review. Besides, we had earlier agreed with the President that there would be no need to challenge the results. This was to prevent a situation where the President-elect would say that he was unable to perform because of the distractions arising from the election petition. Statesmanship has a price. You cannot win on all counts.

• • •

CHAPTER FOURTEEN

THE AFTERMATH

On the evening of Monday, 30 March 2015, when the results coming in were clearly not going our way, I went to the Presidential Villa with a request from the FCT Judicial Service Commission for the appointment of Hon. Justice Ishaq Bello as the Acting Chief Judge of the FCT. I was in the lounge with Dr Ahmadu Ali, one-time National Chairman of the PDP who served as the Director-General of the presidential campaign; Chief Ifeanyi Ubah, a political associate of the President; and a few others.

The First Lady, Dame Patience Jonathan, came out and acknowledged the usual courtesies from everybody except me. Stunned, I repeated the greeting with emphasis. "Your Excellency I am greeting you," I said. She asked why I was greeting her after betraying her husband. She went on to make some uncomplimentary remarks which seemed to suggest that I didn't give the President enough legal support to overcome his political challenges, especially with the opposition party.

I was jolted. But I was happy the First Lady voiced out her misgivings to me head-on. I was not unaware of conjectures in some quarters insinuating that I was sympathetic to Buhari and that I was a closet APC supporter. Possibly, there may also be others who could be spreading the theory that I was a Northern Muslim secretly working to support another Northern Muslim to take over power from a Southern Christian.

I had been accused of not supporting the various calls to prosecute or issue fiat to prosecute Buhari for certificate forgery. I had been accused of not backing the exhumation of the judicial murder of 1984, and of not handing Buhari over to the ICC for prosecution for electoral violence. I had also resisted attempts by some highly placed persons to obtain a restraining order to stop the counting of the votes and release of the results when it became obvious that we were going to lose. All these probably culminated in the conclusion by some people that I handed power to Buhari.

I appreciated the First Lady for dressing me down in public, for telling me her mind, for not offering me a plastic smile and pretending that all was well. I was embarrassed, truly, but that was not the worst thing that could happen to a human being. Being dressed down in public by the First Lady was the least of my worries. I still managed to respond: "Madam First Lady, I served the President creditably well. I would have been astonished if this came from the President himself, but since it is coming from you, I take it as a statement that was made out of place."

When I eventually went in to see the President, my mind was still unsettled. Presenting the letter from the FCT Judicial Service Commission to him, I sat there quietly ruminating on the encounter with the First Lady. He noticed that I was disturbed.

"My Attorney-General, what is the matter?" he asked.

I narrated the incident to him. In his humble and humane manner, he apologised on her behalf. "It is one of the hazards of office. Please let go," the President pleaded. I did. As far as I was concerned, the President had apologised. That settled everything.

• • •

I was to face more in-house attacks after my humiliating encounter with the First Lady. I was constantly described as a "Buhari boy." It seemed the President was beginning to believe the gossips, because, for once, he confronted me with the allegation. I cannot remember any other occasion on which the President confronted me with allegations made by gossips.

After the elections had been concluded, the National Assembly curiously passed into law the Constitution Fourth Amendment Bill 2015 and sent it to the President for assent. I had travelled out of the country when this happened and on return discovered that the bill had not been forwarded to me for review as was the practice with President Jonathan. On getting wind that the President was about to transmit his assent to the National Assembly, I quickly placed a call to the Senior Special Assistant to the President on Administration, Mr Matt Aikhionbare, to confirm if, indeed, the President had signed the bill.

Upon confirmation that he had, I requested Aikhionbare not to transmit the instrument to the National Assembly as I needed to discuss some of the amendments with the President. I felt I owed a duty to the nation to prevent such a calamity as the amendments were fraught with irregularities and were done without due process. I immediately rushed over to the Presidential Villa. I met the SGF, Anyim, with the President. When I asked the President if it was true that the National Assembly had sent the Constitution Amendment Bill to him and if he had signed it, he confirmed that he assented to the bill "a few minutes ago."

I informed him that there were many contentious provisions in the amendments. Some of the provisions, in my humble view, were purely self-serving. For one, the bill sought to take away the power of the President to assent to constitutional amendments. That meant that the legislature would, on its own, amend the Constitution and it would become operational without the consent of the President of the Federal Republic of Nigeria. Two, the bill sought to make Presiding Officers of the National Assembly life members of the National Council of State. Only former Presidents/Heads of State and Chief Justices of Nigeria were permanent members. Three, the bill sought to put Presiding Officers of the National Assembly on life pensions irrespective of the duration of their service. Four, the bill also granted immunity to lawmakers in the same vein as the President, Vice-President, Governors and Deputy Governors.

I further enumerated some other lapses in the bill, including the fact that the thresholds for amendments in respect of provisions of Chapters Two and Four were not met; some policies verging on the fundamental objectives and directive principles of state policy which are not justiciable, being in Chapter Two, were moved to Chapter Four, which made them justiciable. Moreover, I pointed out the economic and financial implications of the items being introduced by the bill.

The clauses seeking immunity for the lawmakers, life pensions for their Presiding Officers, and life membership of the National Council of State had apparently escaped the vigilance of the President. Nor had he averted his mind to some of the far-reaching implications that the amendments connoted, such as the bifurcation of the office of the AGF and Ministry of Justice portfolio. Reminding him that I was an advocate of the bifurcation, I, however, drew his attention to the clumsy manner in which the provisions had been drafted without showing clearly which of them would be the Chief Law Officer of the nation.

The President looked genuinely surprised and promptly withdrew his assent. He directed me to prepare a memorandum elucidating all the issues I had raised and why he would have to veto the bill. Then I pressed him for the reason he had not sent the bill to the Ministry of Justice, contrary to the usual practice. His response showed that he was put under pressure by certain Senators to sign the bill as time was of the essence. Even as he made that explanation and handed me the bill to review, it still left a bad taste in my mouth to think that he would sacrifice the benefit of a sound legal advice on crucial amendments to the Constitution on the altar of exigency.

A former Senator, who stood to benefit from the amendment in form of life pension and life membership of the National Council of State, tried to prevail on me to back down on my opposition to the presidential assent. But I reasoned that the amendments would be taken in bad taste as the President had just lost the election and would be vacating office in less than three weeks. If he had won, he would probably not have assented to a bill that sought to, among other things, make 'legislative tyrants' of the National Assembly and weaken the powers of the President.

I suspect, till date, that it was this former Senator that leaked my position to the Principal Officers of the National Assembly. It generated a lot of controversies. The National Assembly threatened to override the President's veto. That was to bring me in direct conflict with the National Assembly and the then Senate President, Senator David Mark, who once jokingly referred to me as the "all-powerful Attorney-General." I was a bit upset by the development. Senator Mark was my boss, a friend and one of those people who had supported me throughout my tenure as Minister of Justice. I felt terrible that I could not explain to him the rationale behind my objection.

I also learnt that Senator Esther Nenadi Usman, a Senator from Kaduna State who had served as the Director of Finance of Jonathan's re-election campaign, was delegated by the Senate to prevail on the President to reconsider his stance. She had bragged to her colleagues that she had a tremendous influence on the President and would ensure a reversal. She went to the President to completely misrepresent the good intentions behind my objection to the Presidential assent.

She said I confessed to Senator Ike Ekweremadu, the Deputy Senate President, that I was a 'Buhari boy' and that I was determined to protect Buhari to ensure that he was not robbed of the powers vested in him by the Constitution. She said I had bragged to Ekweremadu that I was going to stop the President from signing the bill into law. While I actually spoke with Ekweremadu on the amendments and the reasons why the President could not assent to the bill, I never boasted I would stop the assent. I never at any time told him that I was a sympathiser of Buhari.

On the contrary, it was President Jonathan I was trying to protect as he had just gained significant political mileage, being the first presidential candidate ever in Nigeria to accept defeat despite the flaws in the elections that could have been legally challenged. I was later to find out that Senator Usman was one of those that pressurised the President to sign the bill in the first place. She had argued that since we were all leaving office, there was no need for the Attorney-General to look into the various amendments. That argument swayed the President into signing. But, fortunately for me, it had not been transmitted to the Senate, and I was able to step in and persuade the President to withdraw his signature.

I had explained my reservations about the amendments to Ekweremadu. I had given him the necessary respect by calling him earlier to explain to him that the proposed amendments would be offensive to the Constitution if passed the way they were. There was a need to have them redrafted. I had emphasised that the most offensive were the areas which would have created legislative tyranny by doing away with presidential assent. In other words, they were vacating Section 58 of the Constitution which stipulates that the President must assent to all bills. I informed him that in respect of constitutional amendments, the President's assent would no longer be required if the amendments were allowed. I felt the usual checks on the exercise of legislative powers as provided by the Constitution through presidential assent were being unduly whittled down. This was more so as there was no provision for a referendum to enable Nigerians evaluate and decide on the utility or otherwise of the proposed amendments.

If such amendments were allowed to go through, Nigeria would have been subjected to the tyranny of the legislature as the legislators could wake up one day and legislate the Office of the President out of existence and the President would not need to sign for that to be! Situating the scenario within our recent history, we could, with all modesty, feel proud of the proactive steps we took to avert a serious constitutional problem. Just imagine what the National Assembly would have done with such a power! All they needed to do was to summon 24 speakers, and before you knew it, they would have amended the Constitution with limitless possibilities at their fingertips.

• • •

On 12 May 2015, we held the last National Security Council meeting under the Jonathan Administration. After the meeting, the President asked me to see him in his office. There, he confronted me with the accusation that he was told I had prevailed on him to withdraw his assent to the amendments because I was a 'Buhari boy'. I found the allegation ridiculous. I was being accused of disloyalty by the very President to whom I had given my total and unalloyed loyalty! I was devastated and sad.

Within myself, I went down memory lane, recalling some instances when I could have betrayed him but had stood firmly by him. For instance, I was approached by one of the Principal Officers of the current National Assembly to contribute to the Buhari campaign election fund, but I refused to, reiterating I would swim and sink with President Jonathan. To that person, I was on a suicide mission as many of my cabinet colleagues, including those known to be close to the President, had made donations to Buhari's campaign. Those involved included heads of agencies. A Principal Officer of the National Assembly from the PDP was to later confess publicly that he donated N5 million to the APC during the elections. I never donated a farthing to Buhari.

Similarly, one of the frontline ambassadors in the country had attempted to prevail on me to consider the possibility of working for President Buhari. But I declined instantly, insisting that I was not only a frontline member of the outgoing administration, I was also too close to Jonathan to contemplate serving under Buhari.

I had just suffered the indignity of being accused of disloyalty by the First Lady, and now the President was confronting me with another allegation. I felt humiliated. I told him: "Mr President, whatever I do, I act in your best interest. And I swear by everything I hold so dear in my life that I would be the last person to be a Buhari boy because you have given me what Buhari could not have given me. God used you to make me the Attorney-General of the Federation for over a period of five years. What else is Buhari coming to give me? What other office is there? Only the offices of the President, the Vice-President, the Senate President and the Speaker are more prestigious and important than the office of the AGF. Why would I now want to sell your trust for a mess of pottage?"

After listening to me, he seemed to have believed me.

He wrote a letter to withhold his assent and the National Assembly started grandstanding that they were going to override the President. They demanded the original copy of the bill, which had the President's signature.

But we ignored them. We advised that they should review the bill, but they could not as time was, indeed, short. They also threatened to impeach the President. In fact, they started assembling themselves to begin an impeachment process. We ignored them and stood our ground.

When I realised that they were about to engage in legislative rascality, I went to the Supreme Court to slow them down. Even though the legal process I was about to take was an inchoate process, considering the bill had not become law, I nonetheless saw it as necessary in the nation's interest. We filed papers at the Supreme Court, making the matters subjudice, thus slowing down the process. The Supreme Court, however, asked all parties to go and reach a settlement. I was not averse to that.

We set up a team. The National Assembly team was led by Ekweremadu, with Ihedioha, Senator Victor Ndoma-Egba, and some others as members. My team comprised Chief Bayo Ojo, Alhaji Ahmed Yola and my aides. I didn't attend the meeting because I would be the person that was going to advise the President. I didn't want to be bound by the outcome of the committee's deliberation. My team calmly took them through the proposed amendments, detailing their implications and impacts contrary to specific provisions of the Constitution, such as Section 9 on the procedure for the amendment of the Constitution and Section 8 on state creation, etc.

My team deconstructed what the National Assembly sought to achieve with the amendments. They finally realised their errors and mooted the idea of a compromise. We did arrive at a settlement after they agreed to expunge most of the offending provisions. However, they didn't touch the areas of life membership of the National Council of State, life pensions and immunity. We refused to budge. Nigerians were already complaining about the immunity accorded to the executive arm of government. The public would never stand for immunity for the legislature as well.

After the agreement, they were supposed to clean up the bill and send to us so we could take it to the President for assent. When they reverted, I had a reservation about the process: it was not legitimate, legal and constitutional for a committee of the National Assembly to be sent on an errand to negotiate to bind the legislature to a law it passed – without going back to the whole house for a ratification of the decision.

Rather than effect the amendments both teams agreed on, they cunningly did some cosmetic changes and preserved the entire principal provisions that we agreed should be deleted. Instead of sending it to the AGF, they sent it directly to the President, thinking that he would say since we had negotiated, he would sign. But the President, in his wisdom, refused to sign out of abundance of caution, and sent the bill back to me.

When the President returned it to me, there were only 48 hours remaining for us to leave government. I noticed that all the infractions we had complained about were still in place. I wrote back to the National Assembly to state that what was before me was a violation of the agreement both teams had reached. I insisted that until those amendments were reflected, I would not be in a position to advise the President to sign. They were really surprised that the President still sent it to me.

I also posited that I would be most guided if they could advise me on whether or not the agreement reached between the teams obviated the necessity for the ratification of the members of the National Assembly. I purposely left out the need for ratification by State Houses of Assembly, not wanting to be accused of becoming a deliberate stumbling block. They then made some quick changes by ensuring that the appropriate corrections were effected. However, they still retained the clauses on membership of the National Council of State and life pensions for principal members.

As at the day they sent it to me, we had only 24 hours left. They kept calling me frantically to find out if the President had signed it, and I kept giving excuses. But I knew I was not going to advise the President to sign that bill. I knew that if the President had signed it, he would have signed himself into trouble. I knew that many stakeholders would have gone to court to challenge it. I refused. As at the night we went for the dissolution of FEC, it was too late for the President to sign. I told him that the amended version was actually sent to me but that it was too late for him to sign. I advised him to allow the bill go to the next assembly to do the proper thing.

That was how the self-serving bill ended up not being signed.

• • •

PART IV

•

THE CHALLENGES,
THE CONTROVERSIES

CHAPTER FIFTEEN

THE IMPEACHMENT MENACE

July 2014 appeared to have kicked off Nigeria's festival of impeachments. The first was the successful impeachment of retired Rear Admiral Murtala Nyako, Governor of Adamawa State, by the House of Assembly. Nyako had been President Jonathan's fierce opponent who had gone to the extent of declaring that the Federal Government was behind the Boko Haram insurgency. To cap it all, Nyako had even defected to the APC. Ordinarily, Jonathan should have been happy that his 'enemy' was removed from office. But that wasn't the case. I can't recollect what misgivings the President had about it.

Perhaps the President was conscious of a possible constitutional crisis, given that the Deputy Governor, Chief James Nggilari, was forced to resign at the same time. The President might have known that there was a political scheme afoot. It was not an ordinary impeachment. Removing Nyako and Nggilari at the same time would automatically make the Speaker, Alhaji Umaru Fintiri, the Acting Governor. At that time, there was a lot of indiscipline in the PDP. The Adamawa legislators had their way and illegally and wrongfully forced Nggilari to resign and subsequently removed the Governor.

Fintiri was sworn in as Acting Governor while INEC prepared for a bye-lection. But Justice Adeniyi Ademola of the Federal High Court, Abuja, ruled that Nggilari's resignation was invalid. It was addressed to the Speaker rather than to Nyako, who was still the Governor at the time of the resignation. Nyako should have had the benefit of acting on the letter, either rejecting or accepting the resignation, according to the court. Nggilari had not been on good terms with Nyako. He had refused to defect with Nyako to the APC and was still in the PDP. Fintiri and most members of the House of Assembly also remained in the PDP.

With Justice Ademola's judgment, Nggilari was sworn in as the substantive Governor of the state. INEC had to call off the scheduled byelection.

• • •

The Nyako impeachment story seemed to have opened the eyes of PDP politicians to another instrument for removing opposition Governors. In Nasarawa State, a move was commenced to remove Governor Tanko Al-Makura, who was a member of the APC. The Nasarawa House of Assembly was controlled by the PDP, so it was supposed to have been an easy ride. Having lost five governors to the APC at one go in November 2013, PDP was about to regain its numerical strength, it seemed.

Having passed a resolution approving Al-Makura's impeachment, the House of Assembly invited the Chief Judge of Nasarawa State, Justice Suleiman Dikko, to constitute an investigative panel – as required by the Constitution. Apparently, Al-Makura, unlike Nyako, was on top of his game. While Nyako could not influence the choice of members of the panel that investigated him, Al-Makura was more proactive. When the panel was constituted, members of the Nasarawa House of Assembly were disappointed and angry. They accused Justice Dikko of having picked the panel in cahoots with Al-Makura rather than selecting an "independent panel of men of credible and unbiased integrity" as outlined in the Constitution. The suspicion was that Al-Makura simply forwarded a predetermined list to the Chief Judge. The committee, not surprisingly, cleared Al-Makura of any wrongdoing. By the letters and the spirit of the Constitution, that was the end of the impeachment move. To Al-Makura's credit, he had done a lot to contain the situation. He had reached out to people everywhere to intervene on his behalf.

The PDP National Chairman, Alhaji Ahmed Mu'azu, came under fire from the Nasarawa State lawmakers for not supporting the impeachment bid. But Mu'azu stood his ground. He insisted that there was no need to heat up the polity. The Nyako case had generated considerable political tension already. The lawmakers began to make all sorts of allegations against Mu'azu himself. When the information reached the President, he decided to invite members of the Nasarawa State House of Assembly to a meeting at the Presidential Villa, perhaps to calm frayed nerves and work out the way forward.

Shortly after that, a former member of the House of Representatives from Nasarawa state, Alhaji Aliyu Wadada, who used to be the Chairman of the House Committee on Securities and Exchange Commission (SEC), came with the Principal Officers of the House of Assembly to see me in my office. They said they had been told that the President would be calling a meeting, so they came to solicit my support to enable the impeachment move to succeed. Although the investigative committee had submitted a no-case report, the legislators still were pressing for the impeachment of the Governor! They accused the Chief Judge of misconduct and wanted him removed and replaced with another judicial officer who would be more amenable to their cause.

Later that afternoon, the Chief of Staff to the President, retired Brig-Gen. Jones Arogbofa, called to inform me of a meeting scheduled for the next day at which the President expected me to be in attendance. According to him, that meeting was going to be a political one. I guessed the President needed my attendance for any legal issues that might arise. On arriving the Presidential Villa, I met the members of the State House of Assembly already seated in the First Lady's Meeting Room. The President sent for me in the ante-room where he was sitting with Vice-President Namadi Sambo, Senate President David Mark, Brig-Gen. Arogbofa, Senator Anyim and Alhaji Mu'azu. We discussed the impeachment.

My analysis of the critical issues presented to them a simple case: the Committee had already submitted its report in accordance with the Constitution; it was not permissible to discuss the report any further as the issues had been rested. In the light of the constitutional provision, there was nothing that could be done. The only option available to the legislators was to start the entire process afresh. That, I opined, would in itself be a wasteful exercise and could even be viewed as a witch-hunt. They agreed with my opinion and it was resolved that the legislators should be advised to sheathe their swords in compliance with the provisions of the Constitution.

With this resolve, we proceeded to meet with the legislators. At the invitation of the President, I addressed the meeting, reiterating my earlier opinion to the smaller group. One of those at the meeting was a one-time Deputy Governor of Nasarawa State who had expressed a contrary opinion to mine. He, in effect, supported the contention that the Chief Judge could be removed in the manner the legislators had proposed. But I contested his position, pointing out that if he thought the Chief Judge had misconducted himself, the proper procedure would be to petition the National Judicial Council (NJC). It was within the remit of the NJC to set up a committee to investigate the allegation of misconduct.

Even if that was done, the report of the investigation would still have to be submitted to the NJC, the only body empowered to recommend the removal of the Chief Judge. A House of Assembly had no such power. Citing the example of Kwara State where the Chief Judge, Justice Raliat Elelu-Habeeb, was removed by the Governor, Dr Bukola Saraki, in 2009, I pointed out that the Supreme Court had reversed the removal and held that the Governor was not empowered to remove the Chief Judge in the manner it was done.

The agitated Nasarawa legislators boisterously refused to see reason. It was their contention that if the President backed them, and if they had the cooperation of the security agencies, they could easily set aside the panel's report and go ahead with the impeachment. All I could do to rein them in was to remind them that the President was presiding over the meeting and would not condone indiscipline. Reiterating my earlier take on the matter, I spoke on the President's behalf on the illegality of their plans, washing our hands off any involvement. The President gave his firm support to my position, and on that note, brought the meeting to a close.

• • •

As I stated earlier, the President had been against the impeachment *ab initio*. It only got fuelled by some of the officials in government, as well as some interest groups, with eyes on the politics of 2015. They pushed the argument that the President stood better chances of succeeding in 2015 if he had more states under control of the PDP. But the President consistently preached respect for the rule of law and the Constitution. His stand was that if they met the constitutional threshold to remove the Governor for an impeachable offence, they would have his support. Everything must be done according to the law, he insisted.

Moreover, the impeachment process outlined in the 1999 Constitution, though somewhat vague and open to misinterpretations, spells out the requirement of "gross misconduct." If an allegation of "gross misconduct" has been established, a President, Vice-President, Governor or Deputy Governor can be removed from office. But the undefined term "gross misconduct" leaves the room for abuse. What if a Governor is found to have committed an impeachable offence "in the opinion of the House," but in the opinion of the investigative panel, he has not done anything wrong? Such vagueness, in my view, makes impeachment as a political sanction tool virtually impossible. There is clearly a need for an amendment of the Constitution in this area.

In the Nasarawa case, for instance, there were sharp political differences between the Governor and the lawmakers, but they could not proceed with the sanction. The rules guiding impeachment proceedings or processes to be used by the investigative panel set up by the Chief Judge had not been put in place either. That lacuna cast a shadow on the process. While I am not arguing in favour of deploying impeachment at the slightest provocation, the process could do with some clarity so that the objectives are not defeated as a result of legal loopholes.

Perhaps, too, the framers of the Constitution, in their wisdom, and knowing the whimsical nature of politicians and their tendency to take advantage of situations, decided to create all these complexities so that it would be virtually impossible to remove a Governor or a President through the process of impeachment. If we aim at getting it right, I am of the firm view that we revisit the American Constitution from which the provisions of impeachment were lifted. In the American system, the judiciary is involved only to the extent that the Chief Justice presides over the impeachment trial while the Senate acts as the jury and judge. I believe that the Chief Justice of Nigeria or the Chief Judge of a state should not be involved in the mechanism of impeachment processes.

In the US, the article of impeachment is triggered from the Congress; if the House of Representatives impeaches the President, it is passed over to the Senate – just as it happened in case of President Bill Clinton in 1998. The Senate then conducts the trial to decide if the President should leave office or not. In the US, impeachment is an indictment, to say one is not fit to continue to be a President or Governor. But if the Senate decides not to remove the President or the Governor, that is the end of the process. Our own arrangement in Nigeria is too complicated and needs to be simplified.

CHAPTER SIXTEEN

THE STATE OF EMERGENCY

On 13 May 2013, the President declared a State of Emergency in three of the North Eastern states of Adamawa, Borno and Yobe owing to the Boko Haram insurgency that was ravaging those areas. The security situation was getting out of hand in those states, despite the efforts of the Armed Forces to contain the terrorist group. There was already political tension in Northern Nigeria arising from the 2011 presidential election. Some politicians had been credited with inciting statements, including that they would make the country "ungovernable" if Jonathan won. They claimed that he had "stolen" the turn of the North. With the unrelenting insecurity and violent situation, which, in fact, worsened two years after the 2011 elections, Nigeria found itself in disequilibrium. The President needed the declaration of State of Emergency in the troubled states in order to deal with the insurgency.

When the issue came up, there were discussions as to the extent the President could go. However, since the insurgency was not spread all over those states, the local government areas most affected were identified. Rather than declare total emergency in the states, the President limited it to those local government areas so that security manpower could be concentrated there to contain the situation. He also did not remove or suspend any Local Government Chairman or Governor. For the first time in Nigeria's history, an emergency was declared with the political leadership in place.

I had advised the President that he was free to declare a full or partial State of Emergency as provided in Section 305 of the Constitution which states that the President may, by an instrument published in the Official Gazette of the Federation, issue a proclamation of a State of Emergency in the Federation or any part thereof. Subsection 2 states that the President shall, after the publication, transmit the Gazette containing the proclamation, including the details of the emergency, to the President of the Senate and the Speaker of the House of Representatives, each of whom "shall forthwith convene a meeting of the House to consider and decide whether to pass a resolution approving the proclamation."

The Constitution specifically stipulates that the President shall have powers to declare a State of Emergency only when the Federation is at war, is in imminent danger of invasion or is involved in a state of war, and there is an actual breakdown of public order in the Federation or any part, to such extent as to require extraordinary measures to restore peace and security. That is, the occurrence of imminent danger or disaster, or natural calamity affecting a community, or a section of the community in the Federation, qualifies as emergency warranting such a proclamation. Under Subsection 4, the Governor of a state may, with the support of two-thirds majority of the state House of Assembly, request the President to issue a proclamation of emergency in the state, when there is in existence any of the listed situations.

• • •

President Jonathan, predictably, came under criticism from commentators who felt he should have removed the Local Government Chairmen as well as Governors in the affected states. Why declare a State of Emergency and retain the Governors? That was what many commentators said. The opportunity for Jonathan's foes to describe him as a weak leader emerged yet again! Historically, State of Emergency was employed more as a political weapon to settle scores with opposing forces, not necessarily to address issues of actual or imminent threat to security. Nigerians were more familiar with that nefarious employment of the provision. The fact that Governors in Nigeria cannot be held responsible for any breakdown of law and order is lost on these critics. Governors are the Chief Security Officers of their states only in name; they do not have the requisite constitutional power of control over the security agencies. Removing them during emergency, to my mind, was simply illogical.

The mentality that a Governor must be removed was most likely derived from what happened in 1962 when, owing to a crisis in the Western Region, government structures broke down. The Premier, Chief S. L. Akintola, had refused to vacate office for his replacement, Alhaji Dawodu Soroye Adegbenro, after being removed by the Regional House of Assembly. The Federal Government had stepped in and appointed Dr Moses Majekodunmi as the Administrator of Western Region, rather than allow Adegbenro to take over as Premier. It was a highly tense political situation. Although Akintola was still a member of the Action Group (AG), his sympathy for the Northern Peoples Congress (NPC), which controlled the Federal Government, earned him a restoration to office.

Another situation was when President Obasanjo removed Chief Joshua Dariye as Governor of Plateau State in 2004 after declaring a State of Emergency in that state. Chief Akin Olujinmi, then AGF, sought to justify the removal by referring to the Emergency Powers Act of 1961, which provided for the removal of a Premier, the equivalent of a Governor. On 25 May 2004, he was reported to have stated:

"Well… you are looking at the Constitution. There are other laws that you have to read along with the Constitution. We have what you call the Emergency Powers Act of 1961. That power was evoked in 1962 in the old Western region, when we had a similar declaration made, and we had Dr Majekodunmi appointed as administrator of the Western Region at that time, so that law is still in existence today. Under that law when you declare a state of emergency, you can appoint an administrator to run the affairs of the state." (*THISDAY* newspaper, 25/05/2005, page 40).

I respectfully disagree with that contention. The Emergency Powers Act of 1961 was derived from the 1960 Constitution. They did have an enabling law that gave the Prime Minister the power to declare a State of Emergency and, in the process, remove the Premier and appoint an Administrator to superintend the management of the Region's affairs. By the time Chief Olujinmi was invoking the Act in 2004, it had become spent.

Because declaration of State of Emergency had been wrongly used by Obasanjo to remove Governors whom he had political differences with, those who thought they loved Jonathan more than he loved himself kept clamouring for it to be used to checkmate Governors. But when I came into office, I took cognisance of the fact that I swore to an oath to abide by the Constitution. I also vowed that as the custodian of the Nigerian Constitution, who must be the legal adviser to all arms of government, I must do what was right.

Irrespective of the pressure, I refused to allow the political persuasion of the government of the day to colour my judgment. I advised the President that while he could declare a State of Emergency, that did not warrant the removal of a Governor. The Governor is the Chief Security Officer of the state, but the Police is centralised under the leadership of the Inspector General. That means Chief Security Officer is nothing but a ceremonial description.

Also, to remove a Governor could bring the President into conflict with the National Assembly. It is not in the interest of the President to take a decision that would not be approved by the National Assembly. That would tend to diminish his executive powers. He must jealously guard his turf and ensure that whatever he does is constitutionally justified. There was no way we would have been able to constitutionally justify the suspension or removal of a Governor through the instrumentality of the proclamation of a State of Emergency, having regard to the provision of Section 305 of the 1999 Constitution.

• • •

The issue of the State of Emergency has always been hugely controversial. The essence of declaring an emergency, as we know it, is that there is an extraordinary situation that has defied the standard laws, processes and procedures for restoring order. And to restore order, one is forced to resort to exceptional measures. It was never meant to be used as a political instrument to punish and remove recalcitrant or 'disloyal' Governors. The issue ought to have been settled by Attorneys-General over the decades, but probably because of the many years Nigeria was under military rule, no one has paid any serious attention to it.

While the 1961 State of Emergency Act allowed for the removal of Premiers, as Chief Olujinmi alluded to, the 1979 Constitution and, subsequently, the 1999 Constitution, spelt out how to declare a State of Emergency. The removal of a Governor is definitely not included in the provisions. Obasanjo, still thinking State of Emergency could rightfully be used politically and illegally the way he had applied it during his tenure, tried to mount some pressure on President Jonathan in his early days in office in 2010 to apply it to the crisis in Ogun, his home state.

In that case, the Governor of Ogun State, Otunba Gbenga Daniel, had fallen out with Obasanjo over who would control the state executive of the PDP ahead of the 2011 elections. The House of Assembly had also been divided, so Otunba Daniel could not function effectively, especially regarding getting the approval necessary for the N100 billion bond he wanted to get from the capital market. All the intrigues raging through Ogun State had led to a shutdown of the House of Assembly Complex. Government practically ground to a halt.

Obasanjo tried to exert a lot of pressure on Jonathan, urging him to declare a State of Emergency. He wanted Jonathan to suspend Daniel and appoint an Administrator to return things to normalcy. When the President asked for my view, I felt the crisis had not reached a boiling point where he would need to declare a State of Emergency. I further pointed out that there were enough provisions under Section 11 of the Constitution to deal with situations where a House of Assembly of a state is unable to sit. The Constitution provides for the functions of such a State Assembly to be taken over by the National Assembly.

Also, even if there were a need to declare a State of Emergency, it would have been to give some extraordinary powers to the Governor and suspend parts of Chapter 4 of the Constitution which relate to fundamental human rights, as opposed to the removal of the Governor. As I pointed out earlier, the removal of a Governor is nowhere provided for in the mechanism for implementing a State of Emergency. It would have amounted to employing extra-constitutional means to remove a Governor.

One of the arguments I used in convincing the President was to draw his attention to the fact that he also had the power to declare a State of Emergency all over the Federation. I then asked that: "For instance, Mr President, if the country is at war, and you have to declare a State of Emergency, would you remove yourself from office and appoint an Administrator to oversee the affairs of the country?" He agreed with me. He could see that it was illogical to remove a Governor on account of a State of Emergency being declared.

• • •

Since we had successfully warded off the use of State of Emergency as a political tool in the Ogun case, it was not too difficult applying the same principles to other suggestions from the marauding hawks. There was still a big battle ahead, nevertheless. As the Boko Haram insurgency continued unabated in the North-East, the hawks told President Jonathan that the State of Emergency, declared by him in May 2013 and renewed in November of the same year, was not effective because the Governors of Adamawa, Borno and Yobe were not removed. Ironically, the three Governors were all of the APC, the leading opposition party.

The potential political gain was glaring. The hawks piled pressure on the President to extend the State of Emergency by another six months and remove the three Governors. This would take us into 2014, when the politicking for the 2015 general election would be in top gear. Two Ministers even drafted a Declaration of Emergency speech and took it to the President. They named three retired Generals to be appointed as Administrators of the affected states. President Jonathan then decided to ask me to make a presentation to the FEC on my position, apparently because he did not want to do anything illegal.

When I got to Council, I marshalled my argument that removing a Governor was not part of the constitutional provisions in declaring a State of Emergency. I told them I do not play politics with matters of law. I also said declaring an emergency was, constitutionally, a shared responsibility between the President and the National Assembly, with the legislature having a superior dominion. While the President can trigger the process, it must be approved by the National Assembly within two days if they are in session and a maximum of ten days if they are not, in which case the President would request that they reconvene to approve his declaration. If the lawmakers refused to approve it, I warned, that would be the end and it would appear to diminish the powers of the President.

A heated debate broke out. Two Ministers, one of them a lawyer that never practised and the other a full-time politician, stood up to me and started an unnecessary argument, insisting that the President could do and undo. The President had to call the house to order as emotions ran high. In the end, President Jonathan decided that he would not violate the Constitution. He did not extend the emergency, much less remove the Governors. In any case, as the Commander-in-Chief of the Armed Forces, he could deploy troops without the approval of the National Assembly.

I became an enemy of many people in government who accused me of misleading the President. After the FEC meeting, some ministers began instigating the Ijaw leader, Chief Edwin Clark, against me. They said it was "one man" with a "bogus title" of "Attorney-General of the Federation" who prevented the President from removing the Governors and replacing them with Administrators. From what filtered to me, Clark was very angry with me and even suggested that the President "should remove that Attorney-General." But the President always had my back.

With such a President as your boss, you would always be confident to tell him the truth. If he had resorted to using State of Emergency as a political bazooka, he probably would have had his way as a bully, but he could never have written his name in the hearts of millions who still adore him – especially when they compare him with other Nigerian leaders who used their powers to terrorise and subjugate their perceived political opponents. It must be a compliment to President Jonathan that President Buhari has also avoided deploying the State of Emergency as a tool in Rivers, Kwara and Akwa Ibom States, despite the political benefits. It is a worthy legacy.

CHAPTER SEVENTEEN

THE JUDGMENT DEBT SCAM

The news of my nomination as a Minister in March 2010 – even before confirmation by Senate – was enough to activate the hidden transactional aspects of the Ministry of Justice. I had received a number of proposals from friends and acquaintances on how the Office of Attorney-General of the Federation could be turned into a money-making machine. I became quite disgusted and at a point called my driver and trusted friend, Saidu, to help me decipher the situation.

"Do I look like a thief, Saidu?" I asked him awkwardly.

He was startled at the unexpected query.

"What happened?" he asked, bemused, ironically proffering question in lieu of answer. Then he heard my explanation and without hesitation, declared: "They don't know you." That was all the validation I needed. I rallied from the effect of the assault I had been suffering. Feeling lighter from Saidu's validation, I was able to bring up the issue more casually with my friend, Damian Dodo, who also laughed and declared: "They don't know you!" That was doubly comforting. People who were close to me and knew me well trusted me. That was my joy.

After the swearing-in, one of the first briefings I had with the Permanent Secretary was regarding the judgment debts scam.

I told him: "Permanent Secretary, I heard that people are stealing money from judgment debts. We are going to take a holistic look at judgment debts during my tenure."

Not long after that, a man came to my office. I had left a standing instruction for my secretary that I was available to anybody that needed to see the Attorney-General. My office was that of the Public Defender. The secretary described the visitor as "a friend of the Ministry and a friend to every AGF before you." Curiously, I awaited the "permanent friend" only to discover he was someone I had known since 2005, a businessman notorious for chasing judgment debts with the ardour of a game hunter. He stepped into my office, smirking delightedly, feeling really at home. Declaring that he came to welcome and congratulate me, he made to present me with a pen.

Looking straight into his face, and without allowing him a word, I admonished him: "I'm aware that you are one of the perennial claimants of judgment debts in this ministry. I have done some homework and I can tell you that judgment debt has become a cesspool of corruption around here and you are part of the racket. If you have brought this pen to me with the expectation that I will be using it to sign judgment debt claims for you, then you are on a failed mission. Out of politeness, I will not reject your pen, but I will, in your presence, right now, give it out to one of my aides. Please make sure whatever you are bringing to this Ministry is something that has merit, and must be justifiable. I will not accept the kind of bogus claims you people have been making on the Federal Government."

The man smiled smugly, probably thinking that I was bluffing.

Two weeks later, he came back to the office with a long list.

"What is this?" I asked him in a less-than friendly tone.

"Sir, these are the claims I have," he replied.

He was wielding the very long list like a sword.

"How come only you have so many claims against the Federal Government of Nigeria? Tell me what this is all about," I demanded.

He sat down, unprompted, and tried to explain that he was actually a collection agent for a lot of people who were being owed judgment debts by the government. His role was to compile the list, do the legwork through his contacts in the Ministry, get the debts paid, and then take his own cut. I reminded him of my vow that I would not encourage such practices. I reiterated that he must learn to follow due process if he had genuine claims. That was my last encounter with the man while in office. Interacting with him had revealed that he was, in fact, the face of that racket which had established itself in the Ministry through the years. He was later seen going around town disparaging me.

• • •

To tackle the sleaze, I reconstituted the standing Presidential Committee on Judgment Debt with the SGF/PS as Chairman, and representation from the Presidency by the State House Counsel, the EFCC, the Nigeria Police Force, Ministry of Finance, Accountant General of the Federation and the

Nigerian Bar Association. The Director, Civil Litigation, served as Secretary and her office was the secretariat for the Committee. The idea was to inject more transparency and accountability into the process as well as ensure that the incidence of collusion was drastically reduced, if not eliminated.

There were so many judgment debts against the Federal Government. The Committee was to scrutinise these debts for possible collusions, conspiracies and connivance of any sort, and where they were found unjustified, recommend actions. One of the methods employed in these cases, as I discovered, was where people would file frivolous suits joining government agencies. Then there would either be no representation or inadequate representation by the Ministry, and default judgments would be entered against the government.

I also discovered that many government lawyers did not go to court, not only out of conspiracy but because some were overwhelmed with work. The number of lawyers employed by the Ministry was insufficient to attend to all the cases that were daily pouring in against the Federal Government. There wasn't enough money to engage external solicitors to defend our cases either. More so, individuals and entities were now very much aware of their rights in a democracy. The Federal Government was being sued for every infraction on democratic rights of expression and sanctity of contracts. One lawyer would be assigned to handle five to six cases in different courts. Since it was humanly impossible to be in six courts at the same time, some cases naturally suffered.

It also came to light that a substantial part of the budgetary allocation made for solicitors' fees was being paid out to only two or three private solicitors. There was a case of a former Attorney-General that was paying a senior advocate N50 million for each case he handled! In one particular year, the entire solicitors' fees of about N1 billion were paid to only two prominent lawyers. Conversely, I also discovered that law officers in the Ministry were not being paid their allowances and out-of-pocket expenses. There was disenchantment among these lawyers who felt neglected. Moreover, they were also not being trained.

I needed to adopt a cocktail of approaches to resolve these issues. Fortunately, when I approached the President, he graciously approved some money for some of the cases that were on ground. From then on, we decided that no SAN would be paid more than N5 million for a brief; any other lawyer, who was not a SAN, would receive a maximum of N2 million. As soon as we activated that process and procedure, we were able to farm out a lot of the cases in order to reduce the workload. We employed the monies set aside for solicitors' fees to also pay for the transportation and other allowances of in-house lawyers, treating them as solicitors also.

As soon as we did that, we were able to drastically reduce the non-appearance of Ministry lawyers in court. At the same time, we were able to provide a buffer to engage more solicitors. We were satisfied with the results. Understandably, not everybody was happy with us. A case in point was one lawyer that complained that he could not understand why he should be paid N5 million when, in the past, he would have earned N50 million. I firmly informed him he was not obliged to continue working for the Ministry if he was not satisfied with what we were offering as fees.

But then we still needed to address the issue of the judgment debts. We started negotiating with the creditors through the Committee. We told them that we knew what they were up to. So many claims were bogus but since it was an organised scam, they were getting away with it. We adopted the stick-and-carrot approach and we were able to reduce the judgment debts substantially. But again, there were too many people interested in judgment debts. We were getting calls from all manner of people, including members of the National Assembly. Actually, some National Assembly members were making appropriation for judgment debts based on an understanding with the debtors. It was a conspiracy against the national treasury.

To further curb the corruption and malpractices associated with judgment debt, I took a memorandum to FEC proposing the decentralisation of payments. The memo provided that each ministry should be responsible for the payment of debts incurred by it and that the payment of such debts would be from the statutory appropriation to the Ministry. The effects of the memo were: one, there would no longer be a centralised judgment debt allocation administered by the Ministry of Justice; two, while the Judgment Debt Committee would continue to scrutinise and validate the claims, it was no longer going to be saddled with the responsibility of paying the creditors as that responsibility was ceded to the Ministry of Finance; three, since the Ministries were responsible for their debts, they would pay more attention to defending suits against them and these would in turn reduce the incidence of collusion.

The President directed that a circular to that effect be issued by the SGF. That reduced the incidence of judgment debts while we were in government. In the end, we resolved that we were no longer interested in the handling of judgment debts because of the various powerful interests we had to contend with. At every opportunity, they would resort to blackmail, using the instrumentality of 'public hearing' by the National Assembly to waste our time, while also scandalising and demonising us. We resolved that it was not worth the trouble. That was how we finally did away with handling the judgment debt issues in the Ministry during my time in office.

Someone had asked me if moving the judgment debt to another ministry had been a good idea or even a lasting solution. I could not say for certain whether it was, but the collusion had been so extensive we just had to make that radical move. There were enough issues to battle with at the Ministry without getting bogged down with wrestling with the National Assembly all the time.

It was not very easy initially but we saved Nigeria a lot of money. A case in point was the Ajaokuta Steel Company matter. An award was made against the Federal Government of Nigeria. I had to go with a team of lawyers to Houston, USA, to negotiate for reduction of the debt. It took all of 28 hours of intense negotiation before we were able to get the payment substantially reduced. I got the President's approval to pay. The creditors had already attached the Federal Government account in New York. When I pleaded the doctrine of sovereign immunity in respect of those accounts, the Court of Appeals in New York rejected my argument based on the fact that the said accounts were being used for commercial transactions. We were, therefore, estopped from relying on the doctrine of sovereign immunity to avoid liability.

In another case, one company, Continental Transfert Technique Limited, got an award of about N40 billion against Nigeria. They had begun the process of executing the award by attaching the assets of the Federal Government and the accounts of the NNPC abroad. We were able to negotiate it down to about N15 billion. We went with Mr Humphrey Abbah, then Minister of State for Interior, against whose Ministry the transaction was connected. We ensured that our national interest was safeguarded and protected in all our negotiations.

CHAPTER EIGHTEEN

THE HALLIBURTON SCANDAL

The Halliburton and Siemens bribery scandals involving high-profile Nigerians rank among the most celebrated corruption cases in Nigeria's history.

From 1994 to 2004, TSKJ allegedly paid bribes in excess of $180 million to Nigerian government officials to secure contracts worth $6 billion for engineering and construction works at the Nigerian Liquefied Natural Gas (NLNG) in Bonny, Rivers State.[5] TSKJ is an international consortium of companies including KBR, which itself was a subsidiary of Halliburton until 1998. The bribes were allegedly paid in tranches of $60 million in 1995, $37.5 million in 1999, $51 million in 2001 and $23 million in 2002.[6] Some of the people mentioned in the bribery scheme were the high and mighty of the Nigerian political landscape, including a former Head of State and a former President.

The bribes were reportedly channelled through a British lawyer, Mr Jeffrey Tesler, who was said to have operated a secret network that delivered the cash to Nigerian government officials. Tesler, reportedly, started the bribery payments by transferring small amounts of money through Switzerland in July 1996. However, he was said to have, in one fell swoop, packaged $1 million in cash to be delivered to officials of NNPC which owned a 49 per cent stake in NLNG. The scandal blew open on 6 February 2009 when the US Justice Department announced that KBR had been charged with paying bribes to Nigerian officials in violation of the Foreign Corrupt Practices Act (FCPA).[7]

The Justice Department filed the charges in a Houston Federal Court.

---

[5] Oyeyemi, Remi, 'Halliburton Bribery: Chronology of a Nigerian Scandal', TheNews, 20-08-2015, available at https://www.thenewsnigeria.com.ng/2015/07/halliburton-bribery-chronology-of-a-nigerian-scandal/ [retrieved 20-07-2018]
[6] 'Halliburton settles Nigeria bribery claims for $35 million', CNN.com, 22-12-2010, available at http://edition.cnn.com/2010/WORLD/africa/12/21/nigeria.halliburton/index.html [retrieved 20-07-2018]
[7] Fitzgibbon, Will, 'Files Open New Window On $182-Million Halliburton Bribery Scandal In Nigeria', ICIJ, 10-02-2015, available at https://www.icij.org/investigations/swiss-leaks/files-open-new-window-182-million-halliburton-bribery-scandal-nigeria/ [accessed 20-07-2018]

KBR pleaded guilty and was ordered to pay $402 million in criminal fines. Halliburton, which was the parent company of KBR when some of the reported bribes exchanged hands, paid most of the fines on behalf of KBR. The US Securities and Exchange Commission (SEC) then filed a civil action under the FCPA, forcing KBR and Halliburton to pay another $177 million in disgorgement of profits. Mr Albert Jackson Stanley, the CEO of KBR when it was a subsidiary to Halliburton, entered into a plea bargain and was sentenced to 30 months in prison for his role in the sleaze.[8]

However, back in Nigeria where the offences were perpetrated, nobody faced any form of punishment. Instead, all the Nigerian lawmakers did, sometime in 2004, was merely to ask that TSKJ and its partners be banned from getting future oil contracts in the country. That was it. The fact that some of the officials who collected the bribes were powerful Nigerians did not help matters.

When I assumed office in 2010, one of the issues that bedevilled the administration was corruption. I was in Geneva, Switzerland, with Mr Onovo Ogbonna Onovo, then Inspector General of Police, when he raised the Halliburton issue with me. Mr Onovo is one person Nigeria has forgotten too soon! Nobody seems to talk about him much, but that gentleman did a lot for the country in the fight against corruption. He offered to synergise his office with mine in order to help the government execute its anti-graft war, starting with the Halliburton case.

His predecessor, Mr Mike Okiro, had done substantial work on the investigation of the scandal already and produced an Interim Report. Added to that, Onovo identified someone we could work with: Mr Ahmadu Ali, whom he described as an intelligent and outstanding Commissioner of Police and who was the anchor of the investigation. Onovo was confident we would deeply dent the armour of corruption in Nigeria. I was very impressed with his commitment. We simply struck a chord of kindred spirit from that moment.

On arriving Nigeria, he directed Ali to bring the Interim Report to me. I read it through in attempting to catalogue the activities of some companies that were used as conduit to pass slush funds to both government officials and other influential Nigerians. While still contemplating how best to go about the matter, I was approached by Mrs Farida Waziri, then Chairman of EFCC. She

---

[8] ibid

167

said some American lawyers could file a civil action in the US with a view to getting the indicted companies in the Halliburton case to pay fines.

She pressed for me to immediately enter into an agreement with the lawyers after I had interviewed them in her presence. But I resisted that move. It wasn't my method to take such decisions without running the matter by the President since I already had the proposed terms of engagement from the lawyers. Besides, I had established a culture of involving Nigerian lawyers in international transactions rather than farming out legal work exclusively to foreign lawyers. I trusted the broad spectrum of competences available among Nigerian legal practitioners. To enlarge their range of experience and develop their practice was a duty I owed my profession.

• • •

Under the terms of agreement proposed by the American lawyers, they would be entitled to thirty-three one-third per cent of whatever they recovered as fines for the Federal Government. I found that condition bizarre! I regarded the percentage they were demanding to be excessive for a developing country like Nigeria. My zeal to protect my professional turf became firmed up against approving any such 'double dipping' by lawyers from the same jurisdiction with the elements that instigated the massive bribery scandals in the first place. They were also asking that I cede my power as Attorney-General to them so that whatever they negotiated with the affected companies would be binding on me. That was tantamount to them making whatever decision that suited them and foisting it on Nigeria with no right of objection whatsoever by us. This was simply unacceptable to me, so I rejected their proposal.

There had to be better ways of handling such matters without signing away Nigeria's sovereignty. The template that readily came to my mind at that point was the resolution of the Pfizer case in Kano State. In that case, in 1996, the world's biggest research-based pharmaceutical company conducted trials for two drugs on 100 children in Kano State following an outbreak of Africa's worst ever meningitis epidemic. The experimental oral antibiotics, Trovan and Ceftriaxone, led to the death of 11 children, amidst claims that Pfizer had not obtained proper consent from their parents prior to the trial.

After a prolonged court case, Pfizer reached a tentative out-of-court settlement with the Kano State Government in 2009 and agreed to pay $65 million. I was one of the lawyers that represented Pfizer while Chief J. B. Daudu was the Lead Counsel for both the Federal Government and Kano State Government. Prof. Yemi Osinbajo, Nigeria's current Vice-President, Mrs Maryam Uwais, now Special Assistant to the President on Social Investment Programme, and some other associates of Osinbajo were on Daudu's team. They were briefed by the duo of then Attorney-General of the Federation, Chief Bayo Ojo, and the Attorney-General of Kano State.

The Pfizer template comprised, first of all, the initiation of criminal proceedings against the company and joining individuals connected to the alleged crimes. From what I had garnered from the Interim Report, there was sufficient evidence in the Halliburton case to put both the companies and certain individuals on trial. We jettisoned the proposal from the American lawyers and Waziri was not happy about that. I could tell from her visage when I conveyed the decision. She later consented to nominating Mr Emmanuel Akomaye, then Secretary of the EFCC, following my advice that the Commission should coordinate the team of Nigerian lawyers that would work on the case. She further nominated Mr Godwin Obla to the team, while I nominated Chief Daudu, Damian Dodo and some other lawyers.

One of the companies the team went after was Julius Berger, the construction giant. Immediately the charges were filed, I got a call from a former National Security Adviser cautioning me that there were national security implications in filing charges against the company. He said prosecuting the company would not be in the national interest and therefore advised that we consider the possibility of settling the matter out of court. He also discussed this with President Jonathan, who asked me to reconsider our decision. We could enter a 'deferred prosecution' agreement based on defined terms, I reassured the President.

A committee was set up to negotiate with Julius Berger. The President nominated retired Gen. Aliyu Gusau, former NSA, to chair the Committee, a task Gusau delegated to retired Col. Kayode Are, who was then Deputy NSA. Alhaji Abdullahi Ibrahim, a one-time AGF, led the team of lawyers that represented Julius Berger Plc. Negotiations took place and an agreement was brokered.

Mr Rowland Ewubare, then Executive Secretary of the National Human Rights Commission who was also part of the Pfizer case, was co-opted for his vast experience practising law in the US, to guide the Committee through the negotiations. According to him, the practice in America was to compel the accused persons not only to disgorge the money involved but also to pay a penalty worth three times that figure. I disagreed with him on that. I thought three times the figure would not be substantial, and suggested and, in fact, insisted that they be made to pay five times the amount. This Julius Berger did.

I adopted the template that was used in paying the prosecuting lawyers in the Pfizer case. I asked Julius Berger to negotiate a fee with the lawyers and pay them directly – to save the Federal Government from bearing any legal costs. In addition, we requested a refund of the sum of $1 million already expended by the Federal Government on investigations. In all, Julius Berger had to cough out about $30 million in fines for its alleged role in that bribery scandal.

Waziri reportedly made snide remarks about the issue. The American lawyers also wrote to complain that payments had been made on the case based on their template, thereby entitling them to professional fees. Waziri even suggested I got the President to approve about $1 million as payment to the Americans. I would have none of that. They had suggested a civil litigation but what we did was a criminal trial. Dismissing their claims, I pointed out that there was a clear distinction between a civil suit and a criminal prosecution. They didn't give up. They went further to approach the President, through Gen. T. Y. Danjuma. When the President called my attention to it, I explained the nature and modality of the transaction, apparently to his satisfaction.

While we could get Julius Berger and five other companies, including Halliburton itself, to pay fines of over $200 million, it was difficult prosecuting the individuals that were named. There wasn't enough evidence to charge them to court. What the police had on them was not sufficient for a robust prosecution. We still managed to charge a couple of individuals to court but we could not touch the big masquerades. It was not as if we were not empowered by the law to do so, but the political situation in Nigeria at the time desperately needed stability. Two of the former leaders that were named were playing the lead role in stabilising the country. Caution was common sense. Jonathan had just assumed the position of President after the death of President Yar'Adua. The polity had been poisoned along ethnic and religious lines and needed an ointment, not a purgative.

I was also advised by several foreign missions in the country that some of the persons involved were icons of Nigeria's democracy who must be condoned despite certain dark patches in their past. According to them, actions taken for the broader interest of the society were often to be reckoned above certain criminal infractions. I had to exercise my discretion in the public interest.

• • •

Another messy case was the Siemens bribery scandal.

In 2007, the German telecommunications company was accused of paying out more than $100 million in bribes to officials in Nigeria, Russia and Libya in order to secure contracts. Nigerian officials, including three former Ministers of Communication, were said to have received $14 million between 2001 and 2004.[9] Siemens agreed, late in 2008, to pay $1.3 billion in penalties to the US and German authorities over the scandal. In Nigeria, just as in the Halliburton case, the government simply banned Siemens from getting contracts. In November 2009, it cancelled an existing $1 million contract for the supply of electrical systems. But we succeeded in extracting a fine of over €50 million from Siemens when we waded into their case.

In the final analysis, we got all the companies that were fingered in these scandals to pay fines to the Federal Government. Curiously, our success in executing that effective model kept irking the EFCC. For refusing to patronise and pay outrageous fees to their foreign-designated lawyers, I became a marked man. They were happy enough to appoint lawyers at their pleasure to handle the cases, yet they would later go into a feverish search for dirt to plaster on me. I became the enemy rather than a patriotic Nigerian doing his best in the service of his country. I made money for Nigeria rather than squander its resources. I brought criminal elements that exploited Nigeria to account. The EFCC, who should encourage such transparent conduct in national life, turned on me!

My relationship with the EFCC further deteriorated when I sought to make regulations prescribing some operational modalities for them, especially with respect to management and disposal of assets recovered by the Commission. Although I acted pursuant to the powers conferred on the AGF by Section 41 of the EFCC Act, the resistance to change was enormous. In an effort to push back on the altruistic objectives of the regulations, the

---

[9] 'Nigeria probes Siemens bribe case', BBC.com, 21-11-2017, available at http://news.bbc.co.uk/1/hi/world/africa/7105582.stm [retrieved 20-07-2018]

EFCC, in their media-instigated trials, claimed they had investigated and discovered that the monies recovered in the Halliburton case were diverted to personal accounts. It was false, needless to say.

• • •

CHAPTER NINETEEN

THE BAKASSI HANDOVER

In trying to make Nigeria look like a responsible country in the comity of nations, I was accused of being a saboteur.

On 10 October 2002, the International Court of Justice (ICJ) ruled in favour of Cameroon in its century-old land and maritime boundary dispute with Nigeria, which included the oil-rich Bakassi Peninsula. Nigerians were disappointed but the country had already submitted to the jurisdiction of the ICJ and was bound by the outcome of the case. On 12 June 2006, President Obasanjo of Nigeria and President Paul Biya of Cameroon signed the "Greentree Agreement," negotiated by Mr Kofi Annan, then UN Secretary-General. The Agreement provided modalities for the implementation of the ICJ judgment. It essentially spelt out the terms of a transitional period for the implementation of the judgment.

However, the Nigerian Senate in November 2007 – six months after Obasanjo had left power – sought to impugn the Greentree Agreement, citing violations of Section 12(1) of the Constitution which provides for legislative approval of treaties entered into by the executive before they can become locally implementable. Section 12(1) of the Nigerian Constitution stipulates: "No treaty between the Federation and any other country shall have the force of law except to the extent to which any such treaty has been enacted into law by the National Assembly." Their argument did not sway President Yar'Adua, President Obasanjo's successor. His government therefore formally handed over the administrative and political control of the Bakassi Peninsula to Cameroon on 14 August 2008.

In 2012, with less than six months remaining to approach the ICJ for a possible review of the judgment, there was increased campaign for it. In September 2012, while the "Take back Bakassi" campaign was raging, President Jonathan led the Nigerian delegation, of which I was a member, to the 67th United Nations General Assembly. We paid a courtesy call on Mr Ban Ki-moon, then UN Secretary-General. It was the Office of the Secretary General of the UN that set up the Cameroon-Nigeria Mixed Commission

(CNMC) to oversee the demarcation of the land and maritime boundary in accordance with the ICJ judgment. The Secretary-General directly supervised the process through his Under-Secretary, Ambassador Said Djinnit.

Ki-moon inquired from the President whether Nigeria was indeed contemplating a request for the review of the 2002 ICJ judgment. Being the leader of Nigeria's delegation to the Follow-up Committee on the Implementation of the Greentree Agreement and the Cameroon Nigeria Mixed Commission, I was directed by President Jonathan to brief the Secretary-General. I outlined the progress so far made in the implementation of the Greentree Agreement and reassured the Secretary-General of Nigeria's irrevocable commitment to the implementation of the ICJ judgment. Having given that commitment, we returned to Nigeria.

The clamour to rescind the agreement waxed stronger, unabated. In fact, it was reaching a crescendo. Senator Liyel Imoke, then Governor of Cross River State, and Senator Victor Ndoma-Egba, then Senate Leader, also from the state, approached me with a request to appeal the ICJ judgment. I informed them that Article 60 of the ICJ Statute foreclosed any appeal. But application for a review of the judgment was possible under Article 61 where new facts have emerged that were not available as at the time the case came before the ICJ.

The materials they were presenting as new facts were already available and canvassed by the Nigerian legal team before the ICJ. It would, therefore, amount to a worthless exercise to reopen the matter which would only constitute an embarrassment to Nigeria. The President had given an irrevocable assurance to the UN Secretary-General that we were not going back on the issue of Bakassi. I informed them that as a member of the UN, Nigeria was bound by Article 103 of the UN Charter to respect the judgment of the ICJ, which is an organ of the UN.

• • •

I was later to discover a hidden political agenda to the clamour when I received a letter from some groups reiterating the possibility of applying for a review. All that was needed, they claimed, was for the Federal Government to pay them $17 million to conduct a research to unearth new and fresh facts that would form the basis of evidence to be presented for a review. It dawned on me at that point that the agitation was nothing but a grand scheme to make money!

When the President called me, I told him my mind. But the clamour became more deafening. Senator Imoke came to me again and I maintained my position on it. He said his Attorney-General had told him otherwise but I said what they wanted was impossible and that as the Attorney-General of the Federation, my duty extended to advising him too. I also said that he was a lawyer and ought to know better. Governor Imoke's response was instructive: "Attorney-General, I know you are right, but you are not a politician. All we want you to do is to file an appeal, and even if we lose the case, we would have satisfied our people that we did our best." I let him know that I was not prepared to subject my professional integrity as Attorney-General as well as my membership of the International Law Commission to question.

A meeting was convened at the instance of the President. Prince Bola Ajibola, a former Attorney-General and Judge Advocate in the ICJ, and Principal Officers of the National Assembly were invited. Although Prince Ajibola endorsed my views, Hon. Femi Gbajabiamila, a lawyer and member of the House of Representatives, raised the issue of the non-domestication and non-ratification of the Greentree Agreement by the National Assembly. He obviously didn't know that the Greentree Agreement did not fall within the contemplation of Section 12 (1) of the Constitution. How do you domesticate an Agreement to implement an ICJ judgment?

The objective of the Agreement was to cushion the pains on the Bakassi population who would have been adversely affected if immediate effect was given to the judgment delivered in 2002. The people that would have been most affected by an immediate implementation of the judgment were Nigerians. Within the given timelines, the Agreement had recognised the rights of these Nigerians to choose either to become Cameroonians or to remain there and continue to do their businesses with their human rights respected, subject to their compliance with Cameroonian laws and regulations.

Still entertaining the possibility of applying to the ICJ, the President constituted a committee to further review the issue and nominated me to chair it. He wanted us to review the case and come up with a position to advise him. We met at Senator Ndoma-Egba's house in the morning of the next day but no satisfactory outcome was achieved. Ndoma-Egba, apparently unsatisfied, insisted that the rights of the people would be circumscribed if they were denied the right to appeal. He said we should go on appeal even if we were going to lose. I disagreed with him, reiterating my earlier position to the effect that the ICJ Statute had no provision for appeal of its judgments.

I, therefore, proceeded to brief the Senate President on why it was not advisable for Nigeria to proceed on the ill-fated move of seeking a review of the judgment. The Senate President, agreeing with me, observed that he had cautioned Ndoma-Egba on the need to take a realistic view of the issue so as not to unnecessarily raise the expectation of the people.

In reality, we had already handed over the administrative and political control of the affected communities to Cameroon. Even if we so decided to apply for a review of the ICJ judgment, how would we retrieve the political authority and physical control of the area from them? Would that not be calling for a war? In my discussion with the Senate President, we had reasoned that in the event of a war, Nigeria might be at a disadvantage as it would be viewed by the international community as a country that had reneged on its international obligations and commitments. Militarily, Cameroon had a subsisting defence pact with France while Nigeria did not have such with any foreign power.

In the course of discussing the issue with the President, Mr Femi Falana had alluded to the fact that the human rights of the people of Bakassi were not being respected by Cameroon. I then urged Falana to raise a complaint, in that case, to the UN Human Rights Committee. I offered to engage him as a solicitor to take up the issue of the alleged abuse of the human rights of the Nigerians living in the Bakassi Peninsula and instructed him accordingly. However, he never reverted to me on that matter before I left office.

There was so much tension building up around the Bakassi area on the border between Nigeria and Cameroon. Killings were allegedly going on and could have been worsened if we had made the mistake of initiating an application for a review of the judgment. It appeared to me that generally, the tendency was for people to canvass issues without a deep understanding of specific and vital facts which are available to state actors. These things may not be in the public domain but, nonetheless, they guide leaders in the process of decision-making. Some elements that were hellbent on causing disaffection went about spreading falsehood about me and calling for my dismissal. They called me a saboteur. On my part, it is always preferable to be rejected for doing what is right than for doing that which is wrong.

• • •

I briefed not only the Senate President but also the Speaker of the House of Representatives, Rt Hon. Aminu Waziri Tambuwal, to get his buy-in. With the necessary consultations with the Principal Officers of the National

Assembly concluded, I proceeded to brief the President on the outcome of our deliberations. The President agreed with the steps taken and authorised that a public statement be issued by me to inform the general public that the country would not be seeking a review of the judgment. With less than 24 hours to the expiration of the deadline, we issued the statement. I have reproduced the entire statement below.

> *It will be recalled that on 10th October 2002, the International Court of Justice (ICJ) delivered judgment in Land and Maritime Boundary between Cameroon and Nigeria, which covers about 2000 kilometres extending from Lake Chad to the Sea. It will also be recalled that before the judgment was delivered, President Olusegun Obasanjo, GCFR of Nigeria and President Paul Biya of the Republic of Cameroon gave their respective undertaking to the international community to abide by the judgment of the Court.*
>
> *The commitment and undertakings given by both Heads of Government were confirmed by the establishment of the Cameroon-Nigeria Mixed Commission (CNMC) pursuant to the Joint Communiqué adopted at a Summit Meeting on 15 November 2002 in Geneva. The CNMC is composed of the representatives of Cameroon, Nigeria and the United Nations and is chaired by the Special Representative of the United Nations Secretary General for West Africa.*
>
> *The CNMC has held 29 Sessions since its inception and has peacefully, amicably and successfully:*
>
> *(a) brought Cameroon and Nigeria back to negotiation table;*
>
> *(b) supervised the handing over of 33 ceded villages to Cameroon and 1 to Nigeria in December, 2003 and received 3 settlements and territory in Adamawa and Borno States Sectors from Cameroon in 2004;*
>
> *(c) initiated the Enugu-Abakiliki-Mamfe-Mutengene Road project as part of the confidence-building measures between the two countries;*

(d) supervised peaceful withdrawal of Civil Administration, Military and Police Forces and transfer of authority in the Bakassi Peninsula by Nigeria to Cameroon in 2008 in line with the modalities contained in the Greentree Agreement signed by Cameroon and Nigeria in 2006 which the United Nations, Germany, USA, France, UK and Northern Ireland witnessed; and

(e) commenced the emplacement of boundary beacons/pillars along the land boundary and initiated final mapping of the whole stretch of the boundary. It is instructive to note that about 1,800 kilometres of the boundary have so far been assessed for Pillar Emplacement leaving only about 220 km to complete the assessment of the entire boundary.

The Greentree Agreement was also signed by H. E. Paul Biya, and President Olusegun Obasanjo GCFR, on 12 June, 2006, in Long Island, Greentree, New York, USA; reaffirming their willingness to peacefully implement the judgment of the ICJ. The Agreement contains the modalities for withdrawal and transfer of authority in the Bakassi Peninsula by Nigeria to Cameroon in pursuance of the ICJ Judgment. The Follow-Up Committee comprising representatives of Nigeria and Cameroon was established to monitor the implementation of the Agreement and settle any dispute regarding the interpretation and implementation of the Agreement. Nigeria handed over the Bakassi Peninsula to Cameroon in 2008.

The Statute of the International Court of Justice provides that the Judgment of the Court is final and without appeal. However, following the resolutions of both Houses of the National Assembly calling on the Executive to take steps to apply for a review of the judgment, President Goodluck Ebele Jonathan called a Stakeholders meeting comprising the leadership of the National Assembly, the Governors of Akwa Ibom and Cross River States, the Members of the National Assembly from both States, the Secretary to the Government of the Federation, the Attorney-General of the Federation and Minister of Justice, the Minister of Foreign Affairs and Director General, National Boundary Commission to review the situation.

The Stakeholders Meeting after due deliberations constituted a Committee comprising the Secretary to the Government of the Federation, the Attorney-General of the Federation, the Minister of Foreign Affairs, Director General, National Boundary Commission and Members of the National Assembly namely: Senator Victor Ndoma-Egba, Dr Ali Ahmed and Nnena Ukeje to examine the issues in contention and available options for Nigeria including, but not limited to the application for review of the ICJ Judgment, appropriate political and diplomatic solutions.

Although the judgment of the ICJ is final and not subject to appeal, the ICJ Statute provides for circumstances under which its judgment can be reviewed. The relevant provisions are:

(a) Article 61 (1) which provides that the Court can review its judgment upon the discovery of some fact of such a nature as to be a decisive factor, which fact was, when the judgment was given, unknown to the court and also to the party claiming revision, always provided that such ignorance was due not to negligence;

(b) Article 61 (4) which stipulates that application for revision must be made at least within six months of the discovery of the new fact, and

(c) Article 61(5), which provides that no application for revision may be made after the lapse of 10 years from the date of the judgment.

The implication of the above provisions of the ICJ Statute is that a case for revision of the judgment of the court can only be successful if:

(a) the application for revision is based on the discovery of a new fact;

(b) the fact must have existed prior to the delivery of the judgment;

(c) the newly discovered fact must be of a decisive nature; and

(d) the party seeking revision (Nigeria) and the Court, must not have known of the fact at the time of the delivery of the judgment.

The Committee proceeded to examine the case for revision against the requirements of Article 61 of the ICJ Statute and was constrained to observe from the oral presentations made to it by the proponents of the revision that the strict requirements of Article 61 could not be satisfied. This is because their presentation was unable to show that Nigeria has discovered a decisive fact that was unknown to her before the ICJ judgment, which is capable of swaying the Court to decide in its favour. This is more so as most of the issues canvassed in support of the case for a revision of the ICJ judgment had been canvassed and pronounced upon by the ICJ in its 2002 judgment.

The Federal Government also retained a firm of international legal practitioners to advise on the merits and demerits of the case for revision. The firm after considering all the materials that were placed at its disposal against the requirements of Article 61 of the ICJ Statute came to the reasoned conclusion that "an application for a review is virtually bound to fail" and that "a failed application will be diplomatically damaging to Nigeria."

In view of the foregoing, the Federal Government is of the informed view that with less than two days to the period when the revision will be statute barred (October 9, 2012), it would be impossible for Nigeria to satisfy the requirements of Articles 61(1)-(5) of the ICJ Statute. Government has therefore decided that it will not be in the national interest to apply for revision of the 2002 ICJ Judgment in respect of the Land and Maritime Boundary between Cameroon and Nigeria.

Government is however concerned about the plight of Nigerians living in the Bakassi Peninsula and the allegations of human rights abuses being perpetrated against Nigerians in the Peninsula and is determined to engage Cameroon within the framework of the existing implementation mechanisms agreed to by Nigeria and Cameroon in order to protect the rights and livelihoods of Nigerians living in the Peninsula. Nigeria will also not relent in seeking appropriate remedies provided by international law such as the invocation of the compulsory jurisdiction of the ICJ; Petitioning the United Nations Human Rights Council and good offices of the United Nations Secretary General which has played a pivotal role in ensuring the peaceful demarcation and delimitation of the boundary between the two countries and other confidence building measures and calls on the United Nations to continue to provide assistance to the affected populations.

Finally, the Federal Government wishes to assure all Nigerians especially the people living in the Bakassi Peninsula of its determination to explore all avenues necessary to protect their interests including but not limited to negotiations aimed at buying back the territory, if feasible, the convening of bilateral meeting of the Heads of State and Government to ensure protection and development of the affected population. In the meantime, we call on all well-meaning Nigerians in the Bakassi Peninsula to be law-abiding and to allow the various initiatives being undertaken by the Federal Government to bear fruitful results.

• • •

As soon as the statement went out, I felt the boulder under whose weight I had struggled finally hefted off my shoulders. I was very proud of myself. I received commendations from the French Ambassador, the British High Commissioner and the American Ambassador. To date, I feel very justified about my role in the Bakassi matter. A lot of those who felt differently were not aware that Nigeria had had the option of not submitting to ICJ jurisdiction *ab initio* when the matter was initiated by the Cameroonian government. That meant Nigeria became bound by the terms of the judgment.

I was not oblivious of the implications of handing over Bakassi to Cameroon. Indeed, Imoke was justifiably concerned for his people. If Bakassi was taken away, Cross River State would lose revenue as it would no longer be classified as an oil-producing state. That was the reality that dawned on that State in 2002 when the ICJ delivered its judgment. Besides, losing Bakassi would also render Cross River State landlocked.

I informed Imoke of the possibility of a lifeline by pointing him towards the Economic Stabilisation Fund of the Federal Government which could be used to cushion the loss of revenue. The Governor accordingly applied to the President for the grant. The request was referred to a committee chaired by Vice-President Namadi Sambo. The committee recommended that the sum of N15 billion be approved for Cross River to stabilise its poor funding resulting from the loss of revenue from the oil wells in the Bakassi Peninsula. The

President eventually approved N12 billion to be paid in three equal instalments. Despite this, I was still labelled a saboteur.

With the "Take back Bakassi" campaign now out of sight, we began to make tremendous progress in putting the Nigeria–Cameroon issue to rest. We saw to the successful implementation of the Greentree Agreement. We also substantially improved the work of the CNMC. The Nigerian High Commissioner to Cameroon, Ambassador Hadiza Mustapha, an articulate and brilliant career diplomat, was helpful to us in making substantial progress, leading to the signing of the Unitisation Agreement regarding the oil wells straddling between Nigeria and Cameroon.

Before the Unitisation Agreement, the CNMC, with the Vice Prime Minister of Cameroon, Mr Amadou Ali and Prince Ajibola of Nigeria as co-chairmen, had had issues with accessing funds and obtaining requisite authority to act on matters requiring presidential approval. These had constituted impenetrable roadblocks, resulting in little progress in the work of the Commission.

With the expiration of the deadline to apply for a review, the first thing the government did was to disband and reconstitute the Nigerian Committee. I was appointed to lead the Nigerian delegation to the CNMC. In my humble opinion, we made substantial improvements as I was able to access funds and obtain requisite approvals from the President for the work of the Commission. The Nigerian Boundary Commission, which had the technical expertise on boundary demarcation, served as the Secretariat for the Commission in Nigeria. The National Security Adviser also used his office to facilitate the work of the CNMC.

When people talk about the ICJ judgment, not many talk about the enormous gains Nigeria derived from it. For instance, Nigeria gained a lot of landmass particularly in the northern boundary with Cameroon. This is in addition to the fact that a good number of the oil wells ended up in Nigerian territory.

I was able to curtail the activities of civil servants who didn't want the assignment to come to an end as it would dry up the financial benefit they drew from the estacode payments! Between Vice Prime Minister Amadou Ali and myself, we drove the process to a very significant point. Djinnit commended me on that when he was leaving office. The former President of the ECOWAS Commission, Dr Mohamed Ibn Chambas, was appointed to take over from Djinnit in September 2014 to complete the assignment.

• • •

CHAPTER TWENTY

A COCKTAIL OF CONTROVERSIES

One week, one trouble. Leadership is a burden, no matter how one views it. Its challenges and controversies become more daunting as they often occur in bits and pieces, practically sprouting steadily out of the woodwork. Dealing with these often requires unconventional skills. Certain government actions flow from the peculiarities only those at the most sensitive positions in power alone are privy to. Some actions found necessary might appear perplexing to citizens who are far removed from the theatre of daily governmental realities.

A lot of socio-political considerations play a huge part in decision-making – which clearly cannot please everybody. The issues are exacerbated by the fact of Nigeria's cultural diversity, with differing economic, political and social concerns. A decision made that is viewed as being in favour of one part of the country often reverberates in another. The guiding principle of fairness, backed by the rule of law, remains the only safeguard that government can call in at all times.

In this chapter, I shall discuss the motley of controversies that we had to deal with in the line of duty and offer explanations on the chosen course of action.

• • •

PARDON FOR ALAMIEYESEIGHA

One of the most controversial decisions of the Jonathan Administration was the pardon he granted Chief DSP Alamieyeseigha, his benefactor and predecessor as Governor of Bayelsa State. To put things in context, Chief Alamieyeseigha made Jonathan his running mate in 1999, leading to him becoming Deputy Governor. When Alamieyeseigha was impeached in 2005, Jonathan replaced him. From there he was made presidential running mate to

Yar'Adua, and when Yar'Adua died in 2010, Jonathan became the President of Nigeria. Expectedly, Jonathan could feel beholden to Alamieyeseigha.

The Metropolitan Police in London had arrested Alamieyeseigha in September 2005 on money laundering charges. After his return to Nigeria in December 2005, he was impeached by the Bayelsa State House of Assembly and arrested by the EFCC. He was detained and put on trial. In July 2007, he was convicted on a six-count charge of corruption by the Federal High Court in Lagos and sentenced to two years in prison. It was a plea bargain, probably one of the first in the history of Nigeria's criminal justice system. He forfeited his assets, both at home and abroad. As part of the plea bargain, he was to be granted presidential pardon by Yar'Adua after his release from jail. This, however, did not materialise as President Yar'Adua fell ill and died.

When Jonathan became President in 2010, Alamieyeseigha renewed his appeal for pardon. President Jonathan was in a moral dilemma. He had helped to broker the deal between Alamieyeseigha and the Federal Government. On the strength of the promise of pardon, Alamieyeseigha had assisted with the peace process in the Niger Delta at the height of restiveness there. Pipeline vandalism had been drastically reduced, thereby significantly improving oil production in the Niger Delta. The Amnesty Programme had also taken root, thereby leading to relative peace and stability in the area. In a manner of speaking, Alamieyeseigha had earned his pardon.

The President passed on the request to me as the Chairman of the Presidential Advisory Committee on Prerogative of Mercy. I, however, advised that the demand of the ex-Governor could not be acceded to at that time; with the mood of the nation, it was bound to boomerang on the government. To begin with, the conviction was based on corruption and the Administration was heading into an election. Such a pardon at that time would become an albatross, with huge electoral implications.

President Jonathan agreed with my reasoning and communicated these sentiments to Alamieyeseigha, outlining why a pardon would not be feasible at the time. By March 2013 when the matter came up again, consideration was given to the fact that there was an earlier agreement between Yar'Adua and Alamieyeseigha and that the former Governor had, indeed, played his part. He had also demonstrated remorse, in addition to acting in the national interest. He deserved the pardon. Upon those considerations, it was agreed that he had paid enough for the crime. Since the President had unqualified power to grant a pardon, there was no reason not to grant it.

President Jonathan consulted with the National Council of State as required by Section 175 of the Constitution. All those that subsequently purported to oppose it did so because of the negative public reaction that followed the announcement. When the backlash started, I still felt that on the strength of the information available to me as the Attorney-General, government had complied with the laid-down procedure by first seeking the input of the Presidential Advisory Committee on the Prerogative of Mercy and subsequently consulting with the National Council of State. I did not have any second thoughts on the issue.

• • •

THE JUSTICE SALAMI SAGA

I had known Justice Ayodele Salami when he was the Presiding Justice of the Court of Appeal, Kaduna Division. Apart from taking personal interest in me, he encouraged me to apply for the rank of Senior Advocate of Nigeria at a time I had given scant attention to it. I could, therefore, not be party to any scheme to humiliate and hound him out of office as was erroneously bandied around in some quarters. The following is my recollection of what happened in 2011.

The Attorney-General is not a member of the National Judicial Council (NJC), but he is a member of the Federal Judicial Service Commission (FJSC). Justice Salami, who was the President of the Court of Appeal (PCA), and Justice Katsina-Alu, who was the CJN, were both members of the FJSC and NJC by virtue of their positions. I was not privy to any undercurrents or so-called 'rivalry' between them. But what I recall was that Justice Salami was absent at one of the crucial FJSC meetings to consider the appointment of new justices. I remember that Justice Katsina-Alu had nominated Justice Salami to the Supreme Court at that meeting, which meant Salami would have to leave his position as PCA.

When Justice Salami heard of his nomination, he wrote an angry letter to the CJN. Among the improprieties he enumerated was that the CJN had attempted to interfere in an election petition case before an Appeal Tribunal. When his complaints went before the NJC, they constituted a panel to examine the issues and submit a report. All I knew of the proceedings was what was available in the public space: that the committee's report was adopted by the NJC, which found Justice Salami guilty of misconduct and demanded that he apologise to the CJN. He refused to do so.

In August 2011, he was suspended and recommended for compulsory retirement. The NJC has the power to discipline any judicial officer found guilty of misconduct. It was their call to make. President Jonathan accepted the recommendation of the NJC and was in the process of transmitting it to the Senate for the required two-thirds majority confirmation when Justice Salami went to court. At that juncture, I advised the President that he could act no further on the matter pending the outcome of the court case. Contrary to my expectation that since the matter was commenced by way of an originating summons, Salami's lawyers would seek expedited hearing, they were, in fact, lackadaisical in handling the matter. They were endlessly seeking adjournments.

I make bold to state categorically that the allegation that President Jonathan hounded Salami out of office was not true. The President was not interested in hounding anybody. Quite the reverse. He was very sad. Even the Northern bigwigs in the profession, both retired and serving, such as Justice Mohammed Uwais, Justice Umaru Abdullahi, Alhaji Abdullahi Ibrahim, Justice Mamman Nasir and Justice Mustapha Akanbi, all attempted to broker peace with no success.

In the interim, because Salami had been suspended, the President had to act under Section 238(4) of the 1999 Constitution, which states: "If the office of the President of the Court of Appeal is vacant, or if the person holding the office is for any reason unable to perform the functions of the office, then until a person has been appointed to and has assumed the functions of that office or until the person holding the office has assumed those functions, the President shall appoint the most senior justice of the Court of Appeal to perform those functions."

That was what the President did. Justice Salami was unable to return to his seat because he was on suspension awaiting retirement or the outcome of the suit he instituted. It was a fairly straightforward case, but because political motives were read into it, many were not convinced that due process was followed.

Later in August 2011, when Justice Dahiru Musdapher became the CJN, he, along with some members of the NJC, tried to see if Salami could be recalled. He did write to the President on it. Regrettably, that line of action did not succeed. Not only did the NJC suspend Justice Salami, the body also recommended his retirement. The President had already acted on the recommendation and was awaiting the determination of the court case instituted by Justice Salami so that the process could be completed.

The NJC, having recommended his retirement, had become irrelevant in the matter and could no longer act on it or take back its prescription. Had it been that it was a mere suspension without the recommendation to compulsorily retire him, the President could have assented to the request of the NJC at the time. The NJC was advised to await the outcome of the court case – but this never saw the light of day owing to lack of diligent prosecution on the part of Justice Salami's lawyers.

$$\bullet \bullet \bullet$$

THE GULF WAR WINDFALL

There was the controversial case of former Military President, Gen. Ibrahim Babangida and the Gulf War Windfall. During the Gulf War from 1990 to 1991, when the US-led Allied Forces pounded Iraq for annexing Kuwait, crude oil prices had spiked, resulting in Nigeria reportedly generating an additional $12.4 billion revenue from oil exports. It was called the "Gulf War Windfall." In January 1994, Gen. Sani Abacha set up the Panel on the Re-Organisation and Reform of the Central Bank of Nigeria, headed by Prof Pius Okigbo and known as the "Okigbo Panel."

What was the connection between the Gulf War Windfall and the Okigbo Panel? Basically, that Panel stumbled on what was known as the "Dedication and Other Special Accounts" that had been set up by the Babangida administration. The first was set up in 1988, before the Gulf War. Gen. Babangida had authorised the dedication of revenue from the sale of 65,000 barrels of oil per day to the account for the financing of "special priority projects" which included the Ajaokuta Iron and Steel Company Limited (ASCL), the Nigerian Iron Ore Mining Company (NIOMCO), and the Shiroro Hydro-electric projects. The account was also to be used for external debt buy-back and the build-up of currency reserves.

In early 1994, while Abacha was in power, the turnover increased to 105,000 barrels per day and later to 150,000 barrels per day. The Federal Military Government further set up a Stabilisation Account for the Gulf War Windfall. Finally, another special account for Mining Rights and Signature

Bonus was created, according to the Okigbo Panel. In all, $12.4 billion accrued to the "Dedication and Other Special Accounts" from 1988 to 1994, overlapping two military regimes. It must be noted that the Gulf War Windfall did not exclusively generate the sum of $12.4 billion. That figure represented accruals to all the "Dedication and Other Special Accounts" and not solely from the Gulf War.

That apart, the Panel, as at 30 June 1994, stated that only a balance of $206 million was left in the account, raising a question as to whether the money was stolen or missing. The Okigbo Panel appeared to have glossed over that question, merely extrapolating that apart from the projects for which the accounts were established, "their use was extended to a wide variety of projects many of which could not be classified as priority. The details of receipts and disbursements on these accounts were, however, carefully maintained, and all payments were duly authorised by the President."

It went further to suggest that if the funds had been regarded as part of the external reserves and had been counted as such, "the impact on the exchange rate in the year under review would have been so significant that the Naira would have been stronger in 1994, in relation to the dollar, than it was in 1985." It then recommended that the "Dedication and Special Accounts" be discontinued, and any existing balances be taken into the external reserves of the Central Bank. The Panel never, therefore, insinuated that money was missing or stolen. Rather, it said the monies were spent on non-priority projects and that the records of expenditure were intact.

When I assumed office as Attorney-General, the Social-Economic Rights and Accountability Project (SERAP) – a nongovernmental organisation – applied to me to prosecute Babangida over the 'stolen' Gulf War Windfall based on the imaginary indictment by the Okigbo Panel. I didn't see the original report. Since they were requesting that I prosecute Babangida I wrote to the SGF who was supposed to be the custodian of such documents, and he replied that there was no such report. I later set up a committee, headed by the Permanent Secretary of the Federal Ministry of Justice, to search for the report, but they could not find one. They also went to the SGF, but nothing was available. Everybody we reached out to declared they had no such record of the Okigbo Panel report.

I wrote back to SERAP requesting that they forward a Certified True Copy of the report to me. They sent me a photocopied document instead. Despite the fact that it was legally worthless, I still took the pain to read it. I discovered from the document that the Okigbo Panel was not even an investigative one but was set up to reorganise the operations of the CBN.

On examining the case, I noticed that there was no basis for such a prosecution. I issued a public statement that there would be no prosecution in the matter, clarifying that the Pius Okigbo Panel Report had been misrepresented and sensationalised for the wrong reasons. There had been no criminal infractions disclosed in it. I also reminded the President that I already placed a memo before him to stop the use of those dedicated accounts. He, thereafter, directed the CBN to close the accounts.

Meanwhile, some individuals had gone on a spin to the President implying that I was dancing to the tune of Northern interests. They were attempting to manipulate him against me. But he listened to my explanations and understood that I meant well. Mr Steve Oronsaye, then the Head of Service of the Federation, also alluded to a possibility of the existence of a White Paper on the Okigbo Panel Report. But no one could produce the rumoured White Paper either. Interestingly, as of that time, I was yet to meet Babangida in person. I did meet him much later, for the first time, during a National Council of State meeting.

• • •

THE AZURA POWER PROJECT

The Federal Government of Nigeria had become susceptible to incurring huge judgment debts from Sovereign Guarantees made in favour of states and private enterprises. Learning its lesson from the losses, the FEC resolved that no further Sovereign Guarantees were to be issued by the Federal Government in favour of private entities. In August 2014, the SGF issued a circular directing that a "specimen indemnity" clause be inserted into all contracts and agreements entered into by the Federal Government with foreign entities. That was to provide additional protection to the Federal Government of Nigeria and some of its separate legal entities, such as the CBN, NNPC and NSIA, whose assets would be liable to attachment in enforcement proceedings in foreign jurisdictions.

The Azura-Edo Power issue came up on the heels of this government's position and in the same year the circular was issued. Azura is an Independent Power Plant in Edo State with plans to generate 461MW of electricity. It is a private company in which the Edo State Government holds a minority stake, based on the 100 hectares of land it allocated to the company. Azura wanted to secure foreign loans for the project, so Dr Okonjo-Iweala sought my legal opinion on the Put-Call Option Agreement (PCOA), which included the Partial Risk Guarantee (PRG) signed with Azura Power. I reminded her of SGF's circular on the need to indemnify the Federal Government and prevent its assets from becoming vulnerable in the event of a default.

I came under serious pressure from Dr Okonjo-Iweala and the Minister of Power, Prof Chinedu Nebo, as well as some other influential Nigerians, on the matter. By January 2015, Prof Nebo wrote a memo to the President seeking a waiver for the Azura project with regards to the circular. He made assurances that all obstacles had been overcome but for the legal opinion from the AGF. The memo was written in a way to make me look like the public enemy. He said inserting the "specimen indemnity" clause would prevent Azura from drawing down on any of the loan agreements that it had signed with a lender group. He cited the involvement of World Bank as evidence that the government should accept to issue Sovereign Guarantee.

I drew attention to the FEC resolution that approved the "specimen indemnity" clause and cautioned on the need to reverse that decision before any action could be taken on Azura's request. I, therefore, advised Okonjo-Iweala and Nebo to present another memo to FEC seeking a review or a waiver. My belief was that such a memo would be favourably considered if they were able to provide justification or exceptional reasons in support of the request. But nobody wanted to take that risk.

Unfair insinuations were made against me – all water off a duck's back. I stood with what was right in the circumstance. Regrettably, as soon as we left office, some people who claimed they had influence in government took advantage of the absence of an Attorney-General, months into the administration of President Buhari. They reached out to Vice-President Osinbajo, who got the Solicitor-General to issue the Sovereign Guarantee. I would have thought the Solicitor-General, having been part of the team that saw the loopholes from all the foregone conversations, would act differently. But he was a civil servant, after all. The Federal Government then signed off its backing of a $237 million World Bank PRG for the construction of the Azura-Edo IPP.

Unfortunately, the Azura Project became an albatross around the neck of the Federal Government because of the ill-advised Sovereign Guarantee. Mr Babatunde Fashola, the Minister of Power under President Buhari, would eventually declare that the Federal Government was no longer keen on providing Sovereign Guarantees to investors interested in building new power plants because of the Azura experience.[10] A part of me felt vindicated. We did many things in office that were derided and criticised, but it is a little gratifying that our critics later came round to our position!

• • •

THE OYINLOLA AND AREGBESOLA SAGA

A few months after assumption of office, I received a letter from the Attorney-General of Osun State for a fiat for a private lawyer, Mr Lawal Rabanna, to prosecute Mr Rauf Aregbesola, the Action Congress of Nigeria (ACN) candidate in the 2010 gubernatorial election, for an alleged offence of forgery of INEC documents.

Aregbesola was at the time challenging the election of Oyinlola at the Election Petitions Tribunal. I declined the request because the Attorney-General of Osun State had already briefed Rabanna who commenced the prosecution at the Federal High Court even before the request was made. There was, therefore, a procedural breach. I was also of the view that a fiat is not granted as of right. Certain criteria must be met. I ought to have been availed the opportunity of appraising the charge and the accompanying police investigation report as well as the proof of evidence before deciding whether or not to grant the request. All these were not done. The request was more or less an afterthought resorted to only when they were confronted with the need to obtain my fiat at the Federal High Court.

Furthermore, I reasoned that Oyinlola might be trying to elicit the support of state institutions to intimidate Aregbesola from asserting his constitutional right to contest the election results. I chose to be circumspect. This angered Oyinlola, who reported to the President that I was an ACN man and a good friend of Lai Mohammed. He alleged that I was a supporter of the ACN and that was why I refused to grant a fiat to prosecute Aregbesola who was "engaged" in an act of "forgery."

[10] Okafor, Chineme and Mozie, Amaka, 'Fashola: FG not Ready to Give Sovereign Guarantees to Power Investors', *THISDAY* 03-12-2018 available at https://www.thisdaylive.com/index.php/2018/12/03/fashola-fg-not-ready-to-give-sovereign-guarantees-to-power-investors/ [retrieved 15-12-2018]

The President sought to know if it was possible for me to oblige them the request. I politely informed him that the Constitution expected me to act in the public interest in such cases and that I felt strongly that a grant of a fiat in that instance would not be in the public interest. The President then allowed me to exercise my discretion to decline the request. Oyinlola was naturally not happy with my stance. He regarded me as an enemy. The, then Honourable Minister of Youth Development, Senator Akinlabi Olasunkanmi, did his best to reconcile us.

Another occasion that I had to decline a request from Oyinlola was during the MTN saga, when it was alleged that the ACN leader, Asiwaju Ahmed Tinubu, was in communication with Justice Ayo Salami, President of the Court of Appeal. MTN was requested to produce the call logs in order to establish that there was improper communication between Tinubu and the judge as alleged. When MTN, for whatever reason, failed to produce the call logs, Oyinlola wanted them prosecuted for obstructing the course of justice.

When I informed him that the materials at my disposal were not sufficient to ground a prosecution, he said he knew but that he just wanted me to commence it so that MTN would come and negotiate with him in order to stem the prosecution. Oyinlola concluded, albeit wrongly, that I was an enemy and as a result, launched an extensive media campaign against me. He even allegedly sponsored a suit in the Federal High Court, Abuja, challenging my refusal to prosecute MTN as evidence that I was not fit to occupy the position of Attorney-General of the Federation. This was amidst orchestrated media allegations that I was a shareholder in MTN and was, therefore, unwilling to prosecute MTN because of possible conflict of interests.

However, I was only following the dictates of the Constitution which required me to exercise the power to initiate a prosecution objectively and in the public interest. On the two occasions that I refused to grant Oyinlola's requests, it was because the requisite criteria were not met. It was not out of ill will. I recall that when Oyinlola won his suit challenging his removal as National Secretary of the PDP, I was one of the first to advise the President that he should be reinstated. Regrettably, he was not reinstated because PDP officials were of the opinion that I was not a politician and that since the matter was purely a party affair, my advice should be ignored.

• • •

PART V

•

THE FOOTPRINTS

CHAPTER TWENTY-ONE

RECOVERING THE ABACHA LOOT

The Abacha family thought they were smart, but they were smoked out by a very simple trick. They had virtually succeeded in blocking Federal Government's efforts at recovering quite a chunk of the funds looted by their patriarch, the former military ruler, Gen. Sani Abacha. Their attitude tended to imply that giving up about $1.3 billion of the loot was generous of them. Nigeria ought to have remained eternally grateful! They felt entitled to retain the rest of the loot to the tune of over $1 billion hidden in different havens in Europe. They had acceded to returning the laundered funds, yet turned tail to orchestrate dodgy schemes despite the fact that the government had kept its part of the bargain. Alhaji Mohammed Abacha, the oldest surviving son of Gen. Abacha, was particularly uncooperative.

Gen. Abacha, who ruled Nigeria from 1993 to 1999, laundered billions of dollars, mostly through European banks, with the aid of his children, a younger brother, and Senator Atiku Bagudu, the current Governor of Kebbi State. These were his fronts. The move to recover the funds was initiated by Gen. Abdulsalami Abubakar, who took over as military Head of State after the death of Gen. Abacha in June 1998. He promulgated the Forfeiture of Assets etc. (Certain Persons) Decree No. 53 of 1999. There was also a clause in the Decree that if assets not disclosed were later identified, the Abachas would forfeit them.

In 2000, under the democratically elected administration of President Olusegun Obasanjo, the Federal Government engaged the services of Mr Enrico Monfrini, a Swiss lawyer, to trace the looted funds worldwide, recover them and facilitate repatriation to Nigeria. In all, Mr Enrico was able to trace about $2.4 billion to various accounts in Luxembourg, Liechtenstein, the UK, Channel Island of Jersey, France and Switzerland. More than half of the identified loot was returned to Nigeria, with Switzerland alone repatriating $500 million in 2005.

As at the time I was appointed Attorney-General in 2010, over $1 billion was still hanging in various accounts across Europe as a result of the pranks being played by the Abacha family. We decided to redouble Nigeria's efforts to recover the monies. Our first step was a holistic review of the strategies adopted by successive administrations since 1999 with a view to streamlining the process for greater efficiency. Then we mounted pressure on the Abachas and engaged with the various jurisdictions where the funds were stashed. Thereafter, we began to see results, despite the challenges. There was a significant increase, both in the quantum and rate, of recoveries.

Liechtenstein gave us the biggest headache. It appeared to have developed cold feet over returning about €185 million located in its jurisdiction, which funds had been frozen by court orders since 2000. Investigators had established that €179 million of the sum was paid as a bribe by Ferrostaal AG of Germany, one of the largest steel traders in the world, to whom Gen. Abacha had awarded the contract for the construction of the Aluminium Smelter Company of Nigeria (ALSCON), Ikot Abasi, Akwa Ibom State. Mohammed and Abba, Abacha's sons, mounted legal obstacles against repatriating the money to Nigeria.

The Liechtenstein Supreme Court ordered its confiscation in 2012, but the Abachas appealed against that. The appeal was finally thrown out in March 2013. Still pushing their luck, they headed for the European Court of Human Rights in Strasbourg, France, and effectively delayed the return of the money to Nigeria. Although everybody knew they would not win the case in Strasbourg, Liechtenstein hung on the excuse of the lawsuit to resist returning the money. That was understandable: Abacha's loot was worth about 25 per cent of the country's annual budget in 2013.

To protect itself, Liechtenstein requested for Sovereign Indemnity, which was promptly signed by Dr Okonjo-Iweala, Nigeria's Minister of Finance, in May 2013. The Letter of Indemnity was worded thus:

The Federal Republic of Nigeria hereby undertakes to indemnify the Principality of Liechtenstein against any financial loss that it might suffer in the event that the European Court of Human Rights should deem that the forfeiture order pronounced on 23 July 2008 by the Land als Kriminalgericht against Glotar Establishment, Nalim Anstalt, and Raw Material Development & Trading S.A., or ensuing proceedings, violated the European Convention on Human Rights, and should order the Principality of Liechtenstein to compensate any of those companies.

Even though the indemnity was given, Liechtenstein still would not budge. They did return €7.5 million against which one of the indicted companies did not appeal. Other complex cases involving Senator Bagudu had also been concluded, and Liechtenstein had repatriated to Nigeria the sums of $65 million in 2003, CHF6.4 million in 2006, and CHF1million in 2007.

There was more drama beyond our expectations, though.

While Monfrini was working day and night to help us get the money back, including negotiating asset sharing as part of the final resolution, Nigeria's Ambassador in Bern, Switzerland, Ms. Fidelia Akuabata Njeze, suddenly showed up on the scene, insisting that she was the only person entitled to conduct the negotiations. That added to the embarrassment being faced by both Nigeria and Monfrini, and possibly contributed to Liechtenstein's reluctance in returning the money.

I left the country along with retired Col. Bello Fadile from the Office of the National Security Adviser, for Geneva, Switzerland, on 27 May 2013 to deliver the Letter of Indemnity to Mr Monfrini and to finalise arrangements for the asset-sharing agreement with the Liechtenstein authorities. The new development forced us to abort the plan in order to give room for consultation with President Jonathan. Ms Njeze really threw a spanner in the works. We needed to rebuild confidence in the Liechtenstein authorities by clarifying who, in fact, should be involved in the negotiations. The Ministry of Foreign Affairs had to write to the Principality of Liechtenstein before we could make a move forward.

Liechtenstein still stuck to their guns. We had to approach the World Bank Group through the efforts of Dr Okonjo-Iweala, who had been a managing director at the Bank before joining President Jonathan's cabinet in 2011. We sought the help of the Bank to break the deadlock. The issue dragged on into 2014, despite high-level meetings between Nigeria and Liechtenstein under the auspices of the World Bank Group. I attended the meetings, along with Dr Okonjo-Iweala. Liechtenstein initially avoided a high-level meeting until the *Financial Times* of London published a story on 10 October 2013 that seemed to paint the government as stalling. Even the subsequent high-level meeting did not prove to be the panacea we craved for.

We had earlier adopted that strategy of 'constructive engagement' with the British Channel Island of Jersey with much success, so we thought Liechtenstein was going to cooperate too. Our approach in Jersey led to the successful prosecution, conviction and sentencing of Mr Raj Arjandas

Bhojwani, an associate of the Abachas, for money laundering offences. They got a confiscation order on proceeds of crime amounting to £26.5 million. I, thereafter, led a delegation made up of officials of the EFCC and Monfrini to St Helier, in Jersey, to negotiate an appropriate sharing agreement. We got £22.5 million repatriated to Nigeria while Jersey got £4 million as reimbursement for costs of investigation and prosecution. All parties left contented.

Not so with Liechtenstein! It kept pleading the need to protect itself from liability in case Strasbourg ruled in favour of the Abachas. In October 2013, Dr Thomas Zwiefelhofer, the country's Deputy Prime Minister, forwarded a proposal to Dr Okonjo-Iweala based on the United Nations Convention against Corruption (UNCAC) treaty to which both Nigeria and Liechtenstein were State Parties. According to Article 57 of the Convention, Liechtenstein was required to return confiscated assets to the requesting State Party, in this case Nigeria. On the basis of that Convention, Zwiefelhofer stated that Liechtenstein was in principle willing to repatriate the assets forfeited to the benefit of Nigeria after deducting reasonable court and procedural costs. However, he said it was not yet able to do so because of the pending complaints by the various companies to the European Court of Human Rights.

He expressed fear at the possible risk of "liability" and "just satisfaction" implications that might befall his country should the European Court for Human Rights rule in favour of the Abachas. He promised that Liechtenstein would repatriate the assets, after deducting costs, to the Federal Republic of Nigeria "quickly" if the Abachas lost the case but that the World Bank should develop solutions on how the recovery would be managed by Nigeria – a veiled remark about the reported mismanagement of previous restitutions made to the country.

The meetings and proposals were essentially a waste of time in the end; all motion without movement. With the Abachas seeming to have successfully frustrated our efforts at repatriating the €185 million loot, I pulled a joker out of the pack. And they were soon brought meekly to their knees.

• • •

Based on the terms of a Global Settlement Agreement entered into by President Obasanjo and the Abachas in 2004, the Federal Government had granted a "complete waiver" to the family on the understanding that they would willingly return all the looted funds traced to them, their companies and their proxies. The family had effectively stalled the Liechtenstein repatriation, as I previously narrated, but I fashioned out a solution: the court. Government initiated criminal proceedings against Mohammed, the treasurer of the family, at the High Court of the FCT, Abuja. He was charged with receiving stolen property, conspiracy to assist in concealing stolen property and concealing stolen property.

He resisted prosecution and raised preliminary objections, arguing that the proof of evidence and the witness statements did not disclose any offence. The trial court did not rule in his favour. He, therefore, lodged an appeal at the Court of Appeal and filed a motion for Stay of Proceedings pending the outcome of his appeal. Part of his argument was that he had immunity to prosecution under Decree No. 53 of 1999. The Court of Appeal ruled in favour of the Federal Government. Dissatisfied, he appealed to the Supreme Court. Unfortunately for him, he also lost the case at the Supreme Court in January 2014.

That defeat left him at our mercy. That was when I pulled the trigger. It was a simple trick. I revived the criminal prosecution against him by briefing Mr Dan Enwelum, who was a member of the original legal team constituted to prosecute Mohammed Abacha. Mohammed could read the handwriting on the wall. He knew the game was up. He had nowhere to hide anymore. He ran helter-skelter, but didn't want to frolic with the courts again.

Mohammed was still smarting from the long battle he had been embroiled in with the Federal Government over the 1994 assassination of Mrs Kudirat Abiola, wife of Chief MKO Abiola. He had been in detention from 1999 to 2002. It was anything but a pleasant experience for him. Although he was discharged by the Supreme Court in 2002 in what many people thought was a political settlement, he was, nonetheless, not ready for another face-off with the Nigerian judiciary. Having lost his current case all the way from the High Court to the Supreme Court, he had no more wriggle room.

After the charges had been filed, Mohammed sent emissaries to me. In a business-like manner, I made it clear that the bottom line was that he should withdraw the cases pending before the European Court of Human Rights, ensure Nigeria's access to the money in Liechtenstein and then all other things would be sorted out. He did precisely that. We entered into a 'deferred prosecution agreement' whereby it was agreed that if he eventually failed to cooperate with the government in the recoveries, the prosecution would be activated.

On 6 May 2014, his lawyers, Abdullahi Haruna & Co., wrote to state that they had instructed their European solicitor to take all necessary steps to bring to fruition the implementation of the Global Settlement Agreement signed in 2004 and withdraw the proceedings pending at the European Court of Human Rights. That was a major victory for Nigeria. It came 14 years after these assets had been frozen by court orders. The journey had been exasperating and frustrating.

Still, the Government of Liechtenstein would not make things easy. They did not release the money without putting up stiff resistance. They came up with one condition after the other. They insisted they needed to know how we were going to spend the money. After a series of tripartite meetings involving the World Bank's Stolen Asset Recovery Unit, an agreement was reached and the first tranche of about $242.2 million was finally paid to Nigeria.

We signed a Repatriation Agreement, dated 14 July 2014, to put a legal seal on all the assurances of cooperation between the Federal Government and the Abacha Family in furtherance of the common objective of ensuring quick resolution of the lingering dispute and the recovery of the outstanding assets. The Abachas undertook to cooperate fully in the legal proceedings to recover the outstanding assets in Luxembourg, the UK and the US. The UK assets to be repatriated, as agreed, were those held in HSBC Bank Plc in the name of Mohammed Abacha; those held in Standard Bank in the name of Standard Alliance Corporation/Mecosta Securities Inc.; and those held in Citibank Private Bank in the name of Navarrio and Morgan Procurement Corporation.

Others included the Jersey assets, held in Deutsche Bank International Ltd, in the name of Doraville Properties Inc., and accounts at HSBC. In France, the assets were identified at Banque SBA SA in the names of Rayville International SA, Harbour Engineering and Construction Ltd and Standard Alliance Corporation. In Luxembourg, the assets were held by Caisse de Consignation of the Grand Duchy in the names of Rilke Ltd, Wambeck Holdings Ltd, Arwood Overseas Ltd, Larbridbe Trading Ltd, Venford Investments Ltd, Savard International Ltd, Junin Finance Ltd, Raw Material Development and Trading Company Ltd, Selcon Aluminium Products Ltd, and MM Warburg & Co. Luxembourg SA. Shares held by Caisse de Consignation were also identified.

All these assets were traced by Monfrini. He was paid 4 per cent of the

$242 million recovered from Liechtenstein and another 4 per cent for the $380 million from Luxembourg as his professional fees, as stated in his contract with Nigeria. Christian Luscher of CMS Von ErlachPoncet Ltd, who acted on behalf of the Abachas, was paid 2.8 per cent as obligatory under the composite agreements. The State of Geneva was paid CHF3 million to cover its expenses. Monfrini was also paid $5 million as a retainer for further action to be brought against MM Warburg & Co. Luxembourg SA and other potential defendants. HBK Investments Advisory SA was paid $750,000 for its services.

Liechtenstein transferred $242.2 million to Nigeria, while the $380 million recovered from Luxembourg was domiciled with the Attorney-General of Switzerland for safekeeping pending when Nigeria would formally apply for it. The net amount due to Nigeria was $321 million after all deductions, although the money was kept in an interest-yielding account. I was not too eager to complete the process. An election was approaching, which we eventually lost. We were being careful. If we had gone ahead to complete the process, the opposition would have said we re-looted Abacha loot. So we concluded that since the job was already done, the in-coming government of President Buhari would take the administrative step of applying for its repatriation.

• • •

With the cases of Liechtenstein and Luxembourg finally settled, things moved on quite evenly. It is worthy of note that the World Bank was impressed with the success we recorded in Liechtenstein and our overall recovery efforts. In June 2014, they wrote us a letter of commendation and promised to work with us in monitoring the utilisation of the funds as we had requested. Meanwhile, the US Department of Justice, perhaps impressed with the progress Nigeria had made, also launched forfeiture proceedings against the Abachas and their associates. That was a welcome development for the Nigerian Government.

The value of assets in question totalled $550 million and £95,910 discovered in ten accounts and six investment portfolios linked to the Abachas in France, the UK, British Virgin Islands and the US. Activating the Mutual Legal Assistance Treaty (MLAT) with Nigeria, the US sent court processes to my office as the Central Authority for the service on Mohammed Abacha,

Senator Bagudu and their associates. The papers were served as requested. On 16 May 2014, I issued a statement affirming Nigeria's support for the effort by the US to recover the looted funds. I confirmed that we had received requests from the US Department of Justice and that we were cooperating fully with them. The US took the lead because the monies passed through their jurisdiction at various times.

In my opinion, Monfrini deserves commendation. Granted he was paid for his efforts, but he had performed excellently on behalf of Nigeria. He effectively traced where the monies were stashed, which was not an easy task. Everybody recognised that it was extremely complex, especially as it included cross-border jurisdictions and a myriad of individuals and companies that had been used as proxies. It was not as easy as just typing 'Mohammed Abacha' into the computer and downloading his accounts. Monfrini was able to create sufficient linkage between those assets and the Abacha family. In appreciation of his service to the country, President Jonathan awarded him the national honour of Officer of the Order of the Federal Republic (OFR) in 2014.

Following President Jonathan's defeat in the 2015 general election, the Abachas began to renege on the agreement they entered into. They probably reckoned that the Buhari government would be less fussy about the Abacha loot. In February 2015, the Government of Jersey had reached out to the Nigerian High Commissioner to the UK, Dr Dalhatu Tafida, to request a meeting to discuss the funds they were preparing to repatriate to Nigeria. The amount involved was $313 million. We held a meeting in Jersey on 27 April 2015, but I came out of it disappointed.

Mr Howard Sharp, the Solicitor-General of Jersey, declared that they could not proceed with the repatriation because Mohammed Abacha had challenged the seizure of $313 million in a Jersey court. Jersey had, in 2003, repatriated $163 million from Bagudu and, in 2011, $22.5 million from Bhojwani as part of the Abacha loot. They could not be accused of bad faith. Mohammed Abacha's legal action was completely in bad faith, but he knew what he was doing.

• • •

I now put this on record for the sake of completeness.

In April 2013, after we had recorded significant success in recovering the looted funds, I got a letter from one Dr Godson M. Nnaka, a US-based attorney, who said he had been briefed in November 2004 by a previous Attorney-General and was now entitled to 33.33 per cent of all recoveries. I thought it was a joke. But Chief Akin Olujinmi, who was the AGF in 2004, followed it up with a letter confirming having given an official instruction to Dr Nnaka "to help with efforts of the Government" to recover Abacha loot. He attached a copy of the Letter of Instruction.

While we were at it, I got a memo dated 9 June 2014 from President Jonathan on the same issue. Dr Nnaka had managed to gain access to the President. I replied the President's memo informing him that Nnaka's claims were false and untenable. I reasoned that if he had an instruction since 2004, where was he for the past 10 years? What did he do with the instruction? Who was he coordinating with? I reminded the President that in August 2012, I made a request to the US Department of Justice for mutual legal assistance for the confiscation of assets constituting proceeds of crimes committed by Gen. Abacha. The request was based on the provisions of UNCAC. The US Government was also duly informed of the appointment of Monfrini as Nigeria's legal representative in connection with the request.

Based on the request, a forfeiture case had been filed by the US Government on 18 November 2013. I explained to him how preposterous it sounded to be receiving a letter from the Law Offices of Nnaka & Associates, with its attached court processes, purportedly for fees and expenses for services rendered to the Government by Nnaka based on a 2004 instruction.

Nnaka was unknown to me, as Nigeria's Attorney-General, in respect of any matter. I was also not aware of any legal services rendered by him since my assumption of office, nor had he ever contacted me with regard to any such services being rendered by him either prior or subsequent to my assumption of office. On the contrary, my inquiries revealed that he had, since 2009, been disqualified from practising as an attorney in the US and was finally disbarred by a court in 2012. The letter of instruction he relied upon expressly provided that he was to be paid for his professional services based on an agreed percentage of sums actually recovered by him.

The forfeiture proceedings in the case were initiated at the request of the Federal Government of Nigeria without any input whatsoever from Nnaka. It was clear from the available facts that Nnaka's claim was not only spurious but also tainted. I advised that such a claim should be discouraged as it had the tendency of being construed as an attempt by Nigerian officials to divert the proceeds of the forfeiture. This might have adverse effects on the repatriation of any forfeited assets to Nigeria.

• • •

This is another important matter for the records. Mr Femi Falana, who would later badmouth me, actually recognised my efforts in the Abacha loot recovery. He not only sent me a letter of commendation, he even made a request to sue the banks that laundered the funds on behalf of the Abachas. In his letter, he alluded to the "important next step" – to seek remedies from those banks. He had premised his letter thus: "I have followed very closely the impressive efforts by the Federal Government ably led by your good self to recover public funds, especially by the late General Sani Abacha. This is highly commendable." *Res ipsa loquitur*? I have nothing more to add.

CHAPTER TWENTY-TWO

THE AJAOKUTA STEEL SETTLEMENT

In 1979, Nigeria set up the Ajaokuta Steel Company Limited (ASCL), National Iron Ore Mining Company (NIOMCO), Itakpe, and the Delta Steel Company (DSC), Aladja, with the big dream of industrialisation. But these have become a nightmare for successive governments. The gigantic ASCL, with four different rolling mills, sits on 24,000 hectares of land. It has become a sitting duck, vulnerable to all sorts of shenanigans over the years. For a steel company that was nearing completion by 1994, it is nothing short of heart-breaking to imagine that Ajaokuta is yet to turn its wheel.

If Ajaokuta were to come fully on stream, the projection is that its multiplier effect would be felt in key sectors of the economy – from construction to transport, agriculture and sundry industries. Ajaokuta was conceived to produce 1.3 million tonnes of liquid steel, yearly, in Phase One. It was to have a built-in capacity to expand to 2.6 million tonnes of flat iron and steel products in Phase Two. By Phase Three, it would produce 5.2 million tonnes of various steel products, particularly heavy plates. The complex has 43 different plants. What's more, it can become a major producer of industrial machines, auto electrical spare parts as well as material for shipbuilding, railways and carriages.

In terms of employment, the steel industry is a notable employer of labour globally. Ajaokuta was to directly engage 10,000 technical staff, plus an indirect employment of 500,000 people. Nigeria has, by some estimates, spent roughly $10 billion on the plant since the foundation stone was laid by President Shehu Shagari in 1980. But stories of woe have trailed the venture from government to government through the years, including reported sleaze in debt buy-back deals under Gen. Abacha. For a plant that has the potential to be the world's fourth largest, it is tragic that Ajaokuta remains forlorn, like the forsaken barren wife of a wicked polygamist. It was proposed at some point that with the injection of just $2 billion more, the plant would come fully alive, but the Federal Government was no longer interested in spending money on it.

In June 2003, President Obasanjo concessioned Ajaokuta to SolGas Energy, a US company, for 10 years. A year later, the concession was terminated as a result of non-performance, according to the Federal Government. SolGas's competence had been questioned from the beginning, but the promoter was said to be close to President Obasanjo's son, so the objections were overruled. President Obasanjo then granted another 10-year concession, the second time around, to Global Infrastructure Nigeria Limited (GINL), a company promoted by the Mittal Group, for a fee of $300 million. GINL was also awarded a concession for Itakpe.

In 2007, shortly before Obasanjo left office, the Ajaokuta concession was converted to 60 per cent equity in favour of GINL under a Share Sales Purchase Agreement (SSPA). When President Yar'Adua assumed office, thereafter, he set up an Administrative Panel of Inquiry to look into the concessions. The report was damning. GINL was accused of committing "breaches" and "unwholesome" practices. The panel reported that GINL failed to submit a workable business plan within the specified timeframe and did not pay the concession fees, in addition to cannibalising the assets. The SSPA was declared null and void because of failure to meet the basic conditions.

The panel also found out that instead of investing foreign capital in the completion of the project as agreed upon, GINL had borrowed massively from local commercial banks, pledging the assets of ASCL as collateral. The panel reported that GINL owed $192 million to the banks. GINL had, in fact, been diminishing the values of ASCL and NIOMCO to buoy up its own fortunes. The concessionary agreements "were largely skewed in favour of the concessionaire, to the detriment of the Federal Government of Nigeria", the panel concluded. Consequently, President Yar'Adua, in June 2008, cancelled both the concession for Itakpe and SSPA for Ajaokuta.

Global Steel Holdings Limited (GSHL), the parent company of GIHL, opted for arbitration against Nigeria a year after.

• • •

When I assumed office in April 2010, one of the first memos the President sent to me was on Ajaokuta Steel Co. Ltd. The memo was based on the report of a committee headed by the Solicitor-General, Federal Ministry of Justice, Alhaji Yola, which examined the dispute that led to the arbitration between

Global Steel and the Federal Government. Upon reviewing the case, the committee recommended, among other things, that the government should pay over $525 million in damages to Global Steel for "wrongful termination of the SPA" in respect of ASCL.

The President directed that I should review those recommendations. I set up a small committee with my technical assistants. Our work revealed that the recommendation made by the Solicitor-General was faulty. I decided to adopt a different approach. I invited the officials of Global Steel for a meeting where I got the chance to appraise them and to discover their underbelly. I challenged them with regards to the compensation they were claiming, making it clear that I was aware that they had taken undue advantage of the negotiations.

Prior to the meeting, I had done my homework and discovered that they had not been paying their taxes. I threatened them with criminal proceedings for tax evasion, in addition to other criminal infractions that they had clearly committed. I also observed that they had cannibalised machines and equipment at Ajaokuta Steel and had taken them to Aladja Steel, which they owned having acquired it through outright purchase, but which, in itself, was faring no better. I pointed out to them that as foreign investors, they were supposed to have brought in their capital and shown evidence of that by a certificate of capital importation but, instead, they had taken local loans and pledged the assets of the company.

When they noticed that I was closing in on them, the prime promoters refused to come to Nigeria for negotiations for fear of arrest and trial for tax evasion. I employed that tactic as a carrot-and-stick approach. To amicably resolve the issue, I insisted that Global Steel should relinquish their interest in ASCL for free without any form of compensation. Before I was appointed Attorney-General, I was Nigeria's nominated arbitrator in the panel that was handling the Ajaokuta arbitration. I had to withdraw from the arbitration and Justice Samson Uwaifo was nominated to replace me. Meanwhile, the arbitration had been put on hold pending further negotiations.

In respect of NIOMCO, Nigeria was apparently in the wrong, unlike in the Ajaokuta matter. The requisite notices had not been given and the procedure for termination had not been followed. It appeared the government and the civil servants, at the time, were too much in a haste to overturn what was done by President Obasanjo and had not followed due process. It was, therefore, not easy to dismiss Global Steel's claims in the manner we could dismiss the claims related to ASCL.

To resolve these claims, the parties (Global Infrastructure and the Federal Government of Nigeria) opted for mediation. It was a preferred option because it guaranteed a win–win outcome for all parties. Such an arrangement would encourage foreign investment as well as safeguard the national interest. We commenced mediation in Dubai, UAE. I led the Federal Government team comprising our retained counsel, Dr Tunde Oghowewe, the State House Counsel, Mr Jalal Arabi, as well as the Sole Administrator of ASCL and relevant officials from the Ministry of Mines and Steel Development and Ministry of Justice.

The highlights of the agreement we entered into in 2013 after mediation were as follows:

Ajaokuta Steel Company Limited: The ownership, management and control of Ajaokuta Steel Company Limited would not revert to GSHL/GINL. Consequently, government would not revalidate the terminated SSPA, which was the subject matter of the dispute. GSHL/GINL accepted this position, including the fact that government would not make any monetary payment to them in respect of any claim that they might have in respect of their alleged investment in the plant.

National Iron Ore Mining Company Limited: Nigeria was at fault in the case of NIOMCO as the termination of the concession was not in accord with the terms of the Concession Agreement signed by both parties in 2004. The Federal Government would rescind the termination and return NIOMCO to GSHL/GINL on the basis of a renegotiated Concession Agreement. Global Steel would guarantee priority supply of raw materials to Ajaokuta by NIOMCO. The Federal Government would restore the period affected by the legal dispute (about five years at the time) to enable GSHL utilise the full term envisaged under the original Concession Agreement.

Global Steel agreed to waive all its rights to damages for any breach earlier committed by Nigeria. In light of the fact that a Presidential Committee had estimated damages payable to them in the region of $525 million, that was a substantial achievement. The negotiation team was able to bargain a higher concession fee payable to the Federal Government from three per cent of turnover to four per cent. That, too, was a substantial and remarkable achievement. The negotiation team was further able to secure the agreement of Global Steel to a renewal of the concession upon satisfactory performance, as opposed to the old model of automatic renewal format. The Concession Agreement would be for the mutual benefit of both parties.

Delta Steel Company Limited: Both parties acknowledged that DSC was not an issue before the Arbitration Tribunal/Mediation Panel. However, in the light of a request by GSHL/GINL, and the need by government to promote the overall growth of the steel sector, the Federal Government would facilitate discussions between GSHL/GINL on the one hand and Asset Management Corporation of Nigeria (AMCON) on the other hand to enable AMCON restructure DSC's debts. That would enable GSHL/GINL regain control of DSC and resume operations.

Railway Concession Agreement: An issue raised by GSHL/GINL in the course of the negotiations was on the status of a Railway Concession Agreement for the Central Railway (Itakpe–Ajaokuta–Aladja), said to have been entered into by the Federal Government (represented by the Federal Ministry of Transport, the Bureau of Public Enterprises and the Nigerian Railway Corporation) on 31 October 2006. The companies tendered a copy of the Agreement, apparently duly signed by the authorised representatives of the government. To prevent another round of litigation, I advised the President that if the Agreement was authentic, Nigeria should abide by it.

The Modified Concession Agreement: The need for a Modified Concession Agreement was one of the outcomes of the mediation held in Dubai. To achieve this objective, meetings were held in London with the promoters of Global Steel with a view to negotiating and drafting a Modified Concession Agreement that enhanced both quality and value derived from the agreement by the Federal Government.

The terms of the NIOMCO Modified Concession Agreement were adopted by both parties in London, on 5 December 2014. I forwarded a memo to President Jonathan on 12 December 2014 apprising him of the terms. I also advised that the terms were acceptable to the parties and would effectively resolve the NIOMCO dispute. I requested that the Minister of Mines and Steel Development, Mr Musa Sada, be directed to execute the Modified Concession Agreement in order to trigger the undertaking by GINL and GSHL to waive their claims against the Federal Government.

Unfortunately, we could not sign it because some people in government had peculiar interests. On the day we were slated to sign, Sada was nowhere to be found. When Dr Kayode Fayemi became Minister of Mines and Steel Development under President Buhari, he simply dusted up the agreement and signed it. NIOMCO was returned to GSHL/GINL in 2016. No credit was given to us for the efforts we made to amicably resolve the dispute. In any event, all we did was for the national interest and not for personal glory.

· · ·

Instead of recognising that some good had been done, Ms. Akpoti Natasha, a lawyer aspiring to be a politician, started a campaign to diminish the achieve-ment. She appeared before the House of Representatives in 2018 uttering all manner of uninformed allegations against me over the concession agreement. She most unfairly stated that I should be held responsible for "successfully assisting" GINL against Nigeria at the arbitration. She declared: "Nigeria was clearly winning the case at the Arbitration Court but the former AGF (Adoke) applied for an out-of-court settlement and Jonathan granted it. The out-of-court settlement brought about the re-concession agreement and the terms stated that Itakpe should be given back to GINL because Nigeria owed them $525 million dollars."

She got a standing ovation for her stunt, and the video soon went viral as she misled millions of Nigerians on a matter she knew nothing about. How on earth could she say I compromised the arbitration? I could not have done so. I didn't start the process of negotiation while the arbitration was going on. Negotiation was already in place, as evident in the recommendation to President Jonathan by the committee led by the Solicitor-General. The committee recommended $525 million compensation in order for GINL/GSHL to terminate the arbitration. That is clear proof that the process of mediation was already on before I came into the picture. How then could I be accused of compromising the arbitration that, in her words, Nigeria was already winning?

It is even disingenuous for her to say Nigeria was winning the case. Arbitration is not a football match where you know the score by the minute. In arbitration, both parties would be heard and their evidence examined before an award is made. How did Akpoti know that Nigeria was winning the case? Did she have access into the minds of the arbitrators? This only shows that she was just playing to the gallery. Not long after her show, she said she was going to run for Senate. She had simply run her mouth for 30 minutes of fame, using me as the punching bag.

• • •

CHAPTER TWENTY-THREE

REFORMING THE JUSTICE SYSTEM

On assumption of office in 2011, I deliberately set out to carry out reforms aimed at improving the effectiveness and efficacy of the justice sector institutions and personnel. This was accomplished through various policy initiatives and legislations. I invited some subject matter experts to assist my aides in fashioning out a reform agenda for the justice sector. Supported by our development partners, we were able to produce a policy document called "Strategy for the Implementation of Justice Sector Reforms" which was launched in August 2011. The Hon. Justice Ishaq Bello, now Chief Judge of the FCT, was appointed Chairman of the Implementation Committee comprising all stakeholders in the justice sector.

The eight-point strategic reform agenda were: (1) reform of the criminal justice system; promotion of legislative reforms and advocacy (2) promotion and protection of human rights (3) improvement of the institutional mandates and structures of justice institutions in line with emerging international developments (4) improved international co-operation mechanisms (5) implementation of the Freedom of Information Act 2011 (6) enhanced welfare services and staff capacity development and (8) improved accountability and efficiency of the staff of the Ministry of Justice and allied institutions.

The implementation of these strategic plans was segmented into short term, medium term and long term. A robust system of reviewing existing laws and proposing amendments where desirable was put in place. This included proposing new legislation to deal with emerging areas of law such as terrorism, financial crimes and cybercrimes.

• • •

REFORM LAWS 2011–2015

During my tenure, the following reform bills were proposed and passed into law by the National Assembly.

The Evidence Act 2011

The Evidence Act 2011 is one of the most significant pieces of legislation passed during my stewardship. Although efforts to reform Nigeria's evidence law began before my tenure, the Act was finally passed into law by the sixth National Assembly and assented to by President Goodluck Jonathan in 2011. The legislation was enthusiastically received by the legal community. Writing on how this milestone was attained in *THISDAY* newspaper in 2011, Prof. Yemi Akinseye-George, a Senior Advocate of Nigeria, stated as follows:

> At last, Nigeria now boasts of a modern Evidence Act after several decades of inertia. Here is how it happened. In Feb., 2011, the Attorney-General of the Federation (HAGF) and Minister of Justice, Mohammed Bello Adoke, SAN conducted a Ministerial Press Briefing. In the course of the meeting, he declared that he was determined to leave behind a legacy of a new Evidence Act. He immediately directed this writer to work with relevant officials of the Federal Ministry of Justice to update the draft Evidence Bill... For now, we say kudos to Mohammed Bello Adoke, SAN for mustering the political will to ensure the passage of the Evidence Act 2011. We thank His Excellency President Goodluck Jonathan for promptly assenting to the Bill and of course, the law makers for rising up to the challenge.

Efforts to enact the Evidence Act began in the 1990s with a Draft Bill by the Nigerian Law Reform Commission. The Draft was updated in 2006 by a Committee Chaired by Hon. Justice SMA Belgore and subsequently adopted by the Hon. Justice Akintola Olufemi Ejiwunmi. It was finally presented to the National Assembly as a private member's bill in 2009 by Hon. Seriake Dickson (now Governor of Bayelsa state). Before the enactment of the Evidence Act 2011, the law in operation was basically a colonial legislation dating back to 1945. It was, therefore, not in tandem with the new developments in information and communication technology and needed to be updated. The major innovations introduced by the Evidence Act 2011 relate to electronically generated evidence, the definition of documents and banker's book, confessional statements and general improvement in the language of the Act.

The innovations introduced by the 2011 Act are meant to assist the courts in the adjudication of complex cases such as financial and cybercrimes that involve the use of technology. The admission of computer printouts, electronic mails, facsimile, and other electronic documents in evidence will no doubt facilitate the adjudication of cases bordering on computer-generated evidence.

· · ·

The Freedom of Information Act 2011

The Freedom of Information Act 2011 (FOIA) was passed by the National Assembly and assented to by President Jonathan on 28 May 2011. It also had a chequered history like the Evidence Act 2011. The ideals of the Act were promoted by a coalition of civil society organisations and civil rights advocates. The fundamental objective of the Act is to facilitate access to information. The Act has 32 sections dealing with various aspects such as the right of access to records, the procedure for making requests for information, circumstances under which requests can be granted or refused, exemptions, judicial review and the Attorney-General's oversight responsibility.

The Act seeks to make public records and information freely available. The idea is to promote open government so as to engender transparency and accountability. It is generally believed that access to information as provided for by the Act will promote good governance and other democratic values necessary for the sustained development of the country.

The FOIA is not just an abstract piece of legislation. Its ideals are firmly rooted in the Constitution of the Federal Republic of Nigeria 1999 (as amended). The Constitution provides in section 39(1): "Every person shall be entitled to freedom of expression, including freedom to hold opinions and to receive and impart ideas and information without interference." Inherent in the freedom of expression is the right to freely access information, which the FOIA promotes.

Given the novel nature of the provisions of the FOIA, it became imperative for me to issue guidelines on its implementation to aid compliance by public institutions. The revised guidelines were issued in 2012. In view of the initial reluctance by public institutions and officials to embrace the new ethos of the Act, I had to issue Advisories to all public institutions to comply with the provisions of the Act.

. . .

The Terrorism (Prevention) Act 2011

The Terrorism (Prevention) Act 2011 (TPA) was enacted in response to the growing incidence of terrorism after the 9/11 attack in the US. There was a compelling need to provide a legal framework that adequately criminalises terrorist offences and prescribes punishment that will serve as deterrence. Dealing with terrorism was certainly a new experience for us. Our development partners were very helpful in assisting us with the draft and review of the legislation to ensure that it compares with international standards and best practices.

The Explanatory Memorandum to the TPA clearly states that the objectives of the TPA 2011 are "to provide for the prevention, prohibition and combating of acts of terrorism, the financing of terrorism in Nigeria and for the effective implementation of the Convention on the Prevention and Combating of Terrorism and the Convention on the Suppression of the Financing of Terrorism."

The TPA is divided into eight major parts. These are: (1) provision of acts of terrorism and related offences (2) prohibition of terrorist funding and seizure of terrorist property (3) provision of cooperation to other countries through mutual legal assistance and seizure of terrorist assets (4) provision of cooperation to other countries through extradition of suspects linked to terrorism (5) investigative powers (6) prosecution (7) power to register or refuse registration of charities and (8) miscellaneous powers.

Despite the commendable provisions of the TPA, after a few months of its implementation, it became glaring that it still lagged behind Financial Action Task Force (FATF) standards and the United Nations Convention on the Suppression of Terrorism in some critical areas. For instance, the provisions of the TPA were adjudged to be grossly inadequate to combat terrorism in line with international best practices. Furthermore, some of the provisions of the TPA did not align with or were in direct conflict with provisions of earlier legislations such as the Economic and Financial Crimes Commission (Establishment) Act 2004 and the National Security Agencies Act 2004. There was the need for a comprehensive review of the TPA to bring it in conformity with international standards set by FATF and the UN Convention on the Suppression of Terrorism.

To cure these defects, the Federal Ministry of Justice embarked on the drafting of a new bill to amend the TPA 2011. During the review period, comments were received from relevant agencies involved in the implementation of TPA 2011 and other international agencies such as the United Nations Office of Drugs and Crime (UNODC), the United States Department of Justice, the United Kingdom High Commission, the UK Home Office and FATF Secretariat.

* * *

Terrorism (Prevention)(Amendment) Act 2013

The Terrorism (Prevention) (Amendment) Act 2013 was enacted to address the defects or shortcomings of the TPA 2011. The Act essentially strengthens the TPA by providing for its extra-territorial application, increasing the number of terrorist financing offences and other issues relating to the effective administration and implementation of the Act. The notable improvements include: the empowering of the Office of the National Security Adviser to serve as the coordinating body for all the security and enforcement agencies under the Act; the increase in the number of terrorist offences from 13 in TPA to 26, to include all offences prescribed by international conventions; investing the Attorney-General of the Federation with the responsibility of ensuring effective implementation of the Act and the power to prosecute acts of terrorism, and the provision for the establishment of a Victims Trust Fund to be managed by a Trust Fund Board.

To give effect to the implementation of the TPA 2011 as amended, I issued the Terrorism Prevention (Freezing of International Terrorists Funds and Other Related Measures) Regulations 2011 in relation to freezing and forfeiture measures. Proscription measures were also taken in form of the Terrorism (Prevention) Proscription Order) Notice 2013 to proscribe both terrorist groups, Jamaa'tu Ahlis-Sunna Liddaawati Wal Jihad (Boko Haram) and Jamaa'to Ansarul Muslimina Fi Biladis Sudan (Ansaru) in accordance with FATF Special Recommendation 3 and the United Nations Security Council Resolutions 1269 (1999) and Resolution 1373 (2001).

• • •

The Money Laundering (Prohibition) (Amendment) Act 2012

The Act was passed in 2012 to further strengthen EFCC's efforts to combat financial and economic crimes. The amendment Act was made to address the shortcomings in the Money Laundering (Prohibition) Act No. 11 of 2011 (the Principal Act) with respect to the predicate offences created under it. The Amendment Act clearly set out the predicate offences under the Act and enhanced customer due diligence in order to effectively combat money laundering in the country. Its provisions include: provision for internal control measures; prohibition of correspondent banking relationship with shell banks; and provision of penalties for money laundering offences. The amendments are no doubt salutary as they have greatly complemented government's efforts in combating money laundering, particularly the ability of the EFCC to prosecute the offences in Nigeria.

• • •

The Economic and Financial Crimes Commission (Enforcement) Regulations 2010

Nigeria's legislative history shows that before 2010, the EFCC had not had the benefit of receiving, through subsidiary legislation, appropriate administrative, operational and prosecutorial guidelines from the Office of the Attorney-General of the Federation. The absence of regulations created a fertile ground for the operations of the EFCC to be conducted sometimes whimsically and capriciously, thereby giving credence to the allegations of selective or double standards against its leadership. The EFCC also faltered on sensitive issues such as plea-bargaining, which saw the imposition of ridiculous sentences by the courts to the chagrin of the public.

Consequently, on assumption of office in April 2010, I had, in the exercise of the powers vested in me by Section 174 of the Constitution of the Federal Republic of Nigeria 1999, ordered a thorough review of the operations of the

EFCC to ensure compliance with the laws. This was necessary because the EFCC was conducting prosecutions on behalf of the Federal Government of Nigeria and the Constitution expressly provides that the exercise of such prosecutorial powers shall be in the "interest of justice" and the need to "prevent the abuse of process."

I consulted widely and constituted a committee with representation from critical stakeholders, including the Nigerian Bar Association and civil society organisations, to prepare draft regulations to fill the gaps identified in the law and operations of the EFCC. To ensure inclusiveness, the Draft Regulations were subjected to further review and a copy was sent to the President for notation and information. It was after these processes were duly completed that on 20 September 2010, I issued the Economic and Financial Crimes Commission (Enforcement) Regulations 2010 to provide for the procedure and process of enforcing and implementing the mandate of the EFCC in the whole or any part of Nigeria.

It is significant to note that although the regulations were duly gazetted and became effective from 20 September 2010, it was later evident in 2011 that they were not particularly welcomed by the EFCC. This was when the debate as to whether or not the EFCC should be merged with the ICPC took centre stage, following the Senate confirmation hearings for ministerial nominees.

In the midst of allegations and counter-allegations as to the efficacy and effectiveness of the EFCC, the regulations that were already in force since 2010 were exhumed and made to look fresh. This generated a lot of media frenzy with views sharply divided as to whether or not the Attorney-General had the power to make the regulations in question; and if he did, whether or not he had overreached it by the regulations.

It is apposite to state that Section 43 of the EFCC Act 2004 provides that "The Attorney-General of the Federation may make regulations with respect to the exercise of any of the duties, functions or powers of the Commission under this Act." A careful reading of the provision would reveal that the lawmakers envisaged a situation where there may be gaps in the framework legislation or the need to provide for detailed procedures required to give effect to the enabling legislation. The rationale for Section 43 is to allow the Attorney-General fill such gaps or provide details of the procedure required to give effect to the Act without the need to revert to the National Assembly. It was therefore clear that I acted properly and well within the powers donated to me by the National Assembly.

Contrary to the impression created by a section of the media and some commentators that the regulations were made to stifle the work of the EFCC or render the agency ineffective, it is clearly stated that the regulations *"are made to provide a procedure for carrying out the mandate of the Commission pursuant to section 43 of the Act and matters related thereto"* while the scope of application of the regulations is limited *"to the procedure for receiving complaints, initiation of prosecution and related matters."*

It was thus my firm belief that given the Attorney-General's overarching oversight over public prosecutions regardless of the prosecuting authority – including the power to initiate criminal proceedings, take over or discontinue criminal proceedings instituted by any other authority – and cognizant of the fact that these powers are exercisable in the public interest, the regulations would ensure that the Attorney-General as the Chief Law Officer is kept informed of cases of public interest and be assured that best practices are being observed by the EFCC in the discharge of its statutory mandate.

It is also necessary to clarify that what the regulations seek to achieve (which is consistent with the EFCC Act and the 1999 Constitution) is to prescribe safeguards which will ensure that the prosecutorial powers of a publicly funded agency are not exercised without the necessary due diligence. In this regard, the regulations, in accordance with best practices, provide that in the preparation of charges, the EFCC shall consider, among other things, the need to reflect the seriousness and extent of the criminality supported by the evidence. This is a practice that is already in place in other countries such as the UK and the US where prosecutorial bodies are similarly guided by the Attorney-General's office.

Contrary to the insinuations that the provisions relating to investigations were meant to stifle the operations of the EFCC and unduly bring its operations under the control of the Attorney-General, the main objective was to ensure compliance with existing constitutional provisions which give the Attorney-General overarching oversight powers over public prosecution. The EFCC is thus required under the regulations to inform the Attorney-General of ongoing investigations and prosecutions. Since EFCC prosecutes on behalf of the state, the Attorney-General needs to be on top of the situation at all times – in view of increasing complaints of abuse of statutory mandate and highhandedness by the agency. Let me reiterate that under the regulations, the EFCC is only required to inform, not seek the consent of, the AGF (as erroneously portrayed to the public) before it commences investigation or prosecution.

Similarly, the regulations relating to plea bargain are meant to forestall situations in which it would be used to defeat the ends of justice as was experienced in the cases involving certain politically exposed persons in which ridiculous amounts were paid as fines without taking cognizance of global best practices which emphasise disgorgement of proceeds of crime and restitution where possible. This is to prevent such convicts from enjoying the proceeds of crime.

On the treatment of confiscated assets, the regulations seek to ensure that proper inventory is done and their disposal handled in a transparent manner. This is against the background of Nigeria's experiences where allegations of lack of transparency in the disposal of seized assets abound. The complaints were that prosecutorial agencies report seizures but the confiscated assets are sold at ridiculous amounts to the detriment of the state or that they do not render proper account as to how such assets were disposed of and whether, indeed, the proceeds of their sale have been lodged into the Consolidated Revenue Fund of the Federation as required by extant laws.

On the receipt of foreign funding, the regulations merely seek to protect national security interests by stipulating that the state be informed within 30 days of the receipt of any foreign grant, especially the amount, purpose and terms and conditions. This is also to prevent the violation of extant laws.

Looking back, I am still very proud of the initiative to make the regulations. The rationale for the regulations was well founded and the objectives totally altruistic. If the EFCC had complied with the regulations, the controversy that trailed the agency when the eighth Assembly started conducting public hearings into the EFCC's activities, especially how it handled the disposal of seized or forfeited assets, would have been avoided.

• • •

The Administration of Criminal Justice Act 2015

The Administration of Criminal Justice Act (ACJA) was signed into law on 13 May 2015 by President Jonathan shortly before the end of his tenure. It was a landmark legislation; the criminal justice system in Nigeria had become fossilised. We needed to do something about it. Nigeria was operating under two different procedures inherited from the colonial era. There was the *Criminal Procedure Code* for non-federal courts in the North, while there was the *Criminal Procedure Act* for courts in the South, as well as the Federal High Court. There were substantive laws on the administration of criminal justice, but we needed to modernise the procedural law in order to ensure effective criminal justice administration in the country.

The journey started in 2006 when Chief Ojo was the AGF. He had set up a National Working Group to critically review the entire justice delivery system so as to introduce the necessary reforms to bring Nigeria up to date with other progressive countries in the world. Ojo left office in May 2007. I continued from where he stopped. In 2012, I appointed the Panel on Implementation of Justice Reform. Three years later, we finally saw the results of almost one decade of work as the bill was passed into law by the National Assembly.

The Administration of Criminal Justice Act 2015 is essentially a 'unifying' law. It is a uniform federal law. By virtue of Section 493, it repealed the Criminal Procedure Act, Cap C41 Laws of the Federation of Nigeria 2004; the Criminal Procedure Code (Northern States) Cap, C42; and the Administration of Justice Commission Act, Cap A3. We set out to achieve two main objectives. One, we wanted to ensure that the system of administration promotes efficient management of criminal justice institutions and speedy dispensation of justice. Two, ACJA is a deliberate shift from punishment as a main goal to restorative justice, which pays attention to the protection of the society, the rights of both the suspect (the defendant) as well as those of the victims of crime. The legal community received ACJA with open arms. It was salutary and far-reaching in its revolution.

So many people would like to claim credit for the enactment of that bill into law, most of them for political reasons. In my reckoning, though, I would commend Ojo for starting the process; Senate President David Mark and Speaker Aminu Waziri Tambuwal for assisting tremendously in ensuring the timely passage of the bill; and President Jonathan, for assenting to it during his last days in office. I would also give honourable mention to a senior Nigerian journalist, Alhaji Yusuf Alli, who drew my attention to a potential flaw in a provision that allowed the President to order the detention of people. Imagine the abuse that sort of provision could have been subjected to if not for Alli's eagle eye.

Dr Ali Ahmad, who was the Chairman of the House of Representatives Committee on Justice, and Senator Umar Dahiru, his Senate counterpart, also deserve special mention. The bill was passed through them to their respective chambers as a private member's bill to avoid administrative bottle-necks in view of its urgency.

The Administration of Criminal Justice Act is, no doubt, one of the most revolutionary laws in the history of Nigeria, but like every law, still far from perfect. Laws are said to be dynamic, lending themselves to regular assessment and review. After we left office and the government that came in started hounding PDP members, I was told that some lawyers started abusing me over the ACJA. I had gone on self-exile when the persecution started. Some high-profile political figures who were in the EFCC custody were reported to have thrown insults my way, saying that having brought the ACJA into being, I should have been around to get a dose of my own medicine! They described me as 'evil' for prevailing on President Jonathan to sign it into law.

Their grouse against me was over the detention of suspects, for which magistrates have power under the ACJA to extend the duration. It was supposed to have been the High Court. When the committee came up with the report that included the Magistrates Court, I had opposed it very strongly. But they had what I thought was a superior argument, being that there are many remote areas in Nigeria without a High Court. At the time I accepted that reasoning, little did I suspect that magistrates were going to set about acting in a very irresponsible manner, even to the extent of issuing undated detention warrants to the EFCC and subjecting the whole process to malignant abuse.

But all is not lost. The AGF, if he is minded to, can always activate the review button that has been provided for in the Act. I am also pleased at the action of the Hon. Justice Ishaq Bello, Chief Judge of the FCT, who, I understand, took steps to address these abuses among the magistracy in the FCT. Incidentally, he was the Chairman of the Justice Sector Reform Committee that midwifed the process leading to the passage of the Act. He is sufficiently aware of the objectives we sought to achieve with the legislation and better placed to point out the abuses in the implementation of the law.

• • •

The Cybercrimes (Prohibition, Prevention, etc) Act 2015

This is another bill that was passed into law by the National Assembly and assented to by President Jonathan a few days to his handing over power to

President Buhari. The Cybercrimes Act 2015 was passed in response to the need to prosecute cybercrimes in Nigeria. While the incidence of cyber-crimes was on the rise in the country, the appropriate legal and institutional framework to deal with the menace was virtually non-existent.

The Act contains three main objectives: (a) to provide an effective and unified legal, regulatory and institutional framework for the prohibition, pre-vention, detection, prosecution and punishment of cybercrimes in Nigeria (b) to ensure the protection of critical national information infrastructure and (c) to promote cybersecurity and the protection of computer systems and networks, electronic communications, data and computer programmes, intellectual property and privacy rights.

The President is empowered to prescribe minimum standards, guidelines, rules or procedure for a number of activities specified in the Act, such as the protection or preservation of critical information infrastructure; general management, access to, transfer and control of data in any critical informa-tion infrastructure; infrastructural or procedural rules and requirements for securing the integrity and authenticity of data or information contained in any designated critical national information infrastructure; the storage or archiving of data or information designated as critical national information infrastructure; recovery plans in the event of disaster, breach or loss, and any other matter required for the adequate protection, management and control of data and other resources. Under the Act, the President may direct the Office of the National Security Adviser to audit and inspect any of the infra-structures to ensure compliance with the Act.

The Act contains a list of prohibited conducts with appropriate penalties. These include offences against critical national information infrastructure, intentional unlawful access to a computer for fraudulent purposes, systems interference, intercepting electronic messages, email, electronic money trans-fers, tampering with critical infrastructure, wilful misdirection of electronic messages, unlawful interceptions, computer-related forgery, and comput-er-related fraud.

Other offences include fraudulent misrepresentation, alteration of infor-mation, theft of electronic devices, theft of ATM, unauthorised modifica-tion of computer systems, network data and systems interference, forgery, fraudulent misrepresentation of electronic signatures, cyberterrorism, iden-tity theft and impersonation, child pornography and related offences such as production, offer and distribution, cyber stalking, cyber squatting, racist and xenophobic offences, attempt to commit offences, conspiracy, aiding and abetting, unlawful importation and fabrication of e-tools, breach of confidence by service providers, manipulation of ATM/POS terminals, non-compliance with employee responsibility, phishing, spamming and spreading of computer virus, electronic cards related fraud, use of fraudulent device or attached e-mails and websites.

The Act places responsibility on financial institutions. They are expected to play pivotal roles in the administration of the Cybercrimes Act, which include preventive measures against commission and corrective measures in the event of commission of crimes to protect victims as well as apprehend offenders. Part IV of the Act provides for the roles of financial institutions which are binding, the breach of which may be penalised as provided for by the Act.

The Cybercrimes Act 2015 is a trailblazer in Nigeria's quest to criminalise and punish cybercrimes. The legislation also lays emphasis on the promotion of cybersecurity in the country in an unprecedented manner. It contains novel provisions designed to protect critical national infrastructure and accords, for the first time, special protection to children and minors from child pornography and related offences in line with the Global Alliance against Child Sexual Abuse Online, which Nigeria signed in 2012. The Act creates obligations on financial institutions with important roles to play in the overall effort to combat cybercrimes.

• • •

Outstanding Reform Bills Awaiting Legislative Action as at 29 May 2015

Although, we had set for ourselves an ambitious legislative agenda to ensure passage into law of essential reform bills, we did not record complete success. As at 29 May 2015 when my tenure ended, a number of Draft Bills were still awaiting legislative action. While part of the problem could be attributed to the cumbersome legislative process under the Constitution, resistance to change and turf wars also contributed to the delays suffered by some of the bills. I nonetheless feel obliged to outline what we sought to achieve for the benefit of the public so as to engender greater appreciation of our sincerity of purpose and the direction we were headed.

The Nigerian Financial Intelligence Centre Bill

This is one of the legislative reform proposals that we did not succeed in getting the National Assembly to pass into law before the end of my tenure in 2015. It was not for lack of trying but because of the resistance or lack of cooperation from the EFCC. The Nigerian Financial Intelligence Unit (NFIU) had operated as a unit under the Control of the EFCC and successive Chairmen of the agency preferred to maintain the status quo. They were, therefore, opposed to any effort to grant the NFIU the necessary autonomy even when it was clear that it was best practice to allow the NFIU to enjoy administrative and operational autonomy.

The bill was drafted with the aim of establishing the Nigerian Financial Intelligence Centre as an autonomous agency with a mandate to gather intelligence, as it relates to suspicious transactions, in conformity with Nigeria's international obligations and laws. It is important to reiterate that the NFIC Bill was designed to, among other things, effectively address the following concerns: the autonomy of the NFIC; the legal, institutional and regulatory framework that ensures transparency, effective and efficient management, administration and operation of the Centre; institutional best practices in financial intelligence management in Nigeria; ability to exchange information with other financial intelligence units, law enforcement agencies, regulators and similar bodies in Nigeria and other countries in matters relating to money laundering, terrorist financing activities and other predicate offences; and the issue of seamless transition from the NFIU to the NFIC, including uninterrupted submission and processing of suspicious transaction reports.

We reasoned that the Centre, despite its proposed autonomy, should be effectively supervised to ensure that it was pursuing its statutory mandate within the ambit of the law. The bill provided for a Board comprising representatives from relevant agencies of government. The Centre was expected to collate information (intelligence), analyse it and disseminate it to relevant institutions with regulatory or law enforcement powers over the information so gathered.

The relevant law enforcement agencies which the Centre was expected to service include: the Code of Conduct Bureau; the Economic and Financial Crimes Commission; the National Drug Law Enforcement Agency; the Nigeria Police Force; the Nigeria Customs Service; the State Security Services; the Independent Corrupt Practices and Other Related Offences

Commission; the Federal Inland Revenue Service; and the National Agency for the Prohibition of Trafficking in Persons. The Centre was therefore essentially an administrative FIU that needed to be effectively supervised to ensure that all the agencies that require information were effectively and efficiently serviced. Consequently, the location of the Centre was important to its effective performance and coordination of the AML/CFT efforts of the Country. The bill as was originally conceived took these into consideration by locating the Centre under the Minister of Justice, who is the focal point for all AML/CFT, issues in the country.

Under the draft bill, the Minister of Justice was charged with the responsibility of recommending the appointment of the Director General for the Centre to the President; conveying the Annual reports of the Centre to the President, making regulations for the NFIC; approving Guidelines made by the Centre and giving general directions to the Centre.

It was, however, disturbing that despite the laudable intentions that informed the location of the original NFIC Bill in the Ministry of Justice, some stakeholders argued against that location and instead preferred to place the NFIC in the Central Bank of Nigeria under the guise of freeing the Centre from interference and ensuring adequate funding for it. I personally felt that this was not ideal, as the CBN was not charged with any responsibility over the Centre in the bill. The CBN didn't have administrative or operational oversight over the Centre. There was therefore no nexus whatsoever between the CBN and the Centre to justify such a proposal to locate it in the CBN. Adequate funding for the agency could be ensured through appropriation, as is the case with other Government agencies such as the EFCC, ICPC, Code of Conduct Bureau, etc. More importantly, the CBN is one of the regulatory agencies that the Centre was expected to be disseminating analysed report to and the Centre should therefore not be located within the CBN. This was the same argument that informed the decision to remove it from the EFCC.

The argument that the Centre's activities would be subjected to interference if located in the Ministry of Justice is not tenable, as the Ministry of Justice was not meant to exercise operational oversight over the Centre as the Board of the Centre was charged with the operational oversight of the Centre. However, to ensure that the Centre kept within its mandate especially in view of the legal issues involved in the exercise of its mandate such as Nigerian's privacy laws, confidentiality laws, money laundering, international cooperation issues, prosecution of terrorism related crimes and terrorist financing, which are matters superintended upon by the Ministry of Justice, there was the need to locate the Centre in the Ministry of Justice. Furthermore, the Minister of Justice by virtue of his constitutional mandate was better placed to seek approval for funding the operational needs of the Centre, ensure effective international cooperation mechanism, and obtain the necessary approvals needed by the Centre to discharge its mandate. These concerns were not adequately addressed before we left office and I was, therefore, not able to achieve the objective of separating the NFIU from the operational control of the EFCC.

The Proceeds of Crime and Asset Management Agency Bill

The bill was proposed against the backdrop of the multiplicity of penal provisions on asset forfeiture in Nigeria. The enabling laws of agencies such as the EFCC, ICPC, NDLEA, Nigerian Customs Act and NAPTIP provide for penal forfeiture in relation to the proceeds of crime. However, Nigeria did not have a single comprehensive legislation on the subject matter. This was despite the fact that since 2011, the Inter-Governmental Action Group Against Money Laundering (GIABA) had advised on the need for Nigeria to enact a single Asset Recovery and Confiscation law to address the weakness in the existing legal framework.

The Proceeds of Crime Bill was drafted in 2014 in response to the advice received from our development partners who were not only concerned about the absence of a comprehensive statue on proceeds of crime, but also the weaknesses of existing legal framework that situated the power of enforcement of proceeds of crime and the management of such assets in the same agencies. They advised that such a practice negates transparency and accountability in the confiscation and management of proceeds of crime. To ensure that these concerns were adequately reflected, the draft bill benefitted from the inputs of various stakeholders and development partners. The bill also benefitted from best practices from other common law jurisdictions such as the United Kingdom, Australia, Canada, Singapore and South Africa.

The major objectives of the bill are to: provide for an effective legal and institutional framework for the recovery and management of the proceeds of crime or benefits derived from unlawful activities; deprive a person of the proceeds of an offence, the instrumentalities of an offence and any benefit derived from an offence committed within or outside Nigeria; prevent the reinvestment of proceeds of unlawful activity in the furtherance of criminal enterprise; harmonise and consolidate existing legislative provisions on the recovery of proceeds of crime and related matters in Nigeria; and make comprehensive provisions for the restraint, confiscation and forfeiture of property derived from unlawful activities and any instrumentalities used or intended to be used in the commission of such unlawful activities.

In essence, the bill, when passed into law, will effectively take from a convicted person the proceeds of crime, thereby rendering the criminal venture unprofitable, empower relevant law enforcement agencies to carry out full financial investigation of the criminal and of criminally acquired proceeds; and ensure adequate measures for the realization, preservation and management of assets.

Although, we had made promises to the international community especially the Financial Action Task Force (FATF) and the Inter-Governmental Action Group against Money Laundering in West Africa (GIABA) of Nigeria's preparedness and political will to enact a robust Proceeds of Crimes Bill as part of the nation's compliance efforts with the recommendations of FAFT, we could not realise this objective before 29 May 2015.

POLICY MEASURES TO REFORM THE JUSTICE SECTOR

The point has been made that the Strategy for the Implementation of Justice Sector Reforms launched in 2011 was the framework deployed to drive my vision for the reform of the justice sector. Apart from the foregoing reform bills, the Committee also worked assiduously towards achieving its objectives by producing the Code of Conduct for federal prosecutors to ensure that prosecutions are carried out professionally, ethically and in conformity with the best traditions of the Bar.

The Committee also worked with our development partners, especially the UK Department for International Development (DfID) to produce the Nigeria Anti-Corruption Strategy 2013–2017 to bring about a coordinated response to the scourge of corruption in the country. The strategy identified the factors responsible for corruption and developed appropriate strategies to be adopted by all the institutions with the mandate to fight corruption.

CHAPTER TWENTY-FOUR

THE MINISTRY OF JUSTICE MAKEOVER

The rule of law is what makes the human society different from the animal kingdom, and woe betide any country whose Office of the Attorney-General crumbles into disarray, or where its staff are demotivated and lacking in professionalism. With these notions in mind, my first move on assumption of office in April 2010 was to carry out an evaluation of the problems of the Ministry. After extensive discussions with the Solicitor-General, the Directors, and a cross section of the staff, I discovered a gnawing situation of acute low morale among staff.

On my first day at work after the swearing-in, I got to the office at 8 am to find most staff not yet in the office. On the second day, I again arrived office at 8 am to the same scenario. Then news went round that the new Minister was in the habit of coming to work early, and that he usually went around to inspect offices to check for punctuality. To my bewilderment, the staff sent a delegation to complain that I was embarrassing them! I was not expected to be in office before 9 am, they said. The standard working hours were 8 am to 4 pm; everybody acknowledged that. I resisted the temptation to dismiss them as I recognised the plausibility of their complaint.

One of the major issues confronting the staff was transportation. A significant number of them depended on public transportation, with its attendant inefficiency. Even for those who owned cars, it was a struggle to keep them on the roads. While the excuses were not acceptable by the Civil Service rules, pragmatism was the only option I could adopt in aid of the objective of improving punctuality. I immediately began seeking solutions to the problem. I was able to source for funds outside of the Ministry to buy three buses for the Law Officers Association. The buses conveyed staff to and from work. That worked an instant miracle! By 8 am on any given day, offices in the Ministry were full and brimming over with activities. That meant more red tapes were removed and files got treated more expeditiously. One hour, particularly in the morning, is vital to productivity.

Another source of their low morale was the backlog of claims due to the staff. I made sure such outstanding payments were cleared as soon as we had the resources. On the other hand, staff demanded the harmonisation of their salaries as professionals in line with what was obtainable in other institutions of government. I took immediate steps to tackle the issues. First, I requested presidential intervention, which was granted. We increased the robe allowance of lawyers and made sure that they were paid. We resolved the very depressing issue of harmonisation after a long battle with the Wages and Salaries Commission. We also got the buy-in of every stakeholder, including that of the Minister of Finance. The process got caught up with red tape, but President Jonathan finally approved it in 2015. We could not start paying immediately because it was not in the budget for that year. Actual implementation commenced in 2017 after I had left office.

As a result of the low morale, lawyers in the ministry would collect files and would not go to court. It was also alleged that some would conspire with plaintiffs to get questionable and dubious judgments against the Federal Government. We took a view of the issues confronting the Ministry in terms of immediate, medium and the long-term goals, and devised strategies for addressing them. In the immediate, we tried to re-professionalise and motivate the lawyers by promising that every solicitor going to court could aspire to the rank of SAN under a 'Public Interest Litigation' category.

When I was a member of the Legal Practitioners' Privileges Committee (LPPC) before I became AGF, we had encouraged the conferment of the rank of SAN on deserving lawyers in public institutions, particularly those that appeared in court. In 2011, the then Director of Civil Litigation at the Ministry, Mrs Agatha Mbamali, was conferred with the rank of SAN. That served as a morale booster to lawyers in the Ministry.

RECRUITMENT AND TRAINING

We also considered the Ministry of Justice to be deficit in terms of training. The Federal Civil Service Commission had graciously acceded to our request to recruit more lawyers. As soon as we recruited more lawyers and they assumed duty, we made sure they underwent induction courses. Our development partners, such as the British High Commission, the European Union and the American Embassy, were very helpful in manpower training. We retooled the staff and provided them with the skills that helped in re-professionalising the Ministry of Justice, particularly to meet the demands of the ever-complex emerging areas such as terrorism and cybercrimes. They were trained on how to gather evidence and prosecute such cases.

We also entered into an arrangement with an agency under the Ministry, the Nigerian Institute of Advanced Legal Studies (NIALS), to assist in the training of our lawyers in modern techniques of legal drafting and prosecution of cases. We brought faculties from the UK to train our lawyers. We sent lawyers to attend seminars and courses abroad as well. As an incentive, we secured a yearly grant from the President, which was managed by the Solicitor-General, to enable lawyers attend the International Bar Association conferences. That initiative allowed them to interact with lawyers from all over the world. This was a big boost to their knowledge and confidence.

We also noticed that before that time, most of the staff who were sent for training abroad got away with skipping actual attendance of those courses. They were wont to sign into such courses and thereafter go shopping. We tackled that effectively by demanding a written report of any training attended. In addition, we organised meetings at the auditorium where such lawyers would share the knowledge they gained from the seminars with the rest of the staff. It became very clear that they had to take the trainings seriously. The worst aspect before then was that some would collect all their allowances for foreign training but fail to travel. Some would receive funds to attend to cases in Lagos and would not go. We developed a monitoring system and raised the bar of accountability. That helped control the bad behaviour.

LEGAL ADVISERS

One major challenge that we faced was that many of the ministry's lawyers preferred being posted to other ministries as legal advisers. Once they went, they never wanted to return. Some lawyers had been posted to the Ministry of Finance for upwards of 15 to 20 years. It was the same for the Ministries of Petroleum Resources, Education and Works and Housing. They never got recalled nor reassigned from those ministries. A cartel developed around that, a protectionist one.

Determined to end that, I recalled all the legal advisers. A new benchmark was set requiring that anybody who had been out as a legal adviser for three years must return to the Ministry of Justice. Further critical evaluation brought us to a realisation that some ministries did not need us to assign legal advisers to them on a permanent basis. We also realised that we could not achieve our manpower needs if we continued to deplete the numbers available by assigning them out as legal advisers.

Only key ministries could thenceforth be sent legal advisers. These included the Ministries of Finance, Agriculture, Petroleum Resources, and Works, etc. We stated that any ministry that needed legal advice should forward their request directly to the Ministry of Justice so that we could advise them appropriately. That strategy helped us give exposure and experience to as many others as possible. In spite of political pressures against withdrawing certain individuals from their comfort zones, we succeeded in breaking the cartel-like operations through that strategy.

A reporting standard was set up whereby fortnightly reports must be sent to the Ministry of Justice by such legal advisers detailing activities in such ministries. As representatives of the AGF, they were required to work in tandem with my office. It was important to me that I receive briefings on decisions and advice rendered on my behalf to avoid situations where I would go to FEC to raise objections or observations to matters which had received the advice of my representatives. There was, therefore, the need for synergy, proper coordination and management of legal issues involving the Federal Government.

SAVINGS CULTURE

I realised that the Ministry was living from hand to mouth. There were no savings. Coming from the private sector, I found that bizarre. There never was enough money for anything! From the overheads, I found it imperative to cut out whatever was superfluous and save whatever we could for the rainy day. A saving formula was developed, depending on how much money was released to the Ministry. We pruned down expenses.

As at 2 June 2011 when I was leaving the Ministry after my first tenure, there was a healthy balance of N1.2 billion in the accounts. That was unprecedented. But as at 2 July 2011 when I returned for my second stint, the account had become empty! All in just one month! Many of the approvals I had given during my first stint, I was to discover, were presented for another round of approval! They were not expecting that I was going to be reappointed as AGF, so they carefully removed all the previous approvals from the files. It took the vigilance of one of my aides to alert me that some files that had been approved before were being recycled. It was incredible how the previous approvals were smoothly diverted.

The N1.2 billion savings were gone, yet the approved solicitors' fees had not been paid. Of course, we investigated these and took a decision to tackle the situation. I made sure that the list of all pending payments and the beneficiaries accompanied the files. This was to ensure that approved payments were not re-routed for payment. I became more vigilant, trusting no one. I was no longer going to suffer fools gladly.

PAYMENT OF SOLICITORS' FEES

Previously, the Ministry did not have a template for the payment of solicitors' fees. There were no specific provisions to grade payments in the Ministry's overhead. They would exploit that opening to give cases to their friends and pay them N50 million for each, while younger lawyers would not have jobs despite the influx of files. Litigation against the Federal Government was on the rise because of the democratic environment which encouraged citizens to sue for breaches of their fundamental rights and contractual obligations. The cases were piling up and we needed more lawyers to handle them.

We created a template that pegged payments at N5 million for senior lawyers, to be paid in three instalments. For young lawyers, we would pay between N1 million and N2 million, depending on the nature of the case. We were able to give cases to more lawyers and, in the process, dispense with outstanding ones. It also reduced the incidence of judgment debt liabilities on the government. We now had a committee that monitored the system. Interestingly, we were attracting lawyers from private law firms to handle our cases. We started getting weekly and bi-weekly updates on all our cases in court.

POLITICAL INSULATION

I believed that if President Jonathan had spent another four years in office and there had been another AGF that would exercise the same level of resistance to political interference as I believed I did, the Ministry of Justice would have become the independent institution desired by Nigerians. That would have helped check most of the abuses attributable to a culture of political interference. Friction would normally be expected to exist between political authorities and the Ministry of Justice, but we laboured to build a culture of independence to strike a balance. We almost got there.

A good instance was on the case of the former FIRS boss, Mrs Ifueko Omoigui Okauru. I had written an opinion on the legality or otherwise of extending her tenure before the dissolution of the cabinet in 2011. Pending the constitution of the new cabinet in July 2011, the President had requested the Solicitor-General to review the opinion. The Solicitor-General had bravely and courageously written back to the President stating that he had looked at the opinion rendered by the Attorney-General and had no reason to depart from it. That was the sort of culture we hoped to build, one where the officers of the Ministry could look political authorities in the face and speak with one voice. That might not appear a tangible achievement to many, but it is *sine qua non* for building sustainable institutions.

PRISON DECONGESTION

Before my assumption of office, the Ministry had become notorious in respect of a scam relating to prison decongestion. The scheme was so poorly handled that even non-lawyers and market women were allocated prison decongestion briefs which they in turn assigned to lawyers. It became such a major scam that some lawyers within the Ministry saw it as a money-making opportunity – a mere handout given to them to cushion the pain of serving in the Office of the Attorney-General where there were no major projects or contract awards to benefit from.

The prison decongestion scheme was created under the Obasanjo Administration and superintended over by my predecessor in office, Ojo. Under it, Ministry officials sought out indigent persons in the prisons, mostly awaiting trial, in order to assist them with legal representation. I suspended the programme, examined its relevance and tried to sanitise its operation. The Solicitor-General took charge of the management of the cases, with instructions that a clear-cut template must be worked out if the scheme must continue. The staff were unhappy. The scheme had benefited them financially. Some considered me a wicked AGF for taking the racket apart.

A committee was set up to evaluate all the cases that had been farmed out under the scheme. We asked for the submission of judgments and periodic reports on those cases. Sadly, we discovered that most of the briefs were not executed, yet payments were made. In all, we noticed that lawyers were forging reports and records of proceedings to enable them make claims on the Ministry. We reported some of them to the police. We debriefed a lot of them and punished their in-house collaborators. I resolved to put an end to the scheme. It had not served the purpose of prison decongestion. In fact, it rather became an unethical violation of the fundamental rights of the prisoners, who would be saddled with such solicitors. In any case, they constituted a usurpation and duplication of the functions of the Legal Aid Council.

The scheme was transferred to the Legal Aid Council as it was within the Council's statutory mandate to provide legal aid to indigent persons. In the interim, we effected payment of genuinely deserving claims. We also set up a committee to go to all the prisons across the six geopolitical zones and identify prisoners who had been convicted and given an option of fine but who could not pay. The committee paid off the fines of these prisoners, gave them some seed capital and entered into arrangements with some civil society organisations to rehabilitate them before they were released into the larger society. This was to reduce the rate of recidivism.

CREATION OF SPECIALISED UNITS

There were five predominant professional departments in the Ministry: Civil Litigation Department, Department of Public Prosecution, Solicitors Department, Department of Legal Drafting and Department of International Law. But because of the specialised nature of our laws, we created specialised units, such as the Central Authority Unit, to manage issues relating to international cooperation especially mutual legal assistance and extradition; the Freedom of Information Unit to deal with issues relating to the implementation of the Freedom of Information Act 2011 because of the centrality of the office of the AGF in its implementation; and the Cybercrime Unit to develop skills required to deal with this emerging area of law. We also set up the Complex Case Working Group under the superintendence of the DPPF to deal with complex crimes such as terrorism.

PARTNERING WITH STATE ATTORNEYS-GENERAL

There were cases in different geopolitical zones that gave us logistical nightmares. We could not be everywhere to prosecute federal offences diligently. We had to issue fiats to Attorneys-General in states to assist in the prosecution of some cases. They did them for free too. That saved us a lot of costs and freed up funds for other uses. Lagos State was particularly helpful when Mr Supo Sasore was AG. Mr Ade Ipaye, his successor, sustained the cooperation. That was a lot of relief for us. The AG of Borno State also did a similar thing on behalf of the Federal Government.

• • •

CHAPTER TWENTY-FIVE

LOOKING BACK, LOOKING FORWARD

While serving as AGF, I had cause to address some topical issues as they came up for consideration directly or tangentially, in the many matters that occupied my attention in that office. These issues continue to be on the front burner of public discourse as the best approach to effectively dealing with them remains a major challenge to the polity. In this closing chapter, I share my thoughts on some of them as they relate to the Nigerian state. The objective is to draw further attention to these burning issues which when dispassionately considered, have the potential of engendering policy, legal and attitudinal change in the polity. While I strongly believe in the potency of my arguments, my views are only generally reflective of my experiences from the vantage position I occupied in government. Some of my reflections on issues contained in the Constitution were expressed as far back as 2012 in the Benue State University Convocation Lecture titled "Amending the 1999 Constitution: Prospects and Challenges for National Development" which I delivered on 7 December that year.

However, my thoughts on other issues as they relate to policy and attitudinal change are fairly recent. Although, many issues deserve mention, I have decided to focus on the following: the separation of the office of the Attorney-General of the Federation from the Minister of Justice; the agitations for state police; the immunity clause under the constitution; the indigene/settler dichotomy; the removal of prisons from the Exclusive Legislative List; the composition of the National Judicial Council; assigning portfolios to Ministers before screening by the Senate; strong leaders vs. strong institutions; and debate on the presidential vs parliamentary system of government.

THE AGF AS THE MINISTER OF JUSTICE

The 1999 Constitution, like its precursor, expressly created the Office of the Attorney-General of the Federation as well as the powers and qualification of the holder of the office. The AGF is both a Minister in the Government of the Federation and the Chief Law Officer of the Federation, or a State as the case may be. Section 150 of the 1999 Constitution states that:

(1) there shall be an Attorney-General of the Federation who shall be the Chief Law Officer of the Federation and a Minister of the Government of the Federation.

(2) a person shall not be qualified to hold or perform the functions of the office of the Attorney-General of the Federation, unless he is qualified to practise as a legal practitioner in Nigeria and has been so qualified for not less than ten years.

The Office of the AGF is unique in the sense that it has a dual role. It is, in fact, the only ministerial office that is specifically mentioned in the Constitution with certain powers donated to it. As the Chief Law Officer, the AGF's responsibilities are unlike those of any other members of the Federal Executive Council. It is contended that the role of the Attorney-General as the Chief Law Officer refers to his overall responsibility as the independent legal adviser to the government, and some have even suggested that it includes the legislature.

As Chief Law Officer, the AGF has a special responsibility to be the guardian of the Constitution. He has a special role in advising the government to ensure that the rule of law is maintained and that government actions pass the acid test of constitutionality. In the discharge of this responsibility, it is important to distinguish the effect of the AGF's policy advice from legal advice. The AGF's policy advice, which would generally reflect his preferences, carries the same weight as those of other members of the executive and may be disregarded by the President or indeed any other person or body. But his legal advice cannot be disregarded lightly in view of his constitutional role.

The AGF routinely advises the President and the government on all matters connected with the interpretation of the Constitution, legislative enactments and all matters of law referred to him by the Government. He also advises the heads of ministries and agencies of Government on all matters of law connected with such ministries and agencies. Often, these issues require the delicate balancing of governmental actions with the dictates of the rule of law. The AGF is obliged to ensure that the rule of law is not compromised in any form. Experience has shown that this is often a great task, given that governmental actions sometimes conflict with the interest of the citizenry.

The power of the AGF over criminal prosecutions is perhaps one of the most publicly scrutinised aspects of his responsibilities. The 1999 Constitution provides for the power over public prosecution under section 174 as follows:

(1) The Attorney-General of the Federation shall have power (a) to institute and undertake criminal proceedings against any person before any court of law in Nigeria, other than a court martial, in respect of any law created by or under any Act of the National Assembly; (b) to take over and continue any such criminal proceedings that may have been instituted by any other authority or person; and (c) to discontinue at any stage before judgment is delivered any such criminal proceedings instituted or undertaken by him or other authority or person.

(2) The powers conferred upon the Attorney-General of the Federation under subsection (1) of this section may be exercised by him in person or through officers of his department.

(3) In exercising his powers under this section, the Attorney-General of the Federation shall have regard to the public interest, the interest of justice and the need to prevent abuse of legal process.

The AGF is required to carry out criminal prosecutions independent of the President and, indeed, any other person or authority. This is important in order to insulate him from partisan considerations and pressures. It is generally believed that the most important role of the Attorney-General is to ensure that the rule of law is upheld at all times and that the formulation of legal policy is in conformity with the constitution. This explains why the AGF should be conscious of the need to balance the interest of the law and society against political expediency. While it is recognised that the President's views, attitudes, and persuasions on law and justice will considerably influence the formulation of laws and administration of justice, the AGF must always resist the temporary expediency of subverting the Constitution in order to please the President and to remain in office.

The enormous powers vested in the AGF call for the appointment of a person with courage, high moral values, integrity and a deep sense of justice.

The merger of the Office of the AGF with that of the Minister of Justice places additional responsibility on the holder of the office. Given the intrigues and underhand dealings that characterise partisan politics in Nigeria, coupled with the 'absolute loyalty to the President' syndrome that pervades the polity, the AGF has to be a saint in order not to be tainted by the views of his party under whose platform he was nominated or those of the President who appointed him.

In view of the foregoing, there is the need to separate the Office of the Attorney-General, which has enormous responsibilities requiring independence of thought, mind and direction, from that of Minister of Justice, who is an appointee of the President with the mandate to assist him in the discharge of his executive function. This is because when acting as Attorney-General, he is answerable to no one but his conscience and the interest of justice, but while acting in his capacity as Minister, he must take directives from the President and do the President's bidding.

This is not healthy especially in our environment. Advanced democracies, such as the UK, and some African countries, such as Kenya and South Africa, have since recognised the potential conflict of interest that could arise from one and the same person performing these functions and have since come to the reasoned decision to separate the offices.

As a past holder of the office, I am of the firm conviction that the time has come for Nigeria to follow suit. Section 150 of the Constitution should be amended to allow for the appointment of the Attorney-General of the Federation as a professional to discharge purely professional duties of proffering legal advice to government, prosecuting cases on behalf of the state and defending actions brought against the state. Such an appointee should have a guaranteed non-renewable tenure of six years. He should not be removed except for misconduct, and this must be supported by two-thirds majority of the Senate. The President should be allowed to appoint a Minister of Justice who will be responsible for policy issues, such as justice sector reforms and liaison with the judiciary, and superintending over justice sector institutions and parastatals of government.

STATE POLICE

Section 214 of the 1999 Constitution (as amended) establishes the "Nigeria Police Force" as a single police force for the entire Federation. It states: *"There shall be a Police Force for Nigeria, which shall be known as the Nigeria Police Force, and subject to the provisions of this section no other police force shall be established for the Federation in any part thereto."*

This provision is consistent with the constitutional pattern which supports centralised security architecture for the country. It is generally believed that the Nigerian Civil War which lasted from 1967 to 1970 severely tested her unity and cohesion, resulting in widespread distrust among ethnic nationalities in the country. The natural response to these challenges has been constitutional arrangements that have tended to favour the unitary structure of our internal security agencies. The military leaders were more familiar with that. They wanted to forestall a situation where the constituent units could deploy regional or state security agencies against the Federation or any part of it in the event of crises.

Consequently, the 1999 Constitution contains elaborate provisions under Sections 214, 215 and 216 on the general direction and control of the Nigeria Police Force with particular reference to its relationship with the political authorities at State and Federal levels. For instance, Section 214(2) prescribes that the force shall be *"organised and administered in accordance with such provisions as may be prescribed by an Act of the National Assembly."* Section 214(2)(c) further provides for the possible enlargement of the scope of the duties of the police force when it prescribes that the National Assembly may make provisions for part of the police force to form part of the Armed Forces of the Federation or to undertake the protection of "harbours, waterways, railways and airfields."

The current debate about the desirability or otherwise of the continued retention of a single Federal Police Force has significantly been anchored on the fact that State Governors who are the chief executives of their respective States do not actually have operational control over units of the Nigeria Police Force deployed in their States. This position appears to be borne out of the provisions of Section 215(4) which, while acknowledging the power of a State Governor to give "lawful directions" to the Commissioner of Police in his State with regard to securing public safety and order in the State, equally empowers the Commissioner, before carrying out such an order, to request that the matter should be referred to the President or any Minister authorised in such behalf by the President. To protagonists of the need for more direct control of the Police Force by the States, the provision of Section 215(4) significantly undermines the capacity of State Governors to maintain law and order in their domains in line with their constitutional role as the chief custodians of security.

Another reason for the agitations for the creation of state police has been the perceived inefficiency of the Nigeria Police Force to combat crime in the country. Governor Abiola Ajimobi of Oyo State was quoted in the *Daily Trust* of Wednesday, 21 November 2012, as saying that "the federally controlled Nigerian Police Force has failed woefully in the maintenance of internal security in the country." He called for the amendment to the 1999 Constitution to accommodate the establishment of state police as a way out of the security challenges currently confronting Nigeria. To Ajimobi, the agitation for the state police had become apt in view of the crime and criminal activities, which had enveloped the country in recent times. It suffices to say that the Boko Haram insurgency, the kidnappings, mob killings, ceaseless armed robberies and assassinations have raised questions on the ability of the police to secure Nigeria.

The Nigeria Police Council, established by Section 153 of the Constitution, remains the highest policy-making organ for the Police Force. Its functions as set out under the Third Schedule to the Constitution are (a) the organisation and administration of the Nigeria Police Force and all other matters relating thereto (not being matters relating to the use and operational control of the Force or the appointment, disciplinary control and dismissal of members of the Force) (b) the general supervision of the Nigeria Police Force and (c) advising the President on the appointment of the Inspector-General of Police.

The composition of the Council reflects a conscious effort to integrate the imperative of a unified Federal Police structure with the reality that State Governors are crucial participants in the task of internal security. Thus, while the President is the Chairman, the 36 Governors of the States as Members dominate the Council. In the light of the current constitutional provisions relating to the police force, it is necessary to ask whether the operational performance of the force has been facilitated or impaired by the current structure as to justify the clamour for State Police. In other words, do Nigerians currently have the efficient and humane police force that they deserve? And if not, could the police force be made to work better if it were decentralised and its component units subjected to the control of each State Government as State Police Forces? Proponents of state police, of course, believe that the present police force has performed below par for several reasons, including its unitary structure.

Deficiencies often cited include: inadequate personnel and material resources to effectively combat crime, a callous and insensitive attitude to members of the public owing to a social disconnect from the people, corruption, inadequate knowledge of local conditions by most police officers deployed to serve in States other than their own, thus leading to abysmal levels of intelligence-gathering and crime interception, as well as the alleged occasional use of the police force by the federal authorities to serve 'Federal' or 'Abuja' purposes, against the interest of the States within which such units of the force are deployed.

Perhaps, from a constitutional point of view, the most potent argument raised by proponents of State Police is the need for State Governments to be substantially responsible for issues of internal security within their States, while the Federal Police Force should only be responsible for the apprehension and investigation of persons suspected of violating federal offences, or to deal with issues relating to cross-border offences. It is argued in support of this viewpoint that greater State control of the police force will lead to the creation of more people-friendly police institutions, conversant with their environment and generally having the trust of the people of the State due to their organic relationship with them. It is canvassed that such an approach will equally encourage or compel States to devote a more substantial part of their revenue to proper funding of the police force, thus eliminating or minimising the present culture of poor funding of the Force, as well as the present ad-hoc 'donation' culture adopted by states to support the work of the police.

On the other hand, it has been argued in favour of retaining the present federal structure that it is a mechanism, like the other security agencies, for enhancing national unity, as envisaged by Section 2(1) of the 1999 Constitution (as amended). Against the backdrop of Nigeria's ethnic diversity which is generally reflected in its 36-state structure, a doomsday scenario is often painted of the different states maintaining 'mini-armies' in the guise of State Police Forces, which in the unfortunate event of tensions, could be deployed by the component units against themselves or against the Federal Government, contrary to the provision of Section 5(3)(c) of the 1999 Constitution which enjoins that the exercise of the executive powers of a State shall not be used in a manner as to "endanger the continuance of a Federal Government in Nigeria."

Meanwhile, the present federal structure of the police has made adequate provisions for the representation of all the States in the running of police affairs in Nigeria. The 36 Governors as members dominate the Nigeria Police Council, as earlier pointed out, with the President and two other federal functionaries being the only other members. The force, like other agencies of Government, is subject to the federal character provisions of the Constitution in terms of recruitment and distribution of sensitive positions, while its internal dynamics ensure the development of an operational ethos which is essentially pan-Nigerian and uniformly applicable across all parts of the country.

There have been passionate arguments by commentators on both sides of the divide on this topic, considering the amount of material which has been generated in the course of the debate – even if assessed only by the volume of memoranda sent to government reviews committees and panels on the issue – which my reflections may not adequately cover in terms of an evaluation of the issues raised. All factors considered, however, it is my opinion that the time for State Police is not now, and that the Nigeria Police Force should continue to serve this country as envisaged by Section 214 of the Constitution.

The realities of our nascent democracy, and the learning curve which many of our political actors are still negotiating, stir a debate as to the likely uses to which they can put State Police Forces, as well as the need to preserve, at this time, certain institutions which emphasise our unity as a nation, such as the police force. These are compelling arguments to retain the existing unitary structure of the police. I am of the view that the debate became necessary in the first place on account of the perceived inadequacies of our present force. Be that as it may, the challenge is to address those inadequacies within the context of the present structure rather than seeking to impose a new Constitutional arrangement which could have significant negative consequences for the polity.

It is instructive that the Federal Government itself realises that there is a need to constantly review and revise the structural and operational modalities of the Nigeria Police Force in order to make it more efficient, humane and people-friendly. The implementation of the Report of the Committee on Police Reforms constituted in 2012 is one sure way by which improvements can be made within the present order. It is also noteworthy that some states have initiated the idea of a Trust Fund to aggregate their resources and other resources from the private sector within the states to complement federal budgetary support for the police as a formal and sustainable response to the issue of inadequate funding.

I must also state that the view often held that the inability of state governors to control Commissioners of Police within their domains creates a fundamental gap in internal security arrangements is often times exaggerated. The relationship, in reality, is more cordial than often admitted by commentators. It is also significant to note that in practically every case, the Federal and State Governments have a common objective in securing law and order within the States, thus minimising any possible area of conflict between the two tiers in relation to the deployment of men and materials of the Nigeria Police Force.

IMMUNITY CLAUSE

One of the provisions of the 1999 Constitution that has elicited a lot of debate and controversy in our effort to amend it is the immunity clause which features under Section 308. It provides immunity for the President, Vice-President, Governor and Deputy Governor from civil and criminal proceedings, arrest and imprisonment, as well as processes compelling their attendance in any judicial proceeding.

Although controversial, this provision has been a feature of our constitutions since 1963 and the rationale has been explained in a number of judicial decisions.[11] In Rt Hon. Rotimi Chibuike Amaechi v Independent National Electoral Commission (2008), the Supreme Court explained: "Section 308 of the 1999 Constitution is not meant to deny a citizen of this country his right of access to the court. It is a provision put in place to enable a Governor, while in office, to conduct the affairs of governance free from hindrance, embarrassment and the difficulty which may arise if he is being constantly pursued and harassed with court processes of a civil or criminal nature while in office. It is a provision designed to protect the dignity of the office."[12]

In Ali v Albishir (2008) the Supreme Court held that "the intendment of the framers of the Constitution was to provide a shield for the President, Vice-President, Governor or Deputy Governor from frivolous or vexatious litigation in respect of personal or criminal proceedings that distract them from the serious business of governance."[13]Similar views were also expressed by the court in Tinubu v I.M.B. Securities Plc.(2001), where Karibi Whyte

---

11 Such as *Tinubu v IMB Securities Plc* (2001) 16 NWLR (Pt.740) 670 and *Fawehinmi v Inspector-General of Police & Ors* (2002) 7 NWLR (Pt. 767) 606.
12 5 NWLR (Pt.1080) 227 at 310, the Supreme Court, per Oguntade, JSC
13 All FWLR (Pt. 415) 1681 at 1710, the Supreme Court, per Belgore, JSC (as he then was)

added that the provision is "a policy Legislation designed to confer immunity from civil suit or criminal process on the public officers named in section 308(3) and to insulate them from harassment in their personal matters incurred before their election."[14]

It may be inferred from the above pronouncements that the immunity clause is a public policy provision aimed at protecting the affected office holders from distraction arising from private matters while in office for the ultimate benefit of the people.

It has been argued by the opponents of this provision that the insulation of the leadership of the executive arm of government from judicial process encourages lawlessness, engenders abuse of power and shields corrupt practices by such leaders. As Ada Ozoemena aptly put it in her article, "Executive Immunity and Public Accountability: The Nigerian Experience", experience over the years "has shown that executive office holders in Nigeria at the state and federal levels of Government have employed the protective shield provided by the Immunity Clause to commit fraud, loot the treasury, subvert the principle of public accountability and engage in sundry acts which undermine the integrity of their office and the interest of the people they govern."[15]

It is on the basis of the foregoing that many have canvassed the need for an amendment of the provision. The suggested amendment ranges from the expunging of the provision in its entirety to allowing for criminal proceedings, especially where it involves matters of corrupt enrichment. These proposals have also drawn from developments in other jurisdictions like the US where the President is only entitled to absolute immunity from damages and liabilities predicated on his official acts as confirmed by the decision of the US Supreme Court in William Jefferson Clinton v Paula Corbin Jones, where it was held that "the President, like all other government officials, is subject to the same laws that apply to all other members of our society. There is no case in which any public official ever has been granted any immunity from suit for his unofficial acts."[16]

There is no doubt that the contending arguments have their merits and demerits. I believe, however, that the ultimate decision to retain or expunge

---

14 16 NWLR (Pt. 740) 670 at 708

15 Ozoemena, Ada, 'Executive Immunity and Public Accountability: The Nigerian Experience', in Guobadia D.A & Azinge E (eds), 'Current Themes in the 1999 Constitution, A Tribute to Hon. Justice S.M.A. Belgore', NIALS, Lagos, 2007, pp. 201-202

16 U.S. Supreme Court No.95-1853

the immunity clause should not just depend on the preponderance of opinion or sentiment or even on what obtains in other jurisdictions. There is need to weigh the contending views on a scale of balance to ensure that any decision taken is one which not only takes into cognizance our socio-economic consciousness but also recognises the uniqueness and peculiarities of our democracy.

It must, however, be observed that expunging or amending the immunity clause is not necessarily a panacea to or a safeguard against the identified ills. Even with the present state of the law, a lot can still be achieved depending on the attitude of the courts and the law enforcement agencies in terms of their understanding and application of the provision. For example, until recently, the attitude was to treat the immunity clause as a bar to investigation of the affected executive officers. This scenario had the effect of slowing down or even preventing criminal investigation against the affected officers, as it was more difficult to obtain evidence required for their prosecution after they had left office.

It took the intervention of the Supreme Court in the case of Chief Gani Fawehinmi v Inspector-General of Police (2002)[17] to appreciate that the immunity clause did not prevent the investigation of the affected public office holders, even though they can neither be prosecuted nor arrested while still in office. This decision has since offered the necessary impetus for law enforcement agencies to investigate allegations of crime against such officers while they are in office and build up files, which could be, and indeed have been, used for prosecution on exit from office. It is thus important to recognise that the protection afforded by section 308 is not intended to be absolute. The immunity, for example, does not protect the affected executive officers in respect of their official actions as they can be sued in respect of such actions whether in or out of office. I am, therefore, of the view that the provisions should be retained in the Constitution.

INDIGENE/SETTLER DICHOTOMY

The 1999 Constitution does not expressly recognise indigeneship in the form asserted and practised in most parts of the federation. The Constitution rather contains provisions relating to Citizenship, although reference is made to "a

---

17 14 NWLR (Pt. 767) 606

community indigenous to Nigeria" in Section 25(1) of the 1999 Constitution where it confers citizenship by birth on "every person born in Nigeria before the date of independence, either of whose parents or any of whose grandparents belongs or belonged to a community indigenous to Nigeria."

The implication of this constitutional provision is that citizenship of the Nigerian state can be determined by reference to membership of an indigenous community. Although, there have been a lot of agitations on the issue of indigeneship of the constituent states in the federation, these agitations do not appear to have constitutional backing. This is because the Constitution only seeks to ensure that no state is marginalised. It recognises and treats all those residing in a particular state, local government or community in the same way and affords equal protection to all.

The federal character principle in the Constitution is to ensure that no state or local government is marginalised in the conduct of government business. In this regard, the relevant provision of the Constitution is section 14(3), which states that the

> ... [c]omposition of the Government of the Federation or any of its agencies and the conduct of its affairs shall be carried out in such a manner as to reflect the federal character of Nigeria and the need to promote national unity, and also to command national loyalty, thereby ensuring that there shall be no predominance of persons from a few States or from a few ethnic or other sectional groups in that Government or in any of its agencies.

The Constitution thus recognises the need to ensure spread and balance in the conduct of government business, but expressly prohibits any form of discrimination on account of place of origin. Consequently, Section 15(2) states that national integration shall be actively encouraged, whilst discrimination on the grounds of place of origin, sex, religion, status, ethnic, or linguistic association or ties shall be prohibited. Section 15(3) further provides that for the purpose of promoting national integration, it shall be the duty of the state to (a) provide adequate facilities for and encourage free mobility of people, goods and services throughout the Federation and (b) secure full residence rights for every citizen in all parts of the federation.

It is, therefore, clear that the Constitution imposes on the government the responsibility of ensuring that its citizens can move about freely and establish their businesses in any part of the federation and where a citizen elects to reside in a particular place, such a person should enjoy full residency rights. The question that arises is whether such a person who has taken up residency in a particular place can actively participate in politics, vote and be voted for in an election? It would appear that the Constitution does not discriminate against such a person.

Thus, subject to performing their civic responsibilities such as the payment of taxes, voter registration and so on, a person should be able to stand for election or be given political appointment on the quota of that state, local government or community where he resides. The Lagos State Government has overtime demonstrated this by its appointment of persons with ancestral ties to other states, but who reside in Lagos, as Commissioners. This is more so when the person has resided in that particular state or local government for several years and has been integrated into the community.

The point being made here is that while the Constitution in the present form does not expressly recognise indigeneship in the form practised in the country, it does not strengthen residency rights to the level required to provide comfort for those who have settled in a particular location for a long period of time so as to enable them freely participate in the socioeconomic and political affairs of their place of abode. The controversy that surrounded the appointment of Justice Ifeoma Jumbo-Ofor to the Court of Appeal amply demonstrates the extent to which indigeneship has been elevated over residency rights. By birth, she was from Anambra State but her husband was from Abia State, where she had served in the judiciary for 14 years. She was initially denied swearing-in into the Court of Appeal as a nominee from Abia State, but reason eventually prevailed.

It is my submission therefore that the Constitution should be strengthened to emphasise residency rights as opposed to indigeneship. Consequently, political appointments should be based on place of domicile rather than state of origin. This will put an end to the nagging indigene/settler dichotomy that has caused a lot of crises/tension in the past to the detriment of our collective endeavour to foster peace and harmony in the polity.

PRISONS AS AN ITEM ON THE EXCLUSIVE LEGISLATIVE LIST

My experience while superintending over the Prison Decongestion Programme of the Ministry of Justice afforded me the opportunity to be directly confronted with the problem of congestion of prisons. Under the present constitutional arrangement, prisons are an item on the Exclusive Legislative List. This means that only the Federal Government can make laws relating to the establishment and operation of prisons in Nigeria. The irony, however, is that most of the inmates are state offenders. The Federal Government is forced by the present constitutional arrangements to make provision for the feeding, health, transportation and other infrastructural needs of prisons nationwide.

The inability of the Federal Government to fully discharge this responsibility has led to the acute shortage of prisons across the country leading to congestion, poor sanitary conditions and general dehumanising conditions. I strongly believe that Nigeria is ripe for decentralisation of the prisons service to enable state governments establish and operate prisons or even privatise the provision of the service or as Private Public Partnerships.

This can be achieved by the alteration of Parts I and II of the Second Schedule to the Constitution relating to the power to make laws with respect to prisons, including the establishment, administration, maintenance and upkeep of inmates hitherto on the Exclusive Legislative List (Item 48) and taking same to the Concurrent Legislative List thereby vesting in both the Federal and State governments, the power to establish and regulate prisons (Second Schedule).This will address the yearnings of some state governments for an enabling legal regime to establish and run their prison system. It will also release the Federal Government from the sole burden and responsibility of maintaining all the prisons across the federation with its attendant cost implications.

THE NATIONAL JUDICIAL COUNCIL

The National Judicial Council (NJC) is one of the Federal Executive Bodies established by Section 153 of the 1999 Constitution with the power to:

(a) recommend to the President from among the list of persons submitted to it by – (i) the Federal Judicial Service Commission, persons for appointment to the offices of the Chief Justice of Nigeria, the Justices of the Supreme Court, the President and Justices of the Court of Appeal, the Chief Judge and Judges of the Federal High Court, the President and Judges of the National Industrial Court and (ii) the

Judicial Service Committee of the Federal Capital Territory, Abuja, persons for appointment to the offices of the Chief Judge and Judges of the High Court of the Federal Capital Territory, Abuja, the Grand Kadi and Kadis of the Sharia Court of Appeal of the Federal Capital Territory, Abuja and the President and Judges of the Customary Court of Appeal of the Federal Capital Territory, Abuja.

The NJC also has the powers to:

(b) recommend to the President the removal from office of the judicial officers specified in sub-paragraph (a) of this paragraph and to exercise disciplinary control over such officers; (c) recommend to the Governors from among the list of persons submitted to it by the State Judicial Service Commissions persons for appointments to the offices of the Chief Judges of the States and Judges of the High Courts of the States, the Grand Kadis and Kadis of the Sharia Courts of Appeal of the States and the Presidents and Judges of the Customary Courts of Appeal of the States; (d) recommend to the Governors the removal from the office of the judicial officers in sub-paragraph (c) of this paragraph, and to exercise disciplinary control over such officers. (e) collect, control and disburse all moneys, capital and recurrent, for the judiciary; (f) advise the President and Governors on any matter pertaining to the judiciary as may be referred to the Council by the President or the Governors; (g) appoint, dismiss and exercise disciplinary control over members and staff of the Council; (h) control and disburse all monies, capital and recurrent; for the services of the Council; and (i) deal with all other matters relating to broad issues of policy and administration.

The NJC is a unique creation of the 1999 Constitution. Before 1999, successive constitutions, starting from 1960 to the one of 1979, did not contain similar provisions. Some of the reasons advanced for the creation of the NJC are to ensure independence of the judiciary, especially in the appointment of judges, and guarantee the remuneration of judicial officers. While the benefits of strengthening judicial independence and integrity cannot be overemphasised, the fact remains that the NJC is a contraption that needs to be completely remodelled.

In the first place, the NJC set-up is totally antithetical to the federal system of government being practised in Nigeria. A federal body should not be appointing judges for states. Under the 1979 Constitution, the Federal Judicial Service Commission was responsible for recommending and disciplining federal judges while the State Judicial Service Commission handled state judicial matters. This was strangely, and perhaps quietly, altered in the 1999 Constitution which centralised the functions under a new body, the National Judicial Council. The NJC took over these functions at both the federal and state levels. This is a gross anomaly that has to be corrected through an amendment to the constitution.

Furthermore, the manner in which the NJC discharges its functions particularly with respect to the recommendation of heads of courts for appointment by the Executive has the potential of occasioning conflicts. Under the present arrangement, the NJC makes recommendations to the Executive for appointment of heads of the various courts and expects that such recommendations should be accepted and acted upon by the Executive. This, in my view, unduly limits the Executive in their exercise of the power of appointment. The potential for conflict arises where the Executive does not accept the recommendation of the NJC and instead desires to appoint another person who may not have been recommended by the body. This is more so as a recommendation is ordinarily not binding on the person to which it is directed.

The conflict that could arise between the NJC and the Executive with respect to the appointment of the heads of courts was glaring in the case of Rivers State. The judiciary was virtually locked down for nearly two years when the Governor, Rt Hon. Amaechi, and the NJC could not agree on who should be Chief Judge. This snowballed into a constitutional crisis, as there was no sitting Chief Judge or Acting Chief Judge to swear in the Governor-elect, Chief Nyesom Wike, in May 2015. It took some ingenuity and sagacity for relevant provisions of the Constitution to be invoked to allow the Chief Judge of a neighbouring state to swear him into office.

The NJC, for all its merits, still remains an anathema in a federal structure. The constituent units of the federation should be allowed the freedom to do certain things that are peculiar to them, including the appointment of judges, without reference to the NJC, which is a federal body. The present system only creates a pseudo unitary judiciary in a federal system with all its attendant negative consequences for the federating units. It is, therefore, my view that Nigeria should go back to the constitutional arrangement under the 1979 Constitution with respect to the judicature, which respected the federal arrangement.

However, if the argument for the retention of the NJC supersedes the desire to strengthen Nigeria's federal arrangement, then some urgent tinkering should be done to change its composition. It is clear that the NJC exercises extensive powers over the affairs of the judiciary especially with respect to the appointment and discipline of judicial officers. There is, therefore, the need for synergy between the NJC – which is the recommending body for the appointment and removal of judicial officers (heads of court and justices of the Supreme Court) – and the Executive arm of the government (President and Governors). The Executive has the constitutional power to make the appointment or accept the removal of judges recommended by the NJC and transmit same to the Senate or State Houses of Assembly as the case may be for approval.

The Attorney-General, who ordinarily is the link between the Executive and the Judiciary as well as a member of the Federal Judicial Service Commission (which makes nominations for the appointment of judicial officers), is not a member of the NJC that makes recommendations to the Executive in respect of judicial appointments. I believe this arrangement is unsatisfactory as it denies the Executive an opportunity of having insight into the recommendations early enough as to avoid confrontations especially where such recommendations by the NJC are not acted upon. One also finds it hard to understand why the Attorney-General who is the official leader of the bar will not be considered for membership of the NJC while other legal practitioners would qualify for appointment into the body.

It is against these observations that I recommend that the Third Schedule to the Constitution be altered to make the Attorney-General of the Federation a member of the National Judicial Council. This will ensure that the Attorney-General, who represents the interest of the Executive in the process of judicial appointments, is there to ensure that the needed checks and balances are observed.

Another worrisome provision that needs to be amended is the power of appointment into the NJC. The Chief Justice has an unimaginable power to pick most members. This is indefensible. He alone is empowered to pick five retired Justices of the Supreme Court or Court of Appeal; five Chief Judges of States; one Grand Kadi from the Sharia Courts of Appeal; President of the Customary Court of Appeal; and two persons who are not legal practitioners but are, in his opinion, of unquestionable integrity.

The only members not appointed by the CJN are himself or herself; the next most senior Justice of the Supreme Court; the President of the Court of Appeal; the Chief Judge of the Federal High Court; President of the National Industrial Court and five members of the Nigerian Bar Association who are recommended by its National Executive Committee (NEC).

Out of 23 members, the CJN alone appoints 14. By the time he or she is added to the number, it becomes 15. Effectively, the NJC is a puppet of the CJN. No single individual should have the power to appoint two-thirds of such a body that handles issues of appointment and discipline. What happens when the CJN also needs to face disciplinary action? The composition and mode of appointment are two issues that have to be critically reviewed and amended.

In my considered opinion, the NJC should not be headed by the Chief Justice. It makes things difficult as it creates a scenario in which the CJN oversights himself or herself. The body should be headed by a retired Justice of the Supreme Court or Court of Appeal, to be appointed by the President. The powers to recommend for appointment and discipline that were vested in the FJSC and SJSC in the 1979 Constitution could be retained in the NJC, but the Judiciary cannot self-regulate. It does not provide for checks and balances and this is against the very nature of the federalism that we copied from the United States of America. The Judiciary cannot be an island.

MINISTERIAL NOMINATIONS AND PORTFOLIOS

The Constitution provides under Section 147 for the Office of Minister of the Government of the Federation. Section 147 provides *(1) that there shall be such offices of Ministers of the Government of the Federation as may be established by the President; (2) Any appointment to the office of Minister of the Government of the Federation shall, if the nomination of any person to such office is confirmed by the Senate, be made by the President.* The appointment of ministers is, therefore, an obligation imposed on the President and in discharging the responsibility, he or she must involve the Senate that is required to confirm the nominee.

While this has been happening since the advent of democratic rule in 1999, views are divided as to the utility of the confirmation exercise carried out by the Senate. Pertinent questions have been raised as to whether the Senate is only required to rubberstamp the nominees of the President or whether all the Senate is required to do is a general background check to ascertain whether the nominee is fit and proper for such a position having regard to his or her educational attainments, state of origin, good standing with his party, known to the Senators from his or her state, etc.

While the answers to these questions are generally useful, what I consider most pertinent is the competence of the nominee which cannot be assessed or determined from the confirmation exercise as presently carried out. This is because the President is not required by the Constitution to specify the portfolio he or she intends to assign to the nominee. This raises the question as to whether the confirmation process is fit for purpose, especially where the Senate is unable to ascertain the portfolio. How, for instance, will the Senate check for relevant educational and professional qualification, cognate experience and track record of performance in the area the Minister is supposed to superintend? How will the Senate prevent the President from putting square pegs in round holes?

In my case, I was fortunate to have been appointed to the Ministry for which I had the relevant educational and professional qualification complemented with reasonable experience. However, it was the President's prerogative to assign any portfolio to me. What if he had assigned me to a totally strange ministry, such as Agriculture? While there are those who argue that a ministerial position is only supervisory in nature and that the Ministry has all the technocrats to assist the Minister to perform in office irrespective of his or educational standing, professional qualification, experience and track record, I hold a contrary view.

My experience while serving as AGF shows that a Minister must have, at least, a basic understanding of the mandate, processes, traditions and nuances of his or her Ministry in order to perform optimally. To make the confirmation process useful, the President should either, as a matter of law or convention, be required to assign portfolios to the list of nominees transmitted to the Senate for confirmation. Where that is done, the confirmation process will assess whether or not the choice was a good one. In the end, the citizens will be better for it as it would enhance transparency, efficiency and effectiveness in government business.

STRONG LEADERS VS STRONG INSTITUTIONS

In recent history, the experience of Nigerians with the performance of public institutions has elicited debate as to whether the polity is better served by strong leaders or strong institutions.

Who is a strong leader? What are his attributes? How does he impact on the polity? My understanding is that a strong leader is one who brings his personal attributes to bear on the workings of state institutions in particular and governance in general. Such leaders often insist that their will should predominate whether or not it is suitable for dealing with a given societal problem. They are overbearing and self-conceited to a point of intolerance to opposing views, no matter how meritorious such views may be. They are dogmatic and dig deep into their trenches and, in the process, shut their eyes to other viable alternatives.

A strong leader may be good at galvanising the people, particularly the masses, in a particular direction. He does not present other alternatives to them. It is easier to follow a one-directional path than one that has two or more options. Such a leader robs institutions of their initiatives, traditions in form of established processes and objectivity. The institutions are railroaded into following the path prescribed by the leader whether or not they agree with it. They defend their action by latching on to the Machiavellian creed that 'the end justifies the means'.

Strong institutions, on the other hand, are, in my opinion, those that hold tenaciously to their mandate, defend it and ensure that their organisational standards, values and processes are not short-circuited by anybody no matter how highly placed they may be in the chain of command. Strong institutions are guided by due process of law. They respect the political leadership but refuse to be teleguided by them in the discharge of their mandate. They hold their staff accountable in much the same way as they hold other members of the society accountable for violations of extant laws and procedures. They are not concerned about the body language, preferences or prejudices of the political leadership.

Our recent history has shown that Nigeria needs strong institutions and not strong leaders to take us out of the woods. Strong leaders and weak institutions have done the nation incalculable harm and have destroyed the fabric of our national life. Today, it has become glaring that regulatory institutions and law enforcement agencies perform below par because of their unflinching devotion to the political leadership rather than their statutory mandates and processes. The rule of law which should regulate their operations has been relegated to the background and the whims and caprices of the political leadership elevated to the level of worship.

Politicians, no matter how altruistic they may be in their thinking and vision, are always swayed by other considerations such as the partisan nature of the polity characterised by different political persuasions and interests competing for dominance in the political space. State institutions must, therefore, insulate themselves from politics and the dictates of the political leadership in order to ensure fairness and accountability in the discharge of their mandates.

PRESIDENTIALISM VS PARLIAMENTARIANISM

In recent years, particularly since the return to democracy in 1999, Nigerians have been complaining about the cost of running the presidential system of government. We have a National Assembly made up of two chambers – 109Senators and the 360 members of the House of Representatives in actual numbers – and a Federal Executive Council that has a minimum of 36 Ministers, going by the constitutional requirement. We also have the offices of the President and Vice-President, Senate President and Deputy Senate President, as well as Speaker and Deputy Speaker. The cost of maintaining all these high-profile offices is a drain on public resources, especially in a developing country that should be making efficient use of its means.

This has been driving agitation for a return to the Westminster parliamentary system of government which Nigeria practised from 1960 to 1966. Under parliamentarianism, the legislature and executive are merged. The Ministers are picked from the Parliament and what they earn more than other parliamentarians is usually marginal. That alone will save a lot of costs. The current system has caused the bloating of government and the resultant humongous running expenses covering salaries and overheads. If we are indeed desirous of pruning the size of government and reducing the bills, we need to carefully consider a return to the parliamentary system.

Similarly, the cost of electioneering in a presidential system is itself a recipe for corruption and waste. Whereas the Prime Minister only needs to contest for a parliamentary seat from his or her own constituency, the Nigerian presidential system requires the candidates to win votes all over the country and, therefore, have to campaign across the federation. It costs billions of naira for a presidential candidate to cover the 36 states – printing posters, erecting billboards, renting campaign offices and appointing campaign teams and polling agents, among several other expenses. Apart from making the process easily capturable by moneybags and political godfathers, presidential electioneering also loads extra expenses on INEC which has to conduct two elections instead of one. These costs run into billions of naira.

There is another complaint about lack of transparency and accountability in the Nigerian presidential system. The executive arm of government is considered to be too powerful and unaccountable by many political commentators. The Nigerian President is often described as the most powerful president in the world while the Ministers are said not to be accountable and transparent in their dealings because they see themselves as appointees of the President, to whom they think they owe their allegiance and responsibility of accountability.

The parliamentary system would checkmate these issues. For one, the Prime Minister is like every other lawmaker. He or she is only first among equals. He or she cannot lord it over them, partly because it is easier to remove him or her than to impeach a President. The process of impeachment of a President is so cumbersome it is virtually impossible. This is one of the factors making the President so powerful. The Prime Minister, meanwhile, has to give account of his or her stewardship to Parliament from time to time, quite unlike what currently obtains in Nigeria where the President is not obliged to give a State of the Nation address to the legislature. The Ministers in a parliamentary system are also dealing with colleagues and equals, so they are compelled to be accountable in parliament.

It is not as if a return to the parliamentary system will address all the problems bedevilling Nigeria, but it has a lot of advantages when it comes to saving the cost of running government, cutting down on electoral expenses and making the elected political leaders and Cabinet more accountable to the people. Certainly, going by the benefits to be derived from the parliamentary system, I would support those who are advancing the argument that Nigeria should jettison presidentialism and return to the system that is perhaps the most popular in the democratic world.

• • •

These then have been my reminiscences, interwoven with thoughts and suggestions on the next steps. In setting them down, it was my wish that the reader, in the best traditions of the law, get to "hear the other side" of the story from the perspective of my personal experience, in the face of rather malignant falsehood. If I have managed to debunk the lies and inaccuracies fed the public by some entrenched interests, I would have achieved my aim. More so, if my thoughts and suggestions based on my experiences as a lawyer and, later, the Attorney-General of the Federation would be of any use in the discourse to improve governance and politics in Nigeria, it would be most gratifying.

ACKNOWLEDGEMENTS

In my life, I have met wonderful people from diverse backgrounds. I have also shared my thoughts with many of them, some of which are reflected in this book. While I may not be able to mention everybody, I want to place on record my debt of gratitude to all my siblings and friends as well as professional colleagues. My interactions and association with them all have made me a better person.

I want to specially acknowledge former President of the Federal Republic of Nigeria, Dr Goodluck Ebele Jonathan, who appointed me to the office of Attorney-General of the Federation and Minister of Justice, a portfolio I held from 6 April 2010 to 29 May 2015. The appointment enabled me to garner experience in public service and contribute my quota to Nigeria's development. I similarly thank the former Vice-President, Arc. Namadi Sambo, former Senate President, Senator David Mark, former Speaker, Rt Hon. Aminu Waziri Tambuwal, and all my cabinet colleagues for their comradeship.

I deeply appreciate my friends who have stood by me through the years, particularly Damian Dodo who is like a blood brother, or, rather, my 'brother from another mother'. I am blessed to have him around me. Ambassador Baba Kamara has become my elder brother through his labour of love and care. I owe him, and his amazing family, a debt of gratitude.

I am forever grateful to Chief Kanu Agabi, former Attorney-General of the Federation, who inspired me while I was in office and has continued to support me thereafter. Chief Godwin Jedy-Agba taught me the practical meaning of true friendship and I will always appreciate him for this. Chief Bayo Ojo and Chief Michael Kaase Aondoakaa, my predecessors, gave the Office of the AGF its place of pride in the power matrix through their courage. I'm glad they prepared the foundation on which I built my own portion as AGF in the development of Nigeria.

Chief Mike Oghiadomhe, former Chief of Staff to President Jonathan, is always available to offer me invaluable advice in challenging situations and I am full of gratitude to him. My heart-felt appreciation also goes to: Prof Fabian Ajogwu (*Odogwu Agu n'eche Ibe of Abbi*, or 'The great man, the lion that protects his people'), Mr Omoruyi Omonuwa (one-time Attorney-General of Edo State), Mr Ade Okeaya Inneh, Mr Dan Enwelum, Mr Abubakar Damisa Sani, Mr Dalhatu Ibrahim Daneji, Amb. Hassan Tukur and Mr Kabiru Tanimu Turaki.

I specially acknowledge Mr Mohammed Rislanudeen, a brother, friend and confidant whom I first met in Kano in 1990. Alhaji Haruna Usman Maikudi has played a major role in my life since I met him in Kano during my national youth service. At every turn, he has always been extremely supportive to me. I am thankful. I thank Major General A.M. Jalingo, my brother-in-law, as well as Chief Uche Secondus, National Chairman of the Peoples Democratic Party (PDP), Mr Emmanuel Audu Bala and Mr Larry Peter Bawa for their various roles in my life.

My tenure would not have been successful without the assistance of my aides. My gratitude goes to all members of staff of the Ministry of Justice, and particular appreciation goes to: Prof Peter Akper, Prof Adedeji Adekunle, Mrs Beatrice Jedy-Agba, Mr Chuzi Egede, Mr Pius Oteh, Dr Taiwo Ogunleye, Mr Bola Odugbesan, Prof. Bem Angwe, Mrs Victoria Mbu, Mrs Clementina Ogunniyi ('Madam Headmistress') who served as my Confidential Secretary and was like a mother figure, Ms Ojochenemi F. Audu (such a selfless and exceptional character), Mr Sani Mohammed Anate, Mr Timothy Katsina-Alu, Mr Shuaibu Umar and Mr Saidu Yusuf, who has been my driver and personal friend for over 25 years.

To my wife, friend and sister, Sa'adatu, I owe the world. She has been a strong pillar of support in the most difficult of times. Her patience and under-standing has kept me going even when it seems to me that my world is crash-ing before my very eyes. I am grateful to my children, Habib, Abdulsamad, Faisal, Husna, Jamila and Binta, and my little nephew, Abba Bello, for their steadfastness and for the sacrifices they have had to make because of my desire to contribute my quota to nation-building. My siblings, Abdullahi, Abdulateef, Bashir, Mukhtar and Aisha, have strengthened me through the years and remain solidly behind me. They have sacrificed for me and endured difficult times with me.

I also wish to appreciate my brother, Abdullahi Rabiu Salisu, my sister, Aisha Rimi, and her husband, Fola Coker, Ms Chinelo Anohu–Amazu and

Ms Nonso Eminigini Ibekwe for their constant prayers, assistance and kindness. I am grateful to Mr Femi Oboro, my solicitor, and Mr Seun Bakare, my friend and brother, for their encouragement. My gratitude also goes to Mr Jimi Lawal for his constant phone calls, Mr Abdulwahab Mohammed, my brother's friend who has taken me as a big brother, and Barbara Garbrah, my adopted sister. Mrs Grace Chia, who was the charge d'affairs at the Nigerian embassy in The Hague, and Mr David Okwor, who was also schooling in The Hague, were very kind to me and I remain grateful to them.

I appreciate retired Inspector General of Police, Mr M.D. Abubakar, who has remained a good friend and brother; Alhaji Yusuf Alli of *The Nation* newspaper who has been there for me in and out of office, and Alhaji Ahmed Abdullahi Yola, who, as the Solicitor-General of the Federation, worked cordially with me. I am thankful to Mrs Yewande Gbola-Awopetu, Prof Desiree Ameze Guobadia, Mr Olukayode Oduyemi Olusheye, Zainab M. T. Waziri, Alhaji Abdullahi Ibrahim (former Attorney-General of the Federation), my cousins Sulaiman Kokori and Raji Adoke, and my family friends – Maimuna Kaleem, Justice Gifty and her husband Maxwell.

Governor Yahaya Bello of Kogi State deserves special mention for his concern for me. I similarly acknowledge the Attorney-General of Kogi State, Mr Ibrahim Mohammed, for his prayers and good wishes. It is gratifying to note that the duo made it a point of duty to call me from time to time to inquire about my wellbeing and encourage me to remain positive in my thoughts, no matter the odds. I thank Mr Adeleke Olutosin Ogunkoya and his wife, Fiona Hughes, who introduced me to my Dutch lawyer and helped me with transportation any time I needed to see my legal team.

Bashorun Dele Momodu, publisher of *Ovation International*, was the first to challenge me to tell my story, reminding me of the late Sir Ahmadu Bello who said "You don't expect someone else to blow your horn." I am grateful to him. Mr Olusegun Adeniyi, Mallam Bolaji Abdullahi and Mr Simon Kolawole have been good to me. They encouraged me to tell my story for the sake of posterity. So also was Chief Solomon Adegboyega Awomolo, SAN, who said writing my memoirs was very important. I appreciate them from the depth of my heart. Special thanks to Dr Reuben Abati, who has been very supportive. I am full of thanks to Mr Dahiru Majeed and Hajiya Zainab Sulaiman Okino. They are problem solvers.

Finally, there are many good people out there who, for reasons of expediency, I cannot mention, especially the man I call 'Global Chairman'. They have rendered invaluable assistance to me in my moment of travail. There are many Governors and Ministers I wouldn't like to name. All the same, I acknowledge their kindness with immense gratitude. Their good deeds towards me will remain indelible in my heart.

May the Almighty God bless all of you most abundantly.

ABOUT THE AUTHOR

Mohammed Bello Adoke was Nigeria's Attorney-General and Minister of Justice from 2010 to 2015, during which he helped resolve the dispute between Royal Dutch Shell and the Nigerian government over a controversial oil licence, saving the country from a potential liability of $2 billion in arbitration. He was also a key player in the amicable implementation of the judgment of the International Court of Justice ceding the Bakassi Peninsula to Cameroon after a century-old dispute with Nigeria.

Adoke was variously educated at the Ahmadu Bello University in Nigeria, the Robert Kennedy University in Switzerland, the University of Nottingham in the UK, and the University of Leiden in the Netherlands. He is a Fellow of the Chartered Institute of Arbitrators, England. As Nigeria's Attorney-General, he was a member of the National Council of State, National Defence Council and National Security Council. He was also a member of the prestigious International Law Commission from 2010 to 2016. He is married to Sa'adatu Mohammed Bello, a lawyer and former Attorney-General of Taraba State, and they have six children.

INDEX

CPSIA information can be obtained
at www.ICGtesting.com
Printed in the USA
LVHW091404110719
623795LV00010B/249/P